THE LUSIADS

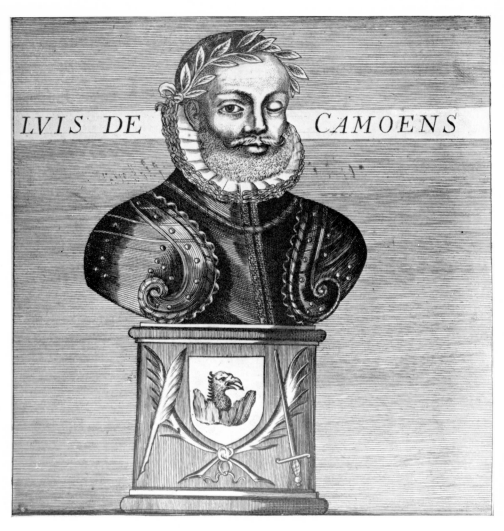

LVIS DE CAMOENS

SPAINE *gave me* noble *Birth:* Coimbra, *Arts;*
LISBON, *a* high-plac't loue, *and* Courtly *parts:*
AFFRICK, *a Refuge when the* Court *did frowne:*
WARRE, *at an* Eye's *expence, a faire renowne:*
TRAVAYLE, *experience, with noe* short *sight*
Of India, *and the* World; *both which I write:*
INDIA *a life, which I gave* there *for* Lost,
On MECONS waues *(a wreck and Exile) tost;*
To boot, this POEM, *held up in* one *hand*
Whilst with the ,other I swam safe to land:
TASSO, *a sonet; and (what's greater yit)*
The honour to give Hints *to such a* witt:
PHILIP *a Cordiall, (the ill* Fortune *see!)*
To cure *my* Wants *when those had new* kill'd *mee:*
My Country (Nothing—yes) Immortall Prayse
(so did I, Her) Beasts cannot browze on Bayes.

LUIS DE CAMÕES

The Lusiads

IN SIR RICHARD FANSHAWE'S TRANSLATION

EDITED AND WITH AN INTRODUCTION BY

GEOFFREY BULLOUGH

SOUTHERN ILLINOIS
UNIVERSITY PRESS

CARBONDALE   ILLINOIS

© Centaur Press Ltd., 1963

Published in the United States by
Southern Illinois University Press
Library of Congress Catalogue Card No.
63-14938

This edition first published in 1963 by
the Centaur Press Ltd., Fontwell, Arundel
and 11-14 Stanhope Mews West, London, S.W.7
Printed in Great Britain by
Villiers Publications, Ltd., London.

To Professor C. R. Boxer, D.Litt.et Phil., F.B.A.

Acknowledgements

In preparing this edition I have learned much from the previous work of Sir Richard Burton, Aubertin, Leonard Bacon, W. C. Atkinson and J. D. M. Ford. and from Sir Maurice Bowra's exciting essay on the *Lusiads*. My interest in Sir Richard Fanshawe's life and work has long been encouraged by Professor E. M. Wilson, Professor Frank Pierce, and Mr. John Crow. Above all, Professor C. R. Boxer has made the work possible. His scholarly caution has saved me from many historical errors; the faults which remain are all my own.

CONTENTS

Plates

Introduction

I

The author of *Os Lusiadas,* Luis Vaz de Camões, was born about the year 1524, probably in Lisbon, of a noble family originally from Galicia and distantly connected with that of Vasco da Gama. His father was a sea-captain who died at Goa after being shipwrecked on a voyage to India; and the boy grew up in a capital which was then one of the great trading ports of the world. Going to the University of Coimbra he became not only a good scholar—with a knowledge of Latin, Italian and Spanish literature—but also a poet. For two years or so after 1543 he mixed with other young aristocrats on the fringes of the court, and celebrated the charms of various ladies such as Caterina de Ataide and Francisca de Aragão. Banished from Lisbon in 1546, perhaps because of a serious love-affair, he lived for some time in the country, where it is possible that he first began to plan a poem "which from hour to hour would increase the glory of Portugal". In 1547 he became a soldier in the garrison at Ceuta in Morocco, losing an eye in battle and gaining a practical knowledge of warfare and a lifelong hatred of the Moors. Back in Lisbon he seems to have become known as an impetuous swordsman, until in 1552, having wounded a Court official in a street-brawl on Corpus Christi Day, he was thrown into prison, and was pardoned apparently on condition that he enter the King's service in India. He sailed in March, 1553, in the fleet of Fernão Alvares Cabral and did not return for seventeen years, during which he suffered many vicissitudes.

He was lucky to arrive in Goa, for three of the four ships that sailed out that year sank on the way. Immediately he was sent out on a military expedition south along the coast of Malabar, and soon he saw service in the Red Sea, Malacca, the Moluccas and Macao, where (according to tradition) in 1556 he was made Trustee for the Dead and Absent in the New Portuguese trading station. Maybe he had already begun his epic, for we learn that when he was relieved of his post in 1559, apparently through the enmity of some of the traders, he was shipwrecked off the Mekong River in Siam and swam to the shore carrying nothing but his manuscript — a pleasant story if nothing more. In Goa he suffered many hardships, including imprisonment first for his actions in Macao, and later for debt, and he criticised bitterly the ignoble activities of colonial administrators and merchants.

In 1567, determining to return home, Camões borrowed money from the new governor of Mozamique, Pedro de Barreto Mobim who gave him a passage there. But being unable to repay his debt the poet remained stranded for two years, until his friend Heitor de Silveira and the historian Diogo de Couto arrived and enabled him to finish the journey. Silveira died as they crossed the bar of the Tagus in April 1570, two years after Dom Sebastião (aged 14) had taken up the government of Portugal.

Os Lusiadas was published in 1572, and the King gave Camões a small pension (15,000 reis) on which he spent his last years in comparative obscurity, dying of plague on June 10, 1580, two years after the disastrous campaign in Africa which ended in the destruction of the Portuguese army and the King himself at Alcacer-Kebir. A few months after Camões' death Philip II of Spain (widower of Queen Mary of England), seized Portugal and it remained under Spain for sixty years.

II

Living through the period between the death of Vasco da Gama and the loss of Portuguese independence Camões knew both the glory of its imperial splendour and its seamy side and swift decline. "All may see", he wrote, "that my country was so dear to me that I was happy to die not only in it but also with it." The appeals to the King in 1.7-18 and in the conclusion of the epic (X.146ff.) are the fruit of Camões' disillusionment and his fear that the great days may be over. But the epic as a whole embodies the triumph of idealism over personal experience; for here is a man who has undergone the worst that the life he describes could afford and yet rises superior to it through his patriotic fervour and generosity of temper.

The *Lusiads* is an epic in praise of a small people whose exploits helped to form the pattern of empire in the western world and opened up the East to soldiers, traders and missionaries. Its hero is Vasco da Gama and its primary topic the story of his first voyage from Lisbon to Calicut; but round this Camões ranged freely—to describe the whole history of Portugal since it freed itself from the Moors until his own time. Since in the poem da Gama is seen in perspective as one contributor to national greatness, it is well here to summarise the story of Portugal as Camões saw it (see also Appendix I).

Like Spain, Portugal grew by gradual expansion from the north as during nearly four centuries the Moors were slowly pushed south down the

Iberian peninsula and Christians settled the territory wasted by war and neglect. The kingdom was first founded round Oporto, and gained independence in 1140. Lisbon was captured with the help of English Crusaders in 1147, and Portugal had driven out the Moslems by 1267, two centuries before the Spaniards took Granada. The Spaniards were the next foe, and were repelled at the battle of Aljubarrota in 1385, with the help of John of Gaunt's archers. Hence the treaty of friendship between Portugal and England in 1386, and the marriage next year of Gaunt's daughter Philippa to King João I. After this the Portuguese developed two ambitions, to capture North Africa from the Moslems, and to explore the coast of Africa as a means of reaching the East. The second ambition brought an illusion of wealth to Portugal though India was in fact an economic burden; the first all but destroyed the country.

Before Vasco da Gama made his first voyage several other mariners had covered parts of his journey. The African coast was well known as far as the Gulf of Guinea and in 1487 Pero da Covilha, having reached India and Calicut through the Mediterranean and the Red Sea, went along the East coast to Safala before returning north. Covilha visited Abyssinia. Also in 1487 Bartolomeu Dias struck south down the west coast of Africa, was blown round the Cape, and then sailed north a short way, but had to return by the 'Cape of Storms', as he named it.

Vasco da Gama, a gentleman at court when Manuel became King in 1495, was chosen as leader for an expedition to follow up Dias's journey. With his brother Paul, and Nicolas Coelho he set sail on July 8, 1497, with two three-masted vessels, an old caraval, and a larger store ship. They had

Sailing South-west by the Madeiras and Canary Islands, they passed the Cape Verde Islands (often called the Hesperides), and made first landfall near Saint Helen's Bay. At times becalmed, at times driven by storms, they rounded the Cape on November 20 after four day's struggle, and in another eleven days passed the great Fish River, where Dias had turned back, and on Christmas Day touched a point they called Natal in honour of the festival. At Mozambique and Mombasa da Gama met serious opposition, for the Moslem settlers and traders, who knew by the experience of their fellows round the Mediterranean the consequences of letting Christian competitors into their markets and sources of supply, did their best to hinder his progress, as Camões relates. At Melinde, a little north of Mombasa, he was more fortunate, and got a pilot for India, but it was the season of storms, and the last twenty-three days of their perilous voyage were difficult in the extreme. They had been nearly eleven months on the way when they reached Calicut on May 20, 1498.

The Great Moguls had not yet conquered the north of India, but there was a Moslem dynasty in Gujarat, and Afghan kings ruled in Delhi and Bengal. At Calicut, although the Rajah was a Hindu, called the Samorin, the Malabar traders were fanatical Moslems, who soon showed open enmity to these Christian intruders who had circumvented their trade route *via* Aden, the Red Sea and Egypt. Da Gama was unable to found a factory, but ran along the Malabar coast before returning home. This journey took another year and many grievous losses, and only 55 of the admiral's companions remained when he cast anchor at Lisbon on August 29, 1499, and went to the church of Our Lady at Belem to offer thanks for a safe return.

King Manuel, delighted at the prospect of a royal monopoly of the Indian trade, invented for himself the resounding style 'Lord of the Conquest, Navigation and Commerce of Ethiopia, Arabia, Persia and India', and the Pope confirmed the title in 1502. Vasco da Gama was loaded with honours and six months later Pedro Alvares Cabral sailed to follow up the exploit with thirteen ships and 1,200 soldiers. Driven west by storms, Cabral reached South America and took possession of Brazil before returning to the Cape and following da Gama's route to Calicut. There he landed traders but they were at once murdered by the Moplas, so after using his cannon on the town Cabral sailed north to Cananor and south Cochin, established factories in those more amiable cities, and returned home laden with pepper and other rare goods.

Vasco da Gama's second journey, with 20 ships, in 1502, was to strengthen Cananor and Cochin. In 1503 Francisco and Afonso de Albuquerque, with Antonio de Saldanha followed with three squadrons of ships. Francisco de Albuquerque was able to help the Rajah of Cochin who was being attacked by the Samorin of Calicut for admitting the Portuguese, and left behind him Duarte Pacheco, who with less than nine hundred men utterly defeated the Samorin and proved to the Indians that the Portuguese were bad enemies and good allies.

King Manuel now decided that the time was ripe to found a strong colony, and sent Francisco de Almeida in 1505 with 32 ships and 1500 soldiers. Almeida fortified Kilwa and Mombasa in S.E. Africa as ports of call for future expeditions and set up his viceregal government in Cochin, whence he waged war against the Moslem merchants along the Malabar coast. When his young son Lourenço, after heroic exploits, was killed at Chaul in 1508 fighting against an Egyptian fleet, Almeida avenged him by routing a large Moslem fleet off Diu in 1509. His successor Afonso de Albuquerque sacked Calicut, moved the capital to Goa which he took in 1510, and sent expeditions to the Spice Islands and occupied Malacca, and Ormuz at the head of the Persian Gulf. Other viceroys maintained or extended Portuguese influence in the Indian Ocean and beyond, and Dom João de Castro, who ruled from 1545 to 1548, won one of the greatest of Portuguese victories against the King of Gujarat before Diu. After him the Portuguese felt secure in India, but their empire was over-extended demographically and economically and by the draining from the centre of so many noble and devoted men, who rarely survived the diseases and dangers of life in the East to bring back to Lisbon the benefit of their experience. The folly of King Sebastião (who dreamed of conquering North Africa for Christ) in invading Morocco in 1578 ended the Portuguese empire when he and the flower of Portuguese nobility and their men were defeated and slain at Alcacer-Kebir. Two years later Philip II of Spain assumed the crown and for sixty years Portugal was under Spanish rule.

Camões was spared the misery of seeing his country lose its independence, and, as the dedication and conclusion to the *Lusiads* show, he hoped that Portugal would be saved by strenuous heroism and by the emulation of such virtuous deeds as he set forth in his great poem, which breathes all the zeal and aspiration of the Renaissance in its physical and social aspects and may be truly regarded as the first great modern heroic poem in the classical manner.

III

What the Renaissance thought such a poem should be was well summarised by Camões' Spanish editor, the historian Manuel de Faria y Sousa:[1] 1. It should not be too remote through great antiquity nor so modern as to seem like yesterday. 2. The action must be heroic, exemplary, and worthy of being imitated. 3. It must be a unity, with one hero. 4. It must not be narrated like a history, but must admit of a fine invention. 5. It must include episodes, figures, imitation, and other adornments to beautify it. 6. The style must be elegant and sublime, yet in its sublimity must not lose ease, suavity and sweetness. 7. The Poet must immerse himself in the personages whom he introduces, speaking according to the quality of each of them and to the material he treats. All these requirements Camões certainly fulfilled, paying special attention to ancient models. The *Odyssey* of Homer, the *Argonautica* of Apollonius of Rhodes, and the *Aeneid* of Virgil had described sea-journeys, but Camões took Virgil for his model, for Aeneas, like da Gama, travelled to found a colony which should carry the civilisation of his people into a distant, unknown land. By calling his poem *Os Lusiadas*, 'the sons of Lusus' (mythical companion of Bacchus), the poet announced his classical intentions and that his poem was about the Portuguese nation, as embodied in the hero and the exploits which opened the way to their empire. Like Virgil he begins his poem *in medias res,* being encouraged to do this no doubt by the fact that until de Gama had passed the Great Fish River he was not ploughing an unsailed ocean but following in Dias's track.   The main story is the journey from Sofala to Calicut and back. Da Gama's difficulties and resourcefulness in overcoming them provide an adequate portrait of the leader, and although his character is not so fully presented as that of Aeneas in Virgil or of Odysseus in the *Odyssey,* he is 'pius' in his patriotism, resolution and religious faith, ruthless when necessary but not cruel, a man of simple nobility and honour.   Like Virgil Camões, having early brought his hero to a resting place (in the *Aeneid* Carthage, here Melinde (Canto II)), looks back on previous events so that Cantos III and IV describe the struggles of the Portuguese against the Moors and Castile, with sketches of the great men of Portuguese history, leading up to Don Manuel's vision which made him commission da Gama to find India.   The retrospect is longer than in Virgil and lasts for most of Canto V.   In Canto VI (as in *Aeneid* IV) the fleet leaves Melinde and the next two Cantos describe the adventures on the Malabar coast, and the enemies encountered there (parallel to Aeneas's conflict with the Latians (IX—XII)).   Some Renaissance critics complained that the poem lacked the strong love-interest provided by Dido and Aeneas in Vergil's Bk. IV. Camões' defenders however pointed out that Canto IX with its luscious account of the 'Isle of Loves' corresponded to that. The passages prophetic of Portugal's future glories in Canto X are parallel to those in *Aeneid* VI and VIII.   Because he was so steeped in the classics Camões felt obliged to introduce the pagan deities who in the *Iliad* and *Aeneid* participated in the conflicts of the human beings, took sides for or against them and influenced the action by aiding or impeding their efforts.   So after the dedication (probably added later) the story begins (I.20) with a scene among the gods, when Bacchus shows his hostility and is restrained by the friendly gods headed by Venus.   The epic action is henceforth assisted by the rivalry between these two deities, and the occasional intervention of Jupiter (e.g. II.56). Some of the finest passages in the poem are concerned with the gods, such as the saving of the fleet at Mombasa when the Nereids keep the ships off the bar with their bodies (II.19-28); Bacchus's descent to Neptune's palace in the sea (Canto VI) and the storm which ensues from their alliance; and the gracious help of Venus and Cupid in providing the erotic isle — a veritable sailors' dream of paradise! (Canto IX).

To some narrowly religious readers the ascription of benevolent powers to the heathen gods was a moral blemish (and over half a century later Faria y Sousa was accused of heresy to the Inquisition for some of his notes on the poem).   The offence was the more manifest since most of *Os Lusiadas*

was historical, and one of da Gama's avowed aims was to spread Christianity
in the eastern hemisphere.   How then excuse the supernatural machinery?
Of course there were good precedents for it; in the Renaissance the classical
literary tradition excused such imitation of the ancients.   Moreover many
of the Fathers had allowed that the pagan deities existed, and if some
believed them to be fallen angels (cf. their appearance in Milton's *Nativity
Ode* and *Paradise Lost*) other more lenient Churchmen allowed them to
have had a permissive function as subordinate ministers of the true God.
Camões used this idea in I.21 where the gods left their sway over the seven
heavens —

> Which by the *Highest Pow'r* to *them* was giv'n;
> The *Highest Pow'r*, who with an eye-brow steers
> The *Earth*, the raging *Ocean*, and the *Heav'n*.

This seems to refer to the Christian God, not to Jupiter, who in the
Ptolemaic universe ruled one of the spheres (X.89).

In Canto X, 76—91, when Tethys displays to da Gama the working of
the Universe a fuller attempt is made to explain the use of pagan deities,
and not content with stating that the Almighty 'rules the round/*World* by
his *Second Causes*' (85), she says that she and the other gods were mere
fanciful creations of the human mind, useful to make poems more delight-
ful, and connected with the planets only by men's thoughts (82).   The
spirits by whom Divine Providence guides the world are Angels, not gods,
and the name 'gods' is wrongly given to the fallen angels. (83-4).

In Canto IX too the luscious joys of the Island of Love and the sea-
goddesses are explained allegorically as 'nothing but the delights of Honour
which make life sublime.' (89.1-4) This summary 'dismissal' of his machinery
after so much has been made of it may be doctrinally orthodox, and may
indeed have been inserted by Camões to meet the objections of ecclesias-
tical censors, but it jars on the modern reader and is inconsistent with the
agreeable and important part played by the deities.   Renaissance readers
would view the matter otherwise.[2]   In 1572 the Censor of the Holy Office
allowed the pagan gods as conventional ornaments of poetic style, while
pointing out that 'all the gods of the heathen are demons'. Although some
bowdlerisation occurred later, this attitude triumphed.   Thus a distinction
like Camões' own was made between truth to theological fact and truth to
poetic custom and beauty; but the two were not incompatible. Faria y
Sousa added a detailed allegorical interpretation by which Jupiter was God,
Venus the Guardian Angel of da Gama, and Bacchus the Devil.   At times
this may be so, and Faria y Sousa probably understood Camões better than
the recent critic[3] who sees the mythological apparatus not only as the most

important feature of the poem but as a direct challenge to Christian morality and Petrarchian chastity. Without following Faria y Sousa into all the ramifications of his allegorical interpretation, we may conclude that reading the *Lusiads* involves shifting between two or more levels of meaning; so the gods are beautiful adornments of the poem's rhetoric; they are also at times secondary agents under the Christian God; and allegorical figures as well, representing in pagan aesthetic terms aspects of Christian doctrine. As in Spenser the emphasis changes from episode to episode, but the allegory is rarely uppermost, and if we do not wish to search for it the poem is still enjoyable.

Apart from this Camões studded his poem with classical allusions and references to Virgil and other poets which could be appreciated by cultured readers. He adorns his work with illuminating similes and analogues from life and art. He has a keen sense of the beauty and terror of nature. He gives some impression of the strangeness of Indian sculpture. He is fully aware of the commercial significance of the voyage besides being learned in geography and history, astronomy and navigation. He describes the peoples encountered and their customs, from the African Kaffirs to the Hindus and people further east. Firsthand knowledge takes the place of the bookish learning found in most modern epics, and gives immediacy to the narrative as he reaches out to all that has been discovered since da Gama's time. The episodes of the voyage itself are chosen and elaborated to serve this teeming diversity — the adventures at Mozambique and Mombasa, the waterspout, the encounter with the giant Adamastor, the storm, the negotiations at Melinde and Calicut, the Moslem plots and the escape from India.

Similarly the historical episodes, whether battles like Ourique, Salado and Aljubarrota, or more romantic incidents like the tragedy of Ines de Castro and the story of the 'Twelve Knights in England', or the portraits of the great kings and their henchman (e.g. Egas Moniz and Nuno Alvarez) and the men who built up the empire (Duarte Pacheco, the Almeidas, Albuquerque, D. João de Castro), all these throw into relief important moments in Portuguese history and give peculiar richness and density to the narrative. Furthermore, as has often been noted, Camões does not portray his country's past as entirely unblemished. He deals out blame as well as praise to kings, queens and viceroys. King Afonso slays the fair Ines; Albuquerque is cruel to the erring soldier; the vices of churchmen and nobles are admitted.

In style Camões achieved a remarkable combination of clarity and adornment. He was a master of rhetoric, of figures, adage and epigram; and of the ottava rima with its adaptable final couplet. Equally at home in the Sublime, the pathetic and plain narrative, he could suit his tone to the moods of all kinds of incident, and shift at need from nautical narrative to lyricism or prophecy. His personal interventions (which often occur at the ends of Cantos) will seem intrusive only if the reader forgets that the Renaissance heroic poet had license to call attention to himself. Though Camões complains of misfortune and ill-treatment, his prevailing tone is noble and generous, and his poem is unified not only by the great story he had to tell, and by his epic machinery, but also by his own vivacious good-humour and humanity.

For us his work has many implications. It presents the stir and discovery of the early Renaissance, the interpenetration of modernity with the mediaeval and the classical, the mixture of mundane motives with lofty idealism, the realisation that a great civilisation was a precarious achieve-ment, not only in the eastern factories which depended on the gallantry and wisdom of so few men, but also in Europe, where danger always threatened, both from Moslem enemies and from a loss of vision and integrity among rulers and people. *Os Lusiadas* is the epic of Portugal; it is also the epic of the European mind in the sixteenth century.

IV

Camões was not translated into English until 1655 when Sir Richard Fanshawe's version was published. Since that time there have been at least nine other versions[4] but Fanshawe's despite its faults deserves republishing as a poem in its own right, especially now that it can be printed with Fanshawe's numerous corrections of the 1655 text.

Richard Fanshawe, sixth son of Sir Henry Fanshawe, King's Remem-brancer, was born in 1608 at Ware Park in Hertfordshire. Sir Henry died in 1616, and the boy was brought up by his mother, who intended him for the law. In London his schoolmaster was Thomas Farnaby, friend of Ben Jonson and editor of Juvenal, Seneca, and Lucan. At Jesus College, Cambridge, his tutor William Beale encouraged his classical studies and his attempts at verse. The many unpublished early poems include translations from Boethius and Martial, Psalm 45, and pieces showing his reluctance to leave poetry for the law. When Fanshawe's mother died in 1632 leaving him £1000 he cut loose and went through France to Spain, returning home after two years for only a brief stay before Lord Aston the new Ambassador to Spain took him back as his secretary in 1635. During the next three years Fanshawe was mainly in Spain, though he made three visits to England on official business. When Aston had to retire through illness, Fanshawe handled English affairs in Madrid until Sir Arthur Hopton could take up the Ambassadorship. After serving with Strafford in Ireland in 1640, he was King's Remembrancer till the Civil War drove him to Oxford, where he was with the King and married Ann Harrison, a neighbour and distant connection.　Probably while in Oxford he made his translation of Guarini's *Pastor Fido* which was published in 1647 with some short additional poems.　With Edward Hyde he was one of those charged with the care of the young Prince Charles, and wandered with him in the South West, the Scillies and the Channel Islands, till after the capture of Charles I the Prince was summoned to France by his mother Henrietta Maria and his father's officials were left to fend for themselves.

Late in 1648, the Fanshawes went to Ireland where Richard worked as Treasurer of the Navy with Lord Ormonde to bolster the Royalist cause. On the death of Charles I, Fanshawe hoped to be made Ambassador in Spain, for the King had promised him the post, but Hyde and Cottington were sent there as Ambassadors Extraordinary.　When Cromwell invaded Ireland and the Royalists had finally to leave, the Fanshawes and their family sailed in a Dutch vessel and, after encountering a Muslim pirate ship, reached Malaga whence they proceeded via Granada to Madrid, arriving on April 13, 1650.　They were unwelcome, however, for their friends were almost without money, and the Spanish authorities, afraid of offending the *de facto* government of England, would not recognise them as Ambassadors of a King, especially after some royalist hotheads murdered a parliamentary envoy, Anthony Ascham, in June 1650.　So the Fanshawes were forced to leave Madrid and, after being shipwrecked near Nantes, went to Paris whence Ann proceeded to London to get money, and Richard went on a mission to Scotland to patch up a quarrel between the new King and his brother James.

In Scotland he was made a Baronet (as from September 2, 1650) for his devotion, and worked usefully during the preparations for Charles's invasion of England.　He was with the King till the Battle of Worcester, then separated from him and was captured at Newport (Shropshire) after destroying his papers, which action, his wife says 'saved the lives and estates of many a brave gentleman'.

After this Fanshawe was held a close prisoner, for a short time in the Tower, then (during his examinations) 'in a little room . . . in the bowling green' at Whitehall where, worn out by his recent experiences, he fell ill with scurvy.　He was solaced by his wife's secret visits before dawn when she stood under his window in the dark and discussed how to get him freed.

He was accused of 'High Treason for adhering to Charles Stuart', but was not in great danger for long.　Cromwell was lenient in victory, and wished to win over the country gentlemen.　He may have known the Fanshawes through Sir Capel Bedell of Hamerton in Huntingdonshire,

Richard's brother-in-law. And he had the same doctor as the Fanshawes, Dr. John Bathurst. Ann approached Cromwell, who asked for a medical certificate that her husband was seriously ill. Given this he persuaded the reluctant Council to allow Fanshawe bail of £4,000. Fanshawe was ill for nearly a year. During his imprisonment he had probably revised some translations from Horace which he had begun in his youth; they were published in 1652 anonymously as *Selected Parts of Horace . . . concluding with a piece out of Ausonius and another out of Virgill*. During the winter of 1652/3, after Ann had had a baby (her seventh), Richard went north, maybe to visit relatives in Derbyshire, and called on his friend William Lord Strafford (son of the great Earl), who in January 1652 had come home after ten years absence to his estate at Tankersley, near Wentworth, north of Sheffield. He offered to rent the Fanshawes a fine house in the Park for £120 a year. Richard got permission to live in Yorkshire on condition that he did not go more than five miles from the house without leave, and in March 1653 they moved in, taking three children, Ann, Richard and Betty, and leaving the new baby at nurse.

At Tankersley, Ann writes, 'we lived an innocent country life, minding only the country sports and the country affairs'. For the first time since their marriage they were not under great political and financial pressure. Here Ann bore another child in October 1653, and Richard busied himself with literature. During the fifteen months of his residence at Tankersley he made three translations of very different kinds; the *Lusiads* of Camões, the Spanish play *Querer por solo Querer*, of Antonio Hurtado de Mendoza, and a slight description of court festivities by the same author: *Fiestas de Aranjuez*. The two pieces from the Spanish were printed in 1671. The *Lusiad* (as he styled it) was published in 1655, and dedicated to the Earl of Strafford with the assertion that 'this Treasure-Trove . . . is so truly a *Native* of Yorkshire, and *holding* of your *Lordship,* that from the hour I began it, to the end thereof, I slept not once out of *these Walls.*' This Epistle Dedicatory was dated 'From your Lordships Park of Tankersley. May 1, 1655.' But Fanshawe was not there then. For on July 22, 1654, his daughter Ann, 'the dear companion of our travels and sorrows' (as her mother wrote), died of smallpox, aged eight. To distract himself from grief Fanshawe began the Latin epistle in which he dedicated his translation of *Querer por solo Querer* to ex-Queen Christina of Sweden. A week or so later the family left Tankersley, fleeing infection, and did not go back. They stayed four months in Huntingdon with Lady Alice Bedell, until he was ordered to London 'there to stay by command of the High Court of Justice, and not to go five miles out of that town, but to appear once a month before them'. The family settled in Chancery Lane, where

Evelyn visited them on November 23, 1654, and there they remained (save for a Christmas visit to Frogpool, Sir Philip Warwick's place in Kent) until Christmas 1655, when they visited Richard's cousin Thomas Fanshawe at Jenkins, Essex. There Fanshawe fell ill again with scurvy on New Year's Day, and they returned to Chancery Lane. He had been unwell intermittently since his imprisonment.

It seems probable then that the Epistle Dedicatory was dated 'May 1, 1654'. If so the poem must have been translated between March 1653 and April 1654, though it may have been revised before being given to the printer after Fanshawe's return to London. The book was entered in the Stationers' Register on 16 August, 1655, for Humphrey Moseley, but advance copies must have been ready before that time, since Fanshawe presented his nephew Sir Thomas Leventhorpe with a copy on July 23rd. 1655. Fanshawe later (1658) regretted that the *Lusiads* and his Latin version of John Fletcher's *Faithful Shepherdess* (*La Fida Pastora*) were 'but ill printed, being at times when I could not be present to overlook the presse.' Since he seems to have been in London most of the time when the poem would be printing, perhaps the book passed through proof-stage while he was away in Kent, or when he was unwell. Certainly the book contained many misprints and misreadings, and it is not surprising that Fanshawe corrected carefully the copy which he gave to his nephew. He also seems to have made one or two corrections in a copy now in the British Museum (G.11,385).

A summary of Fanshawe's later career may fitly come here. After the Restoration he was sent to Portugal in 1661 to co-operate with the Earl of Sandwich in arranging the dowry and other matters concerning Charles II's marriage to Catherine of Braganza. He quickly won the Princess's confidence, and preceded her to England, hoping for a high post in her household. Before leaving Lisbon in December 1661 he visited the English College, where students were trained for the Catholic priesthood. The boys entertained him with a dialogue in which the Genius of Camões praised his translator as poet and diplomat. Apparently owing to sickness in the College the verses were only hastily put together, but they form a pleasant tribute to Fanshawe and an agreeable post-script to his translation, so I give them in modernised form in an Appendix.

Fanshawe attended the private marriage-ceremony between the King and Catherine, but he failed to obtain a post near the new Queen, and had to return to Lisbon in 1662, this time with his family. He was cordially welcomed, but neither the climate of Lisbon nor the chaotic state of Afonso VI's court pleased him, and in January 1664 he was transferred to Madrid. He died there of a fever in June 1666, after failing to make a satisfactory commercial treaty with Spain, and failing also in his strenuous efforts to make peace between Spain and Portugal. The Earl of Sandwich, who supplanted him as Ambassador in Madrid, was more successful on both counts, and in 1668 Spain recognised Portuguese independence.

V

Fanshawe's translation of *Pastor Fido* (1647) had been accompanied by a number of poems relating to Spain which he may have written during his stay there in the thirties. They included a poem on the *Escorial* and translations of several sonnets by Gongora and Argensola. A manuscript in the Bodleian Library (MS. Firth, C.1.) has others. Obviously Fanshawe knew the Spanish language well[5], but he did not visit Portugal until 1661, and it is unlikely that he had studied Portuguese before he began to translate Camões. This was however only a small obstacle. Besides the many editions of *Os Lusiadas* in Portuguese there had been translations into Spanish (e.g. by B. Caldera (1580), H. Garces (1591), L. G. de Tapia (1630)). In 1639 had appeared the scholarly edition by Manuel de Faria y Sousa, in which each stanza in the Portuguese was followed by a prose translation in Spanish with copious annotation and commentary. There was also a long life of Camões and a critical introduction to his epic. That Fanshawe used this edition is almost certain. A feature of Faria y Sousa's edition was its engravings and commendatory poems. After a lengthy prose eulogy by Lope de Vega comes a page on which appear side by side in two columns a bust of Camões on a plinth and one of Manuel de Faria. Under each of these are eulogistic verses. Under the Camões engraving is the sonnet of 'Torquato Tasso en su Parte 6, fol. 47'[6]. This Tasso poem was used in other editions, e.g. the Portuguese edition of 1631, but without the engraving. I have not found this engraving in any other edition. In Fanshawe (see Frontispiece) there is a very similar engraving of Camões, obviously copied from it. The poem below is different (though based on Faria y Sousa's biography); but Fanshawe gives the Tasso poem, and precisely the same reference, together with his translation, at p. 55. The fact that Fanshawe used de Faria y Sousa does not mean that he relied entirely on the Spanish prose 'crib'. On the contrary, he kept close to the Portuguese, and imitated the rhetorical turns of Camões' style in a manner which proves his close reading of the original stanzas.

The 1639 edition may also have given Fanshawe the idea of including some preliminary matter about the nature of heroic poetry. For this he used a translation from the *Satyricon* of Petronius of the remarks of Eumolpus on the nature of poetry and of historical poetry in particular, exemplified by a 'rapture' on the Civil Wars of Rome. This Fanshawe put into run-on heroic couplets in a close-knit style which he had already practised in his poem on the Escorial in 1637. This Petronius fragment may have been written between 1639 and 1642, while Fanshawe was still in London and enjoying a friendship with Thomas May the poet-dramatist and translator of Lucan's *Pharsalia,* the epic of the Civil Wars[7]. May's Lucan had been published in 1627; he completed the unfinished poem in English (1630) and Latin (1640). But he had included the first part of the 'rapture' in a speech by Petronius in his play *The Tragedy of Julia Agrippina, Empresse of Rome,* acted in 1628. May's version is more 'correct' than Fanshawe's, which has a rougher, more 'Metaphysical' cast.

Fanshawe inserted this 'Rapture' because he regarded it as "the *Rule* and *Model,* which (*indubitably*) guided our Camoens in the raising his Great Building". Camões' problem, as Fanshawe saw it, was to reconcile the epic manner with a historical subject — preserving some sense of history without 'striking too close to *truth*'. This had been Lucan's fault, whereas most other epic works, from Homer to Spenser, had produced an effect "wholly fabulous". Petronius alone of the ancients had in his fragment obtained 'a mixt *nature* between *Fable* and *History*', and this Camões also achieved. Fanshawe therefore cited with approval Eumolpus's assertion that the epic poet must not confine himself to 'things done' (that was the historian's field), but must infuse an inspired prophetic spirit through the work, making use of digressions, mythology, and 'fabulous ornaments upon the rack of invention'.

His aim seems to have been to convey the vivacity and rhetorical copiousness of the original. He never explicitly stated his theory of translation, but it was done for him by his friend Sir John Denham, who in 1647 praised Fanshawe for the originality of his *Pastor Fido*:

> A new and nobler way thou dost pursue,
> To make Translations, and Translators too.
> [Others] preserve the Ashes, Thou the Flame,
> True to his sense, but truer to his Fame.

Here Denham was hitting at the word-by-word 'cribs' of teachers, such as John Brinsley's *Virgils Georgicks Grammatically Translated* (1633), and careful 'Metaphrases' such as Jonson's *Ars Poetica,* George Sandys' *Ovid,* and the *Persius* of Barton Holyday. Fanshawe and Denham tried to keep the spirit rather than the letter. As Denham wrote in a *Preface* published the year after Fanshawe's *Lusiad,*

I conceive it is a vulgar error in translating poets, to affect being *fidus interpres* . . . for it is not his business alone to translate language into language, but poesy into poesy; and poesy is of so subtile a spirit, that in the pouring out of one language into another, it will all evaporate, and if a new spirit be not added in the transformation, there will remain nothing but a *caput mortuum,* there being certain graces and happinesses peculiar to to every language, which give life and energy to the words . . .

And as the speech is the apparel of our thoughts, so there are certain garbs and modes of speaking which vary with the time . . . and therefore if Virgil must needs speak English, it were fit he should speak not only as a man of this nation, but as a man of this age[8].

Such a view was highly controversial, but it strongly influenced Dryden when he translated Juvenal and Virgil, and Pope in his Homer. It explains many passages in Fanshawe which depart from the strict meaning of Camões.

In his youth Fanshawe had imitated Spenser somewhat (in his version of *Aeneid,* Bk. IV), but he now wrote as a Cavalier poet, with masculine forthrightness in a style which mingled colloquial expressions with turns of 'metaphysical' wit, more like Suckling than Lovelace or Waller. Partly because he wished to make Camões speak 'not only as a man of this nation, but as a man of this age', partly also because he had difficulty with some of Camões' rhetorical turns, his version missed the lucidity and grace of the original. Mickle (whose own version was less vigorous and poetic) blamed Fanshawe because "in every page, there are puns, conceits, and low, quaint expressions, uncountenanced by the original." This is true, and Southey, who thought more highly of it, pointed out examples of his failure to rise to the epic manner. But though he declared "It was pitched in the wrong key", Southey admitted that "justice requires that he should . . . come off with a good tang i' the end."

Some illustrations of Fanshawe's peculiarities will show the nature of his deviations from Camões.

Sometimes he tries to clarify the original. Thus at IX.2.7-8 he explains a reference. Mecca, in the original a city 'made great by the false and profane superstition of the Mahometan religious water' (a reference to the holy well of Zenizem) becomes the city

> which hath its fame
> From Mahom's superstitious *Lavatory,*
> Promising Heav'n through watry *Purgatory.*

This is probably an instance of Fanshawe's using the commentary of Faria y Sousa. (There was nothing ridiculous in the word *Lavatory,* which meant a place or vessel for ritual washing.)

At I.42.7-8, where Camoes wrote that the sun was entering the sign of the Fish (i.e. in February 1498):

> Queimava então os deoses que Tifeo
> Co temor grande em peixes converteo,

Fanshawe has

> 'Twas in that month, when Sol the *Fishes* fryes
> To which fear'd Brontes turn'd two Deities

— a lapse in taste which does not clear up the obscurity. [Cupid and Venus escaped from Typhon by taking the form of fishes.] The next stanza, when the sea reveals new isles which he girds and laves ('cerca e lava'), adds a gamesome note characteristic of Fanshawe:

> Neptune disclos'd *new Isles* which he did play
> About, and with his billows danc't *the Hay.*

At II.112.5 'Se houve feitos no mundo tão possantes' is turned into "if such *high Boys* as these the world hath had', a mistranslation which nevertheless reflects humorously on the 'soberbos Gigantes' just described.

Habitually Fanshawe intensifies or adds to the content of a stanza. Thus in III.110 when Camões describes the 'false and naked claims' of the Saracens to other men's lands, Fanshawe anticipates what follows, and adds 'reck'ning without their Host'. In the next stanza describing Goliath's mockery of David, where Camões writes that the large-limb'd Giant 'scorned the frail, ill-clad youth' ('Despreza a fraco moço mal vestido'), in Fanshawe the 'big-bon'd giant' 'Scorns the poor Boy, and sends him to his Nurse'. Such changes add concreteness to the Portuguese but at the expense of heroic tone. Thus, 'Que menos é querer matar o irmão' ('For it is little to seek to kill a brother') becomes 'Would never stick to cut a *Brother's* Throat' (IV.32.3).

Again, when Velloso goes exploring up a mountain and has to retreat, da Gama tells how he saw him 'e segundo ao mar caminha,/Mais apressado do que fôra, vinha;' which Fanshawe describes humorously:

> Behold him comming with a vengeance
> Down from the Mountain-top towards the shipps
> And faster homeward, then he went, he skips.

> (V.31.7-8)

This jocularity continues when the negroes attack and are so belaboured

> That (I believe in earnest) with our *Rapps*
> Wee made their *Heads* as *crimson* as their capps
>
> (V.33.7-8)

Only now and then does Fanshawe diminish the power of the original, as when he replaces 'Lá donde as ondas sahem furibundas' with 'There, whence to play their Pranks the *Billows* creep' (VI.8.3). His usual custom is to elaborate with some telling phrase; as when, describing Venus's palace which in Camões is 'adorned with shining metals', he writes 'Which upon *Pillars* of pure *gold* did stand', and transforms 'abundant tables resplendent with noble viands' into 'a most splendid and *Opiperous Feast*' (X.2.4-6).

Fanshawe's love of 'conceits' led him to insert into the poem witty turns and hyperbole characteristic of Caroline court-poets. Thus Venus (II.36) has shoulders 'Whose whiteness smuts the Fleece of unfaln Snow' (Cf. Camões, 'Pelo collo que a neve escurecia'); her breasts, which in the original are 'milky' ('lacteas'), in Fanshawe 'ev'n their own milk excel'. Her 'alva petrina' (white bosom) becomes 'Her Cestos white' (her girdle); then he introduces an obscurity not in Camões, referring to 'those white bellows'. A few stanzas later, when Venus, tearfully appealing to Jove (II.41-2), breaks off overcome by emotion, Fanshawe adds 'making a salt Parenthesis'; and his Jove is 'mov'd by that dumb *Rhet'rick*' (Cf. 'E destas brandas mostras commovido').

He intensifies the appeal to the senses, particularly in the erotic Canto IX. Thus he gives Venus' swans 'long white necks', and describes their 'lascivios bejos' as 'with lascivious Beaks'. The lemons (IX.56) which in Camoes 'imitate virgin breasts', in Fanshawe, 'with their button-Caps/Hang imitating *Virgins'* fragrant *Paps*.' The concreteness becomes absurd at times, e.g. when Cupid 'ayms at *Thetys's* Liver' (IX.48.3).

Now and again he will re-write a set description, as in that of the mountain-streams in the Enchanted Isle (IX.54);

> Tres fermosos outeiros se mostravam
> Erguidos com soberba graciosa,
> Que de gramineo esmalte se adornavam,
> Na fermosa ilha alegre e deleitosa;
> Claras fontes e limpidas manavam
> Do cume, que a verdura tem viçosa;
> Por entre pedras alvas se deriva
> A sonorosa limpha fugitiva.

In translating this Fanshawe turns from nature to art; the grass becomes 'imbroyder'd Hangings', the springs 'crystal' which shatter on the pebbles, the verdure Livery 'laced' by water; and the last line sustains while it denies the idea of a man-made beauty like Aranjuez:

'Such *Musick* never *Water-works* did make.'

In the next stanza (55) he elaborates with Narcissus-coyness on the simple pathetic fallacy of the trees in Camões:

Vendo-se no cristal resplandecente,
Que em si o está pintando propriamente.

Fanshawe rarely goes as far as this. Perhaps out of prudery he avoids Camões' point in IX.74.8, and in St. 82 he makes the Nymph melt with love and fall at the Sailor's feet, whereas in Camões it was he who then 'dissolved in purest love' ('Que todo se desfas em puro amor'). And Fanshawe specifically mentions 'Rites of *wedlock*' which Camões does not (84). His translation is Italianate, Marinistic, the work of a Cavalier poet who loved wit and humour, and who did not take his task too seriously. Translating *Os Lusiados* was a respite from sad thoughts. It reminded him of his own travels and of the seafaring life, and he regarded it rather as a superb sailors' yarn than as a great epic to be approached with awe. He applied to it his new way of translating which allowed some freedom, and he certainly made Camões speak English 'not only as a man of this nation, but as a man of this age'.

It must be admitted that Fanshawe's translation lacks the polish of the late Leonard Bacon's version. But Sir Richard Burton's tribute was fully justified:

'His work is that of a gentleman, a scholar and a soldier. His English, like that of Harrington, is nervous and idiomatic. The sprightly gallant style, the gay and lively tilt, the spring and swing of the verse show that he enjoyed his task. He has life with movement; and the rude energy of his poetic vein has still the power to please because we feel that he is swimming with the stream. Often comic, inverted, savage, tortured as Isaac Walton, he can be as sweet as Camões himself; and, when at his best, he is stirring, dignified and dramatic.' (I.143)

VI

The 1655 edition of Fanshawe's translation has often been thought to have been pirated, since the editor of the poet's diplomatic correspondence (1724) asserted that the book was published without his knowledge, and before he 'could put his last finishing stroaks' to the translation. Now Fanshawe's Postscript to 'Petronius his Rapture' stated that just as Petronius 'had *not added thereto the last hand* . . . neither have I added more to the *English*'. In the preface to his Latin translation of John Fletcher's *Faithful Shepherdess* (*La Fida Pastora*, 1658), he regretted that both this and his *Lusiads* were 'but ill printed, being at times when I could not be present to overlook the presse'. So the epic was not pirated, merely published without his proof-corrections, and this distressed him, since he was a man of great neatness and precision.

Indeed the elaboration of the edition, with its three engravings of Camões, Henry of Portugal, and Vasco da Gama, would be most unlikely in a pirated work. The last engraving is signed 'T. Cross', and probably all three were by that well-known engraver of frontispieces (fl. 1632-82), who must have been loaned Faria y Sousa's 1639 edition of *Os Lusiadas* in order to copy the bust of the poet, which he did closely.

Today the printing seems very odd, with its extravagant punctuation and use of capital letters large and small (GOD is always in large caps., place-names are usually in small). Many words are italicised for no apparent reason, and there are so many commas that an editor is tempted either entirely to modernise the text or (with J. D. M. Ford) to rationalise the punctuation greatly. But having access to the corrected copy given by Fanshawe to his nephew Sir Thomas Leventhorpe I have thought best to give the text largely as Fanshawe corrected it (with a few deviations for clarity). Readers will have little difficulty if they bear in mind these features:

Commas are used to emphasise important nouns, and to mark dependent clauses. *Oratio recta* is introduced by a semi-colon. Most unusually (and irritatingly), in possessives "s' is added to plurals and other words ending in 's'. But this final 's' is not sounded (e.g. 'Foes's'. 'Nereus's', 'the Portugalls's', 'Lusitanians's').

In the Leventhorpe copy Fanshawe corrected many misprints, and amended punctuation. Apparently he did not object to the compositor's practice, and some of his insertions agree with it. He added inverted commas on the left to mark sententious passages and those in which the poet spoke in his own person. He inserted some omitted words and lines (e.g. IV.38.5; IV.60.1; V.74.8), and revised many individual words and some lines which the printer had undoubtedly taken from the 'copy' (II.39.6; III.93.2 and 4; III.96.3; IV.64.8; V.39.7; V.78.7; VI.26.4; X.1.8; X.90.7-8). A complete list of Fanshawe's corrections, and of the errors he missed, is included in the Textual Notes.

The present edition reproduces the illustrations of the 1655 edition, but alters the position of the engravings of Prince Henry and Vasco da Gama, which in the Leventhorpe copy were placed facing each other between the Translator's Postscript and the Tasso poem, leaving three blank pages.

G. Bullough.

---

[1] *Lusiadas de Luis de Camoens . . . Commentadas por Manuel de Faria i Sousa . . . Ano 1639. En Madrid. Por Juan Sanchez, a costa de Pedro Coello.* 4 vols. in 2.

[2] See F. Pierce, 'The Place of Mythology in the Lusiads', *Comp. Lit.*VI.2. 1954, 97-122, for a close examination of the problem.

[3] A. J. Saraiva, *Historia da Cultural em Portugal.* Vol. III (1962), 637-84.

[4] By W. J. Mickle (1776), Thomas Moore Musgrave (1826), Edward Quillinan (I-V. 1853), Thomas Livingstone Mitchell (1854), John James Aubertin (1878), R. ff. Duff (1880), Sir Richard Francis Burton (1880), L. Bacon (1950) and W. C. Atkinson (1952). An edition of Fanshawe was published by J. D. M. Ford (Harvard University Press) in 1940.

[5] The Portuguese Ambassador wrote home when Fanshawe was appointed Ambassador: 'He speaks Castilian but is true Portuguese'.

[6] Taken from the five-volume edition of 1589, *Rime, et Prose del S. Torquato Tasso.* Ferrara (and Venice). Giulio Vasalini.

[7] Fanshawe and May parted company when war broke out, for Fanshawe was faithful to the King whereas May became a secretary to the Parliament and a propagandist, publishing a *History of the Long Parliament* in 1647. He died in 1650.

[8] *Preface to The Destruction of Troy, an Essay in the Second Book of Virgil's Aeneis* (1656). The translation had been first drafted as early as 1636.

THE
LUSIAD,
OR,
PORTUGALS
Historicall Poem:

WRITTEN

In the PORTINGALL Language

BY

LUIS DE CAMOENS;

AND

Now newly put into ENGLISH

BY

RICHARD FANSHAW Esq;

HORAT.

Dignum laude virum Musa vetat mori;
Carmen amat quisquis, Carmine digna facit.

LONDON,
Printed for *Humphrey Moseley*, at the Prince's-
Arms in St *Pauls* Church-yard, M.DC.LV.

Provenance of the Copy Used

The text of this edition is based on that in a presentation copy of the original (1655) edition corrected by the translator. The fly-leaf of this copy bears the inscription

ble
For my hon: Nephew
Sr Thomas Leuenthorp

July 23d   Ric. ffanshawe
1655./

The front paste-down carries the signature of the poet's wife, 'Ann ffanshaws', and the bookplate of 'John Fanshaw Parsloes Essex'. On the title-page is 'I. Fanshaw '(the signature of a clerical member of the family who died in 1763). The Fanshawe arms are stamped in gilt on both covers.

The Leventhorpes originated in Yorkshire and lived at Shingey Hall, near Bishop's Stortford, Herts., not far from the Fanshawes of Ware. Sir Thomas Leventhorpe had married Mary, daughter of Richard Fanshawe's sister Alice (Lady Bedell) in January 1654/5. He died in 1679 after being kicked by his horse while visiting his daughter (wife of John Coke) at Elvaston in Derbyshire. (Cf. H. C. Fanshawe, *Memoirs of Ann Lady Fanshawe*. 1907, p. 320). Because of its personal associations the volume was probably returned to Lady Fanshawe after Sir Thomas's death. It remained in the Fanshawe family until it was purchased by E. W. H. Meyerstein from Quaritch in 1930. Professor C. R. Boxer bought it at the sale of Meyerstein's collection at Sotheby's, 15 December, 1952.

Summary of the Poem

Camões begins Canto I with a claim that his story rivals those of Homer's and Virgil's travellers (3), and is truer than Ariosto's and Tasso's epics (11). He invokes the young King Sebastião (8-18), promising to tell the exploits of great Portuguese of the past. Then he begins his story (19). Da Gama's fleet has already rounded the Cape when the Gods meet in Council and Jove promises the heroes rest after their recent toil (23-29). Bacchus opposes this, but Venus and others are pleased (30-41). The ships reach Mozambique and are at first received courteously (42-63), but on learning that they are Christians the Moslem governor resolves to destroy them (64-70). Bacchus disguises himself and encourages the Moors, who try to prevent the Portuguese from getting water (73-87). The Lusitanians retaliate fiercely (88-93). Guided by a treacherous pilot (94-106) they anchor off Mombasa.

In Canto II the King of Mombasa, helped by Bacchus, deceives them into thinking that there are Christians there (1-15), and lays an ambush (16-17). Venus and the Nereids prevent the ships from passing the bar (18-25) and the Moors reveal their treachery in flight (25-32). Venus prays Jove to save her friends (33-41). He foretells their exploits (42-55) and sends Hermes to tell da Gama to sail to Melinde (56-64). This is done (64-73) and they are cordially welcomed by the King (74-113).

Canto III is occupied with da Gama's account of Europe (6-19) and of Portugal (20-21) and her history to the time of Dom Fernando. High lights are, the fidelity of Egas Moniz (35-41), the Battle of Ourique (42-52), the siege of Lisbon (57-61), the line of kings and their battles, the story of Ines de Castro (118-25).

Canto IV continues da Gama's historical narrative, describing the defence of Portugal against Spain, Nunio's inspiring conduct (14-22), the Battle of Aljubarrota (23-45), and the first overland expedition towards India (60-65). King Manuel's vision of the rivers Ganges and Indus (66-75) leads to da Gama's commission (76-80) and the departure from Lisbon (81-93), with the old man's warning (94-104).

Canto V describes da Gama's voyage to Melinde, the strange peoples seen, the waterspout (18-23), the adventure of Fernando Velloso (26-36), the giant Adamastor, guardian of the Cape (37-60), the way north to Sofala (61-73), scurvy (80-82). The Canto ends with Camões' own comments on these heroic actions and his country's neglect of poets (86-100).

In Canto VI Bacchus, descending to Neptune's palace (6-19), incites the sea-gods against the Portuguese heroes (20-37). Velloso has just told the story of the Twelve Knights in England (38-69) when the storm strikes (70-79). Da Gama prays (80-83). Venus with her nymphs soothes the winds (85-91), and India is seen ahead (92-94). Camões explains how true glory is achieved (95-99).

Canto VII begins by extolling the Portuguese above other nations for their crusading spirit (1-14). India is described, and Calicut (15-22) where Monçaide, a friendly Moor, tells them about Malabar (23-41). Da Gama lands, is welcomed by the Catual (42-46), sees Indian gods and sculpture (47-54), and visits the Samorin (57-65). The Catual visits the flagship (66-77) and admires her pictorial banners. Camões breaks in, complaining of his own wrongs; he will tell the truth (78-87).

Canto VIII continues the description of banners depicting Portuguese heroes (1-42). Bacchus appears in a dream to a Moslem priest and warns him against the Portuguese (45-51). The Catuals work on the King but da Gama's sincerity wins him over (56-78). The enemies however will not let him return to his ships until ransomed by his merchandise (79-96). Camões reflects on the evils of gold (96-99).

In Canto IX da Gama wins the release of two of his factors by seizing hostages, and sails away (1-16). To reward the Portuguese for their endurance Venus prepares a floating island stocked with amorous Nereids (17-63). The sailors are entertained with love (64-88). Camões interprets it all allegorically (89-95).

Canto X ends this delicious respite with feasting (1-7). Camões prays Calliope to let him finish his poem (8-9). A siren foretells future Portuguese triumphs in the East, under Pacheco (12-25), Almeida (26-38), Albuquerque (42-49) and others (-74). On a mountain top da Gama is shown a vision of the Universe and its operation under God (75-90) including the earth and the distant places in east and west to be reached by Portuguese (91-143). The sailors embark and arrive home (144). The poet concludes by urging the young King to revive these glories by his example, and offers his own services (145-56).

To the Right Honorable
WILLIAM
EARL of STRAFFORD, &c.

My good Lord,

I Can *not* tell how your Lordship may take it, that in so *uncourted* a *language,* as *that* of PORTUGALL, should be found extant a *Poet* to rival your beloved TASSO. How *himself* took it, I *can;* for he was heard to say (his great JERUSALEM being *then* an *Embrio*) HE FEARED NO MAN BUT CAMOENS: Not-withstanding which, he bestow'd a *Sonet* in his praise. But, admitting the TUSCAN Superiour; yet, as *He* [said] (with some anger) of GUARINI, when he saw, by the unquestionable *Verdict* of all Italy, so famous a LAUREATE as *himself* by that man's PASTOR FIDO outstript in the *Dramatick* way of *Poetry:* SE NON HAVUTO VISTO IL MIO AMINTA — (because indeed the *younger,* for a *Lift* in this kind, was *beholding* to the *Elder*): So, and for the same cause, might my PORTINGALL have retorted upon *Him* with reference to his own *Epick* way; IF HE HAD NOT SEEN MY LUSIAD, HE HAD NOT EXCELL'D IT.

Since then I find, HORACE, in the days of old, held himself accountable to *his* potent friend LOLLIO for the *profits* of those vacant hours, which *he* past in his *proper Villa,* whilst LOLLIO lay *Ledger* in ROME about that which was the great *Domestick glory* of the ROMAN NOBILITIE of those Times;

Trojani belli Scriptorem, maxime Lolli,
Dum Tu declamas Romae, Praeneste relegi:
Whilst thou (Great LOLLIO) in ROME dost plead,
I, in PRAENESTE, HOMER twice have Read:

(Hor. lib. 3. Epist. 2)

How much more obliged am *I* to bring unto your Lordship this TREASURE-TROVE, which (as to the second *life,* or rather *Being,* it hath from me in the *English-Tongue*) is so truly a *Native* of YORKSHIRE, and *holding* of your *Lordship,* that, from the hour I began it, to the end thereof, I slept not once out of *these Walls?*

And, if the same HORACE proceed;
Qui, quid sit pulchrum, quid Turpe, quid utile, quid non,
Plenius ac melius Chrysippo & Crantore, dicit:

Who, what availes, what *not*, what's *brave*, what *base*,
Clearer and *better* then the Stoicks, says):

Whether this *Poet* also (however *dis-figur'd* in the *translating*, yet still reteining the old *materials*, both *Politicall* and *Moral*, on a *truer* and more *Modern Frame* of *Story* and *Geography* then *that* of Homer:

    — *Et, quamvis plebeio tectus Amictu,*
    Indocilis privata loqui)

shall not be valuable upon the like account, I appeal to your Lordship, whose *devoted* (since he turn'd *Englishman*) he *is*, by the *title* I have already mentioned, and by as many more, as I am

                            My Lord,

From your Lordships
  Park of Tankersley
  May 1. 1655.

                              Your Lordships
                              humble servant
                        RICHARD FANSHAW.

Out of the Satyr of Petronius Arbiter

Petronii Arbitri SATYRICON :
pag. 48

Multos, inquit *Eumolpus,* O juvenes, *carmen* decepit. Nam ut quisque versum pedibus instruxit, sensumque teneriorem verborum ambitu intexit, putavit se continuo in *Heliconem* venisse. Sic forensibus Ministeriis excercitati, frequenter ad carminis tranquillitatem, tanquam ad portum faciliorem refugerunt : credentes faciliùs *Poema* extrui posse, quam *controversiam* sententiolis vibrantibus pictam. Caeterum neque generosior spiritus vanitatem amat, neque concipere aut edere partum mens potest, nisi ingenti flumine literarum inundata. Effugiendum est ab omni verborum (ut ita dicam) vilitate, & sumendae voces a plebe summotae, ut fiat, *Odi profanum vulgus* & *arceo.* Praeterea currandum est, ne sententiae emineant extra corpus rationis expressae, sed intexto Vestibus colore niteant. HOMERUS testis, & *Lyrici,* Ramanusque VIRGILIUS, & HORATII curiosa felicitas. Caeteri enim aut non viderunt viam qua iretur ad carmen, aut versum timuerunt calcare. Ecce *belli civilis* ingens opus! quisquis attigerit, nisi plenus literis, sub onere labetur. Non enim res gestae versibus comprehendendae sunt (quod longe melius historici faciunt) sed per ambages Deorumque ministeria, & fabulosum sententiarum tormentum praecipitandus est liber spiritus, ut potius furentis animi vaticinatio appareat, quam religiosae orationis sub testibus fides : Tanquam si placet his impetus etsi nondum recepit ultimam manum.

Orbem jam totum victor Romanus habebat :
Qua mare, qua terrae, qua sidus currit utrumque :
Nec satiatus erat. Gravidis freta pulsa carinis
Jam peragrabantur. Si quis Sinus abditus ultra,
Si qua foret tellus quae fulvum mitteret aurum,
Hostis erat : satisque in tristia bella paratis
Quaerebantur opes. Non vulgò nota placebant
Gaudia : non usu plebeio trita voluptas.
AEs Ephyraeum laudabat miles : in unda

Out of the Satyr of Petronius Arbiter

Young men, young men, (said Eumolpus) *this same thing called* Poetry *hath deceived many: for if a man have but set a Verse upon it's feet, and swathed his weaker matter with a winding about of words, he thinks himself presently over head and eares in* Helicon.   *Therefore, those who have got the practice of pleading or declaiming in publike, have frequently fled to the tranquility of versifying, as to a gentler port: believing it easier to com-pile a* Poem, *than an* Argument *embelish'd with little sparkling Sentences. But neither doth a more generous spirit affect a tympany, nor a mind conceive, or can be delivered of this birth, that overflows not with a mighty torrent of learning.   There must be a flying all cheapness (as I may say) of words, and such language cull'd out as is above the common people.   This is* to hate the lay vulgar, and to make them know their distance.   *Moreover there must be a* Care *that the* Sentences *do not hang out like tassels from the body of the matter, but shine woven thereinto like gold into a silken-garment; witness* HOMER, *and the* Lyricks, *and Roman* VIRGIL, *and* HORACE *his curious felicity.   For others either saw not the way of Poetry, or (seeing) feared to tread it.   Behold a great Task,* THE CIVIL WAR! *Whoever will touch that burthen (unless abounding with letters) shall sink under it.   For not* things done *should be comprehended in verse, (which is much better performed by* Historians) *but the free spirit must throw it self headlong in digressions, and in personatings of Gods, and in fabulous ornaments upon the rack of invention: that it may seem rather an ebullition of some prophetick truths, amidst a world of pleasant extravagancies, from a breast inflamed with fury; than a deposition, as of sworn witnesses to* tell the truth, all the truth, and nothing but the truth: *As for example, this* rapture, *though it have not received the last hand.*

Now conquering Rome *did all the world controle,*
From East *to* West, *from* one *to* th'other *pole:*
Yet was not satisfied.   The plough'd-up Sea
With brazen keels, was made her common way.
If any nook were hid, if any Land
(Which yellow Gold *afforded) lay beyand,*
It was a foe, *and covetous anger seiz'd*
Whatever *wealth.   No* vulgar *pleasure pleas'd:*
No worn plebeian *joy.   The* Soldiers *disht*

Quaesitus tellure nitor certaverat ostro: 10
Hinc Numidae lapides, illinc nova vellera seres,
Atque Arabum populus sua despoliaverat arva.
Ecce aliae clades, & laesae vulnera pacis.
Quaeritur in Sylvis Mauris fera: & ultimus Hammon
Afrorum excutitur; ne desit bellua dente
Ad mortes pretiosa: fames premit advena classes:
Tigris & auratâ gradiens vectatur in aulâ,
Ut bibat humanum (populo plaudente) cruorem.
Heu, pudet effari, perituraque prodere fata!
Persarum ritu male pubescentibus annis   20
Surripuêre viros, exectaque viscera ferro
In venerem fregêre: atque ut fuga mobilis aevi
Circumscripta mora properantes differat annos:
Quaerit se natura, nec invenit: omnibus ergo
Scorta placent, fractique enervi corpore gressus
Et laxi crines, & tot nova nomina vestis,
Quaeque virum quaerunt. Ecce Afris eruta terris
Citrea mensa, greges servorum, ostrumque renidens
Poniture, as maculis imitatur vilius aurum:
Quae turbant censum, hostile, ac male nobile lignum   30
Turba sepulta mero circumvenit, omniaque orbis
Praemia correptis miles vagus extruit armis.
Ingeniosa gula est: Siculo scarus aequore mersus
Ad mensam vivus perducitur: inde Lucrinis
Eruta littoribus condunt conchylia caenas:
Ut renovent per damna famem: jam Phasidos unda
Orbata est avibus, mutoque in littore cantum
Solae desertis aspirant frondibus aurae.
Nec minor in campo furor est: emptique Quirites
Ad praedam strepitumque lucri suffragia vertunt.   40
Venalis populus: venalis curia Patrum:
Est favor in pretio: senibus quoque libera virtus
Exciderat: sparsisque opibus conversa potestas:
Ipsaque majestas auro corrupta jacebat.
Pellitur a populo victus Cato: tristior ille est
Qui vicit, fascesque pudet rapuisse Catoni.
Namque hoc dedecus est populi, morumque ruina.
Non homo pulsus erat, sed in uno victa potestas,
Romanumque decus: quare tam perdita Roma
Ipsa sui merces erat, & sine vindice praeda.   50

Their meat in Silver: and (from Rivers fisht) 10
The Purple *of the* Land *rivall'd the* Sea's.
Here Lybian stones, *there* silks (*the* new disease)
And their perfumed fields ARABIANS *fleece.*
Lo, other spoils *and* wounds *of injur'd* Peace!
In woods is sought the Mauritanian *beast,*
And AFFRICKS *farthest* Hammon *hunted, least*
That Monster *should be wanting, which is slain*
Because his tooth *sells deare.   Instead of* Graine,
Armenian *Tigers our* Corn-fleets *import,*
To be led stalking in a gilded Court: 20
And quaffe (the people *clapping) humane blood.*
I blush to speak, and broach Fates *violent flood.*
In Persian *guize (yeares ripening to their harm)*
They grub man *up, and with a knife disarme*
The apt for Venus *wars: and, whiles this checks*
Time's *horse in his full speed, lost* nature *seeks*
And cannot find her self: so all *approve*
Male Concubines, *and which, like* Geldings *move*
Broke to a pace: Love-locks *and* Cloaths *which speak*
All Countreys, *and no* man. *Behold they break* 30
Numidian *ground! a* Citrian *board comes out*
On painted Carpets *plac'd, and round about*
A Troop *of* waiters *stand: and, drown'd in wine,*
Upon the floore wallows an herd of Swine.
A Tree *which did a* Patrimony *cost,*
Fetcht (for the ruine of a Land) *to boast*
A new Nobility, *did counterfeit*
With spots *the* cheaper gold: *On which were set*
By the Earth-rounding-Soldier (*that* now *hurl'd*
His Arms *aside) the spoyls of all the* world. 40
His throat *had* wit.   A Terbot, *that did dive*
In Corsick Seas, *rose at* his Board *alive;*
There Oysters *pull'd out of the* Lucrine *lake,*
Onely for Sawce *to lure his hunger back.*
Now Phasian *waves are of their* birds *bereft:*
And the dumb banks (*save* winds) *have nothing left*
To sing amongst the widowed *leaves.   As dire*
Is the field's *fury:* The base Romans *hire*
Their votes *out for the* chime, *and touch of* Gold.
A venal people: venal Senate: sold 50

Praeterea gemino deprensam gurgite praedam
Faenoris ingluvies, ususque exederat aeris.
Nulla est certa domus : nullum sine pignore corpus :
Sed veluti tabes tacitis concepta medullis,
Intra membra furens, hiris latrantibus errat.
Arma placent miseris; detritaque commodo luxu
Vulneribus reparantur : inops audacia tuta est.
Hoc mersam caeno Romam, somnoque jacentem
Quae poterant artes sana ratione movere,
Ni furor, & bellum, ferroque excita libido?   60
    Tres tulerat fortuna duces, quos obruit omnes
Armorum strue diversa feralis Enyo.
Crassum Parthus habet : Libyco jacet aequore Magnus :
Julius ingratam perfudit sanguine Romam.
Et, quasi non posset tot Tellus ferre Sepulchra,
Divisit cineres : hos gloria reddit honores.
    Est locus exciso penitùs demersus hiatu,
Parthenopen inter, magnaeque Dicharchidos arva,
Cocyta perfusus aqua, nam spiritus extra
Qui furit effusus funesto spargitur aestu.   70
Non haec Autumno tellus viret, aut alit herbas
Cespite laetus ager : non verno persona cantu
Mollia discordi strepitu virgulta loquuntur :
Sed chaos, & nigro squallentia pumice saxa
Gaudent ferali circum tumulata cupressu;
Has inter sedes Ditis pater extulit ora,
Bustorum flammis & cana sparsa favilla :
Ac tali volucrem Fortunam voce lacessit.
    "Rerum humanarum, divinarumque potestas,
"Fors cui nulla placet nimium secura potestas,   80
"Quae nova semper amas & mox possessa relinquis :
"Ecquid Romano sentis te pondere victam?
"Nec posse ulterius perituram extollere molem?
"Ipsa suas vires odit Romana juventus,
"Et quas struxit opes, male sustinet. Aspice late
"Luxuriam spoliorum & censum in damna furentem.
"AEdificant auro sedesque ad sydera mittunt.
"Expelluntur aquae saxis : mare nascitur arvis,
"Et permutata rerum statione rebellant.
"En etiam mea regna petunt, perfossa dehiscit   90
"Molibus insanis tellus, jam montibus haustis

Favour: even Age *let her free vertue fall,*
And right by bribes was justled to the wall:
And Majesty *lay flat, with gold sought out.*
Cato *himself repuls'd was by the rout;*
He that o'recame more sad, who blusht to see
That Cato *should have fewer* votes *than he.*
For 'twas the people's *and the* time's *disgrace:*
'Twas not a man, *but* virtue *lost the place,*
And the old Roman honor: *here then lyes*
Rome, *her own* Merchant, *and own merchandise.* 60
Besides now use on use, *mens* principals
So swell'd, it overwhelm'd them.   No man calls
His house his own.   None uningag'd: but debt
Like to a lingering disease, doth fret
Into their barking bowels; being pain'd
They cry to Arms: *and wealth with* ryot *drayn'd*
Must heal with wounds: *safe* WANT *sets all on fire.*
Cast in this sleep, *and rowling in this* mire
What reasons can wake Rome, *but* war *and* blood?
Which till th'are felt, are never understood. 70
    Fortune *had rais'd three* Captains, *all which feel*
In several ways Enyo's *mortal steel.*
In Asia, Crassus, Affrick, Pompey *slain:*
Ungrateful Rome *great* Julius *blood did stain*
And Earth, *to poize her* load *by portions just,*
(Greatness found this respect) divides their dust.
    A wide-mouth'd vault *descends to* Hell's *black-hall,*
'Twixt great Dicarchis *fields, and* Naples *wall,*
Lav'd with Cocytus *streams, whence all the heath*
About is blasted with a Sulph'rous *breath:* 80
Where Autumn *is the mother of no* fruits,
Out of the Summers Turf *no glad* herb *shoots,*
No tender sprigs, *inspir'd by* vernal *songs,*
Are heard to warble with melodious tongues:
But Chaos, *and rocks sweating with black dew,*
Delight in Canopies *of fatal* Ewe.
Here Pluto *rose in funeral flames and smoke,*
And with these words light Fortune *did provoke:*
    "Divine-*and*-humane-*things*-commanding-Power,
"Fortune, *that likest no height that's too* secure, 90
"*That lov'st* new *things, and (gain'd) discard'st them straight,*

"Antra gemunt : & dum varios lapis invenit usus,
"Inferni manes coelum sperare jubentur.
"Quare age, Fors, muta pacatum in praelia vultum
"Romanosque cie, ac nostris da funera regnis.
"Jampridem nullo perfundimus ora cruore,
"Nec mea Tisiphone sitientes perluit artus,
"Ex quo Sullanus bibit ensis & horrida tellus
"Extulit in lucem nutritas sanguine fruges.
   Haec ubi dicta dedit dextrae conjungere dextram   100
Conatus, rupto tellurem solvit hiatu.
Tunc Fortuna levi defudit pectore voces :
   "O genitor, cui Cocyti, penetralia parent
"Si modo vera mihi fas est impune profari,
"Vota tibi cedent, nec enim minor ira rebellat
"Pectore in hoc, leviorque exurit flamma medullas.
"Omnia quae tribui Romanis arcibus, odi;
"Muneribusque meis irascor : destruet istas
"Idem, qui posuit moles Deus, & mihi cordi
"Quippe cremare viros, & sanguine pascere luxum.   110
"Cerno equidem gemina jam stratos morte Philippos,
"Thessaliaeque rogos, & funera gentis Iberae.
"Jam fragor armorum trepidantes personat aures.
"Et Libyae cerno tua Nile gementia claustra
"Actiacosque Sinus, & Apollinis arma frementis.
"Pande age terrarum sitientia regna tuarum;
"Atque animas arcesse novas. Vix navita Porthmeus
"Sufficiet simulacra virum traducere cimba,
"Classe opus est. Tuque ingenti satiare ruina
"Pallida Tisiphone, concisaque vulnera mande.   120
"Ad Stygios manes laceratus ducitur orbis.

   Vix dum finierat, quum fulgure rupta corusco
Intremuit nubes, elisosque abscidit ignes.
Subsedit pater umbrarum, gremioque reducto
Telluris, pavitans fraternos palluit ictus.
Continuo clades hominum venturaque damna
Auspiciis patuere Deum, namque ore cruenta
Deformis Titan vultus caligine texit.
Civiles acies jam tum spirare putares.
Parte alia plenos extinxit Cynthia vultus,   130
Et lucem sceleri subduxit. rupta tonabant

"*Shrink'st thou not yet beneath the* Roman *weight,*
"*Unable longer to support the Tower*
"*Of* Romes *recoyling Greatness?   Their own Power*
"*The* Roman *youth abhor, nor bear the piles*
"*Of wealth they rais'd. See their vast* Lux *of spoyles,*
"*And riches curs'd into a punishment!*
"*They build in Gold, and to the Firmament*
"*Exalt their seats. Here Seas with* stones expel,
"*There let them in with* Sluces, *and rebel*   100
"*Against inverted* Nature. *Not I 'scape:*
"*The earth delv'd through for their wild Heaps doth gape;*
"*The* Mountains *shovell's down: the* caves *now groan*
"*Where, whilst for several uses they dig stone,*
"*The*'Infernal *Ghosts are bid to hope for day:*
"*Then* Fortune *turn thy smiles to dreadful fray:*
"*Possess with rage the* Roman *breasts, and throng*
"*Our Realms with funerals. Methinks 'tis long*
"*Since these* black *jaws have been with Gore imbrew'd,*
"*Since my* Tisiphone *hath bath'd in* blood   110
"*Her thirsty limbs: since* Sylla's *sword was drunke,*
And horrid Earth nurs'd fruits from humane trunke.
   This said, and striving to give her his hand,
With reaching up he brake the cleaving Land:
Then Fortune *thus from fickle bosome says,*
   "*O* Sire, *whom all on that side* Styx *obeys,*
"*If without danger I the truth may tell,*
"*Thy wish is granted thee: nor to rebel*
"*Have I less mind then* thou : *or boyles my womb*
"*With a less rage. All I bestow'd on* Rome   120
"*I hate, and am fallen out with my delight:*
"*The* God *that rais'd these walls, the* same *shall slight.*
"*The sweet of burning* Towns, *of sucking* blood,
"*Is by me also fully understood.*
"*I see* Philippi *with two* Chiefs *there slain:*
"*Thessalian tombs: and funerals of* Spain.
"*The clash of* Arms *now strikes my trembling eare:*
"*The groans of* Libya : *and her* Nile *I hear :*
"*And* Actian *waves: and* Sol *cry, on. Expand*
"*The thirsty Kingdoms of they silent Land :*   130
"*And get more* Furys *help. A boat's too small*

Verticibus lassis montis juga, nec vaga passim
Flumina per notas ibant morientia ripas.

Armorum strepitu coelum furit & tuba Martem
Sideribus transmissa ciet; jamque AEtna voratur
Ignibus insolitis, & in aethera fulmina mittit.
Ecce inter tumulos atque ossa carentia bustis
Umbrarum facies diro stridore minatur.
Fax stellis comitata novis incendia ducit;
Sanguineoque recens descendit Juppiter imbre.   140
Haec ostenta brevi solvit Deus.   Exuit omnes
Quippe moras Caesar, vindictaeque actus amore
Gallica projecit, civilia sustulit arma.

   Alpibus aeriis, ubi Graio nomine pulsae
Descendunt rupes, & se patiuntur adiri,
Est locus Herculeis aris sacer; hunc nive dura
Claudit hiems canoque ad sydera vertice tollit:
Coelum illinc cecidisse putes. non solis adulti
Mansuescit radiis, non verni temporis aura:
Sed glacie concreta rigens, hiemisque pruinis   150
Totum ferre potest humeris minitantibus orbem.
Haec ubi calcavit Caesar juga milite laeto,
Optavitque locum, summo de vertice montis
Hesperiae campos late prospexit, & ambas
Intentans cum voce manus ad sidera, dixit:

   "Juppiter omnipotens, & tu Saturnia Tellus
"Armis laeta meis, olimque onerata triumphis:
"Testor ad has acies invitum arcessere Martem,
"Invitas me ferre manus, sed vulnere cogor,
"Pulsus ab urbe mea, dum Rhenum sanguine vinco,   160
"Dum Gallos iterum Capitolia nostra petentes
"Alpibus excludo: vincendo, certior exul:
"Sanguine Germano, sexagintaque triumphis,
"Esse nocens coepi, quanquam quos gloria terret,
"Aut qui sunt, qui bella volunt? mercedibus emptae,
"Ac viles operae; quorum est mea Roma noverca,
"Ut reor, haud impune; nec hanc sine vindice dextram
"Vinciet ignavus, victores ite ferentes,
"Ite mei comites, & causam dicite ferro.

"For Charon *to waft o're his* souls *withal*:
"It asks a FLEET: *and pale* Tisiphone
"*With the great ruine do* thou *gorged be*:
"*With ragged tushes chaw the tender wounds*:
"*The mangled* world *descends to* Stygian *sounds.*
  Scarce had she spoke, when (cleft with lightning sheen)
Trembles a cloud, and darts squeez'd *fire beween.*
The King *of* Shades *into* earth's *bosome sunk*:
And from his Brother's *thunder frighted, shrunk.*   140
Forthwith the fates of men, *and ills to come*
Heaven *shows by* signes: *for the deformed* Sun
Veils with a mist his blushing face, as far
From giving count'nance to a civil *war.*
The Moon *at full (to leave them groaping) pops*
Her light out too. The palsey'd Mountain-tops
(Supported with weak necks) come thund'ring down.
Nor wand'ring Rivers *run in channels known,*
To dye a natural *death.* Armies *appeare*
*In th'*Ayre, *and* Trumpets *(even in his own sphere)*   150
Alarum Mars. *Now hotter* AEtna *burns,*
And thunderbolts *for* thunderbolts *returns.*
Lo! 'Mongst the Tombs *and disinterred bones,*
The Gastly *shadows send up baleful groans*!
A blazing-Star *draws an unusual train*:
And a new Jove *descends in* bloody *rain*:
Heav'n soon these signes *expounds: for* Caesar *drove*
With his own *speed, and sweet revenges love,*
Threw down the Gallick, Civil *Arms took up.*
  On cloudy Alps, *where, winding to the top,*   160
The rock's *made passable by* Graecian *hands,*
A Temple *sacred to* Alcides *stands.*
'*Tis thatch'd with crusted* Snow, *and blends its gray*
Head with the Stars: *how like the* milky way!
It thaws not with the Sun's *Meridian rayes,*
Nor with the Spring's *warm breath: but pav'd with lays*
Of Ice *and* feathered Rain, *the* Heaven *it beares*:
For it both threatens and supports the spheares.
When He *(the* Soldier *glad) these* cliffs *did tread,*

"Namque omnes unum crimen vocat, omnibus una　　170
"Impendet clades. reddenda est gratia vobis:
"Non solus vici. quare, quia poena trophaeis
"Imminet, & sordes meruit victoria nostra,
"Judice fortuna cadat alea. sumite bellum,
"Et tentate manus, certe mea caussa peracta est.
"Inter tot fortes armatus nescio vinci.
　Haec ubi personuit, de coelo Delphicus ales
Omnia laeta dedit, pepulitque meatibus auras.
Nec non horrendi nemoris de parte sinistra
Insolitae voces flamma sonuere sequenti.　　180
Ipse nitor Phoebi vulgato laetior orbe
Crevit, & aurato praecinxit fulgure vultus.
Fortior ominibus movit Mavortia signa
Caesar; & insolito gressu, prior occupat haustus.
Prima quidem glacies, & cana juncta pruina
Non pugnavit humus, mitique horrore quievit:
Sed postquam turmae nimbos fregere ligatos,
Et pavidus quadrupes undarum vincula rupit,
Incaluere nives, mox flumina montibus altis
Undabant modo nata: sed haec quoque, jussa putares,
Stabant & vincta fluctus stupuere pruina:　　191
Et paulo ante lues jam concidenda jacebat.
Tum vero male fida prius vestigia lusit,
Decepitque pedes. passim turmaeque virique,
Armaque congesta strue deplorata jacebant.
Ecce etiam rigido concussae flamine nubes
Exonerabantur, nec rupti turbine venti
Deerant aut tumida confractum grandine coelum:
Ipsae jam nubes ruptae super arma cadebant,
Et concreta gelu Ponti velut unda ruebat.　　200
Victa erat ingenti Tellus nive, victaque coeli
Sidera, victa suis haerentia flumina ripis:
Nondum Caesar erat: sed magnam nixus in hastam
Horrida securis frangebat gressibus arva:
Qualis Caucasea decurrens arduus arce
Amphitryoniades, aut torvo Juppiter ore,
Quum se verticibus magni demisit Olympi,
Et periturorum disjecit tela Gigantum.
Dum Caesar tumidas iratus deprimit arces:
Interea volucer motis conterrita pennis　　210

And touch'd his wishes, from the Mountains head   170
Stretching his voice, (*the* Latian *fields survey'd*),
And both his hands *to* Heav'n, *thus* Caesar *said.*
   "*All powerful* Jove, *and thou* Saturnian *Land*
"Triumphant *oft,* safe *always* by my *hand,*
"*Witness I come unwilling to this warre,*
"*Unwilling* Clash: *but such my proud wrongs are,*
"*Expuls'd my* Country, *whilst I paint with blood*
"*The* Rhine, *whilst I the* Galls *the* Alps *exclude,*
"*Threat'ning again the* Capitoll. *Exil'd*
"*Farther by conquering* more: *the* Germanes *foyl'd,*   180
"*And sixty* triumphs *are my* crime. *But who*
"*Denounce this war? Blind with our beams! a crew*
"*Of trading* Soules, *step-children to my* Rome;
"*But* they (*I think*) *shall know too* upon whom:
"*Nor shall* mechanick *hands bind* these *with cords.*
"*Go* mine: *Go* victors: *plead the* Cause *with* Swords.
"*We* all *are in one fault: one fate threats* all:
"*You conquer'd* too. *If punishment must fall*
"*On them that* beat, *if* this *our* triumph *be,*
"*Let the* Dye *fall, and* Fortune *judge for* me.   190
"*Take up the war they throw you: try your force:*
"*If overcome,* my *case can be no worse.*
"*But* arm'd, *and with* such *men,* that *ne're can hap.*
   This said, the Delphick *bird her wings did clap,*
(*An* Omen *good*) *and in a* wood *beside*
A Bay-tree *crackling in strange fire was 'spy'd.*
Appolo's *self shone brighter then he us'd,*
And had a golden glory *circumfus'd.*
Stronger then Omens, Caesar did advance,
And with unwonted pace first snatch'd a Lance.   200
First bound with ice, and candyed with the driffe,
The earth was quiet with dull horror stiffe:
But when the Troops the clouds gives off, did take,
And trembling horses the waves fetters brake,
The heat snows melted; streight new rivers burst
Out of the hills: these *also streight were forc't*
To make a stand: whilst (loe!) new ice appears,
And liquid late makes work for Pioneers.
Then first deceiv'd the feet the slipp'ry ground,
And tript them up, Men, Arms, and whole Ranks, (round)

Fama volat, summique petit juga celsa Palati:
Atque hoc Romano attonito fert omnia signa:
Jam classes fluitare mari, totasque per Alpes
Fervere Germano perfusas sanguine turmas.
Arma cruor, caedes, incendia, totaque bella
Ante oculos volitant, ergo pulsata tumultu
Pectora per dubias scinduntur territa causas.
Huic fuga per terras illi magis unda probatur.
Et patria est Pontus; jam tutior est magis arma
Qui tentata velit: fatisque jubentibus actus.   220
Quantum quisque timet, tantum fugit: ocyor ipse
Hos inter motus populus, miserabile visu,
Quo mens icta jubet, deserta ducitur urbe.
Gaudet Roma fuga, debellatique Quirites
Rumoris sonitu maerentia tecta relinquunt.
Ille manu trepida natos tenet, ille penates
Occultat gremio, deploratumque relinquit
Limen, & absentem votis interficit hostem.
Sunt qui conjugibus maerentia pectora jungant,
Grandevosque patres: onerisque ignara juventus   230
Id pro quo metuit tantum trahit. omnia secum
Hic vehit imprudens, praedamque in praelia ducit.

Ac velut ex alto quum magnus inhorruit Auster,
Et pulsas evertit aquas non arma ministris,
Non regimen prodest: ligat alter pondera pinus,
Alter tuta sinu tranquillaque littora quaerit:
Hic dat vela fugae Fortunaeque omnia credit.
Quid tam parva queror? Gemino cum consule Magnus
Ille tremor Ponti, saevi quoque terror Hydaspis
Et piratarum scopulus: modo quem ter ovantem   240
Juppiter horruerat; quem fracto in gurgite Pontus,
Et veneratus erat submissa Bosphorus unda,
Proh pudor! Imperii deserto nomine fugit,
Ut Fortuna levis Magni quoque terga videret.

Tergo tanta lues Divum quoque numina vidit;
Consensitque fugae caeli timor. Ecce per orbem
Mitis turba Deum, terras exosa furentes
Deserit; atque hominum damnatum avertitur agmen.
Pax prima ante alias niveos pulsata lacertos

PRINCE HENRY
OF PORTUGALL

HONI·SOIT·QVI·MAL·Y·PENSE

CEUTA

In heaps deplor'd. *Big* clouds *with tempest's stroke,*   211
Their burthens threw. Nor blasts *with* whirle-winds *broke,*
Were wanting there, or vollyes of gross haile.
The concrete *raine fell ratling on the Mayle,*
Like showres of Arrows from a Parthian *bow:*
The Earth *was overcome with a deep snow:*
The Lamps of heaven *o'recome; with Christal bit*
The Rivers *overcome;* Caesar *not yet:*
But leaning on his speare, that would not yield,
With secure steps he *brake the horrid field:*   220
As when Alcmena's *son marched apace*
Down Caucasus: *or with an angry face*
When Jove *descended the* Olympian *hill,*
With Giants *blood* Phlegrean *plains to fill.*
Meanwhile swift Fame *is born with frighted wings,*
And perching on the Capitol, *sad things*
Tells the affrighted Romans: *that the* Maine
Is swarm'd with ships: The Alps *of a light flame*
With Troops, yet reeking with Sicambrian *gore,*
Arms, Blood, Death, Fire, *and* War *is drawn before*   230
Their eyes from head to foot: which makes them erre,
And see their danger *double through their* feare.
This *flyes by* land, *this* by, *and that to* Sea;
So for no *land his* native *changes* he.
He's safest now, the Chance of war that tryes,
And follows fates instinct: He farthest flyes
Whose feare is longest winged: (A grief to say!).
The people, led by wild amazement, stray
They know not whither: Rome *delights in flight,*
And scar'd Quirites *their sad mansions quite;*   240
At the bare *rumour of approaching* Arms,
Those *clasp with trembling hands their tender* barnes:
These *in their bosomes hold their* Houshould-Gods:
And hurry from their desolate aboads:
And in their prayers *kill the* absent *Foe:*
There are that to their wives *sad bosomes grow,*
And bedrid parents: youths *impatient heat*
Takes onely her, *on whom his soul is set.*
Some all, and to the war *unwisely sweep*
The prey, *for which 'tis made.—*

Abscondit galea victum caput, atque relicto   250
Orbe fugas Ditis petit implacabile regnum.
Huic comes it syncera Fides, & crine soluto
Justitia, & maerens lacera Concordia palla.
At contra, sedes Erebi qua rupta dehiscit,
Emergit late Ditis chorus horrida Erynnys,
Et Bellona minax, facibusque armata Megaera:
Laethumque Insidiaeque, & lurida Mortis imago.
Quas inter Furor, abruptis ceu liber habenis
Sanguineum late tollit caput, oraque mille
Vulneribus confossa cruenta casside velat.   260
Haeret detritus laeva Mavortius umbo,
Innumerabilibus telis gravis: atque flagranti
Stipite dextra minax terris incendia portat.
Sentit terra Deos, mirataque sydera pondus
Quaesivere suum, namque omnis regia caeli
In partes diducta ruit: primumque Dione
Caesaris acta sui ducit. comes additure illi
Pallas, & ingentem quatiens Mavortius hastam:
Magnaque cum Phoebo soror, & Cyllenia proles
Excipit, ac totis similis Tyrinthius actis.   270
Infremuere tubae, ac scisso Discordia crine
Extulit ad superos Stygium caput. hujus in ore
Concretus sanguis, contusaque lumina flebant.
Stabant aerati scabra rubigine dentes;
Tabo lingua fluens, obsessa draconibus ora
Atque intertorto laceratam pectore vestem
Sanguineam tremula quatiebat lampada dextra.
Haec ut Cocyti tenebras, & Tartara liquit,
Alta petit gradiens juga nobilis Apennini,
Unde omnes terras, atque omnia littora posset   280
Aspicere, ac toto fluitantes orbe catervas:
Atque has erumpit furibundo pectore voces:
  "Sumite nunc gentes accensis mentibus arma;
"Sumite, & in medias immittite lampadas urbes.
"Vincetur quicunque latet; non foemina cesset,
"Non puer, aut aevo jam desolata senectus.
"Ipso tremat Tellus, lacerataque tecta rebellent.
"Tu legem Marcelle tene: tu concute plebem
"Curio, tu fortem ne supprime Lentule Martem.
"Quid porro tu Dive tuis cunctaris in armis?   290

—*As when the* deep   250
Is plough'd up by Northwinds, *and her* roul'd *hills*
Are knock'd *together: And the* Seamen's *skills*
Avail not now; one *binds the splitting mast,*
Another *to the quiet shore doth hast,*
A third *to Sea and* Fortune *trusts with all.*
What talk I of small things?   *The* Generall
With both *the* Consuls, *The* great Pompey, *He*
Terror of dire Hydaspes, *and the* Sea,
The Pyrates rock, *whom (thrice triumphing late)*
Jove *trembled at, lest he should shake his state:*   260
Whom Pontus *(having crush'd it's* watry *braves)*
And Bosphorus *ador'd with crouching waves*:
(Oh shame!) deserting the State's *rudder, fled:*
That fickle Fortune *might t'have seen be sed*
Ev'n Pompey's *back.*   *A flight authoriz'd so,*
Involv'd the Gods, *and* Heaven *his back did show:*
See a mild troop of Gods *(loathing the rage*
That reigns *in mortals) take a pilgrimage,*
From a damn'd crew of Earthlings: *And first* Peace
(Beating her snowy Arms) her vanquish'd face   270
Hides with a cask, *and, flying from the* light,
Seeks the husht mansions of eternal Night:
With Her *pure* FAITH; *and* JUSTICE, *(her* sword *broke);*
And CONCORD, *in a rent and mourning Cloak.*
On th'other side, where Hell's *wide jaws respire,*
Grim Pluto's *train springs rife:* Erinnys *dire,*
And fierce Bellona, *and flame-girt* Megeare,
And Death, *and* Fraud, *and multiplying* Feare.
Amongst whom Rage, *like* Bacchus *(his reines broke)*
Runs headlong, and with bloody helm doth Cloake   280
A thousand ugly faces digg'd with wounds
With heavy shafts: a Martial Target *sounds*
Worn with his left, *and, from his* right hand *hurl'd,*
A blazing fire-brand terrifies the world.
The stars are pos'd: light-headed Atlas *reels,*
Wond'ring to miss the weight that poys'd heaven's *wheels.*
The factious Gods come down on earth *to side.*
And Venus *first her* Caesar *justify'de,*
Pallas *with her, and* Mars *that shakes a whole*
Oak for a speare; and with his Sister, SOL: 290

"Non frangis portas? Non muris oppida solvis,
"Thesaurosque rapis? Nescis tu Magne tueri
"Romanas acies? Epidauria moenia quaere,
"Thessalicosque sinus humano sanguine tingue.
Factum est in terris, quicquid Discordia jussit.

The Translator's Postscript

Here Petronius breaks *off* abruptly, *thereby* as well as in many *imperfect places* of his *own Copy*, proving as good as his word, that he had *not added thereto the last hand.* In which thing alone I have translated him to the life, for neither have I added *mine* to the *English*: onely making so much use thereof, as to shew the *Rule* and *Model*, which (*indubitably*) guided our Camoens in the raising his Great Building, and which (except *himself*) that I know of, no Poet ever *followed* that *wrought in great,* whether *ancient,* or *modern.* For (to name no more) the *Greek* Homer, the *Latin* Virgil, *our* Spencer, and even the *Italian* Tasso (who had a *true,* a *great,* and *no obsolete story,* to work upon) are in effect wholly *fabulous*: and Lucan (though *worthily* admired) is as much censured by *some* on the other side, for sticking too close to *truth.* As Fabius for one;—"Lucan *full of flame and vigour, and most perspicuous in his Sentences: yet (that I may speak what I think) rather to be reckoned amongst the* Orators *then the* Poets." And Servius for another, with less manners in his expression; "*That which I said, that the Art of Poetry is forbidden to set down a naked story, is certain: for* Lucan *deserved not to be in the number of* Poets, *because he seems to have compiled a* History, *rather then a* Poem." Amounting to the same which is *objected* above in the *Introduction* to this *Essay* (which glanceth particularly at Lucan) and mended (as the Author thereof conceived) by the *Essay* itself, which is of a *mixt nature* between *Fable* and *History.*

And ATLAS GRANDSON, *and* Alcides (*found*
Like him *in all his acts*). *The trumpets sound,*
And DISCORD *with torn hair, her* Stygian *head*
Advances from a dell, her dim eyes *shed*
Intead of tears a clotted show'r of blood:
Two tire *of brazen* grinders *rusty stood*:
Her tongue *o'reflows with gore*: *her snaky locks*
Hang down over her face: *and through her* Frocks
Wide-gaping Rent, thrusting a bloody hand
About her head *she tost a flaming brand.*   300
She *leaving Hell and where sad rivers joyne,*
Touch'd the high top of noble Appennine:
From whence each realm and sea she might command,
And view the Troops *that roule on every Land*:
Then burst into these words, with fury warm,
    "*Arm all the* world: *with fell intentions arm*:
"*Shoot flames in midst of Towns (who e're he be*
"*That stands a* Newter, *is the* Victor's *fee*).
"*Fight* Boys, *fight* Maids, *fight* Old men *neer your end.*
"*Quake* Earth, *and shattered* stones *rebel.—Defend*   310
"*The laws* Marcellus.*—Do thou* Curio *preach*
"*Up tumults.—*Lentulus, *do not impeach*
"*Thy Martial spirit's working.—What mak't* thou,
"*Julius the while* freezing *in* Armour? *now*
"*Enter the gates, or scale the walls, and break*
"*The* Roman Fisk.*—*Pompey *art thou too weak*
"*To keep* Rome's *Towers*? *to* EPIDAMNUM *pass*
"*The* Ominous Scene, *and dye* Thessalian *grass*
"*With* Roman *blood.   To all that* DISCORD *said,*
EARTH *cry'd 'Tis done*: *and her command obey'd.*   320

TORQUATO TASSO

in his 6 part. fol. 47

VASCO, le cui felici ardite Antenne
  Incontro al *Sol,* che ne riporta il *giorno,*
  Spiegar le vele, e fer colà Ritorno,
  Dove egli par che di cadere accenne:
Non più di *Te* per aspro mar sostenne
  Quel, che fece a CICLOPE oltraggio, & scorno:
  Ne *chi* turbò *l'Arpie* nel suo soggiorno,
  Ne diè più bel *Subjetto* a Colte *penne.*
Et hor *quella* del colto e buon LUIGI
  Tant' oltre stende il glorioso volo
  Che i tuoi spalmati *Legni* andar men lunge.
Ond' a *quelli,* a cui S'alza il nostro *polo,*
  Et a chi ferma incontra i suoi vestigi,
  Per *lui* del corso *tuo* la fama aggiunge.

VASCO, *whose bold and happy ships against*
  The Rising Sun (*who fraights them home with day*)
  Display'd their wings, and back again advanc't
  To where *in Seas all Night he steeps his Ray:*
Not more then Thou, *on rugged Billows felt,*
  He *that bor'd out the Eye of* POLYPHEME;
  Nor He *that spoyl'd the* HARPYES *where they dwelt,*
  Afforded Learned Pens *a fairer* Theam.
And this *of Learn'd and honest* CAMOENS
  So far beyond now takes it's glorious flight,
  That thy breath'd Sailes *went a less Journey, Whence*
  To Those *on whom the* Northern Pole *shines bright,*
And Those *who set* their *feet to* ours, *The boast*
Of thy Long Voyage *Travails at his Cost.*

THE
LUSIAD

OF

Lewis Camões

———————

First Canto

STANZA 1

Armes, and the Men above the vulgar File,
Who from the *Western Lusitanian* shore
Past ev'n beyond the *Trapobanian*-Isle,
Through *Seas* which never *Ship* has sayld before;
Who (brave in *action,* patient in lŏng *Toyle,*
Beyond what strength of *humane* nature bore)
　　'Mongst *Nations,* under *other Stars,* acquir'd
　　A *modern Scepter* which to *Heaven* aspir'd.

2

Likewise those *Kings of glorious memory,*
Who sow'd and propagated where they past
The Faith with the *new Empire* (making dry
The *Breasts* of Asia, and laying waste
Black Affrick's vitious Glebe) And *Those* who by
Their deeds at *home* left not their names defac't,
　　My *Song* shall spread where ever there are *Men,*
　　If *Wit* and *Art* will so much guide my *Pen.*

3

Cease *man of* Troy, and cease thou *Sage of* Greece,
To boast the *Navigations* great *ye* made;
Let the high Fame of Alexander cease,
And Traian's Banners in the East display'd:
For to a *Man* recorded in this *Peece*
Neptune his *Trident* yielded, Mars his *Blade.*
　　Cease *All,* whose Actions *ancient Bards* exprest:
　　A brighter *Valour* rises in the *West.*

4

And you (*my* TAGUS's *Nymphs*) since ye did raise
My *Wit* t'a more then ordinary flame;
If I in *low,* yet *tuneful* Verse, the praise
Of your sweet *River* always did proclame:
Inspire me *now* with *high* and *thund'ring* lays;
Give me them *cleer* and *flowing* like *his* stream:
  That to *your* Waters PHEBUS may ordaine
  They do not envy *those* of HYPPOCRENE.

5

Give me a *mighty Fury,* Nor rude *Reed's*
Or rustick *Bag-Pipes* sound, But such as *War's*
Lowd Instrument (the noble *Trumpet*) breeds,
Which fires the *Breast,* and stirs the *blood* to *jars.*
Give me a *Poem* equal to the *deeds*
Of your brave *Servitors* (Rivals of MARS)
  That I may sing them through the UNIVERSE,
  If, whom *That* held not, can be held in *Verse:*

6

And *you,* a present *Pawn* to PORTUGALE
Of the old *Lusitanian-Libertie;*
Nor the less certain *Hope* t'extend the Pale,
One day, of *narrow* CHRISTIANITIE:
New *Terrour* of the *moorish Arsenale:*
The foretold *Wonder* of our *Centurie:*
  Giv'n to the World *by* GOD, the World to win,
  To give *to* GOD much of the World agin.

7

You, fair and tender *Blossom* of that *Tree*
Belov'd by *Him,* who dy'd on *One for Man,*
More then whatever *Western* MAIESTIE
Is styl'd MOST CHRISTIAN, or CAESAREAN.
Behold it in your *Shield!* Where you may see
Orique's *Battaile,* which ALPHONSO wan,
  In which CHRIST gave for *Arms,* for *you* t'emboss,
  The same which *He himself* bore on the *Cross;*

8

You (pow'rful *King*) whose *Empire* vast the *Sun*
Visits the *first* as soon as he is born,
And eyes it when his Race is *half-way* run,
And leaves it *loath* when his tyr'd Steeds *adjourn.*
You, who we look should clap a yoak upon
The bruitish Ishmaelite, become your scorn;
    On th'*Eastern* Turk, and Gentil who still lies
    Sucking the *stream* which water'd Paradise.

9

That *Majestie* which in this *Brow* appears
(This *tender* one) suspend for a small time,
Already such, as in your perfect years
When Fame's immortal *Temple* you shall climbe.
Those *milder* eys, with which you banish *Feares,*
Bend to the *ground:* on *which,* by num'rous *Ryme,*
    You'l see in *me* a Passion overgrown,
    To make the *Portugal-Atchievements* known.

10

You'l see a strange love to my *Native-soyle,*
Not mov'd with *Vile* but high *immortal Meed:*
For, to be compted is a Meed not vile
The *Trumpet* of the *Nest* where I was bred.
By *That,* their names drawn great, and laid in oyl
You'l see, of whom you are the *Sov'raign Head:*
    And judge, which is the greater *Honour* Then
    To be *King* of the *World,* or of *such Men.*

11

Hear *me,* I say, for not for Actions *vaine,*
Fantastick, Fabulous, shall you behold
Yours prais'd, though *forraigne Muses* (to obtaine
Name to *themselves*) have ev'n *feign'd names* extold.
Your Subjects *true* Acts are so great, *they staine*
And *credit* all the *Lyes* of *others* told;
    Stain Rhodomont, that puffe Rogero too,
    And Mad Orlando, though their deeds were true.

12

For *These*, I give you a fierce Nunnio
Who *King* and *Country* propt, almost alone.
An Egas, a *Don* Fuas, whose worths to show
I wish my *Voice* could reach great Homer's tone.
For the *twelve Peers*, I other *twelve* bestow
That past to England, and Magrizzo one.
  Th'*illustrious* Gama in the Reare I name,
  Who rob'd the *wandring Trojan* of his Fame.

13

Then (if to Match with Charles The Great of France,
Or one you seek to rival Caesar's name)
The *first* Alphonso see, who with his *Lance*
Eclipses whatsoe're *outlandish* Fame!
And *Him*, who by successful Valiance
Rescu'd and snacht his *Realm* from *civil* Flame!
  The *second* John, unconquer'd by the sword!
  The *Fourth* and *Fifth* Alphonsos, and the *Third*!

14

Nor shall my Verses in Oblivion leave
Those Chiefs, who, in the *Kingdoms* of the *Morn*,
Their name in *Armes* unto the *starres* did heave,
By whom your ever-conqu'ring *Flag* was born:
Matchless Pacheco: Two Almeydas brave,
Whom weeping Tagus will for ever mourn:
  Terrible Alburquerque: Castro bold:
  And more, whom *death* had not the pow'r to hold.

15

And whilst I *These* do sing, and dare not *you*,
Great *King* (for I aspire not to that height)
Take *you* your *Kingdomes* reynes your Hand into,
And furnish matter for a loftier flight,
Whilst your new *worth* may meet a *Vein* as new.
Your num'rous *Fleets*, and *Armies* pond'rous weight,
  Let the *World* groan with, and their *terrour* seize
  The Affrick-*Lands*, and Oriental-*Seas*.

16

On you with fixed eys looks the cold MOORE,
In *whom* he reads his ruine prophecy'de:
The barb'rous GENTILE (viewing *you*) is sure
You'l yoak his neck, and bows it to be ty'de.
The silver THETYS offers you in dow're
All her *blew Realm,* and doth the same provide.
  Took with your *Face* (where *love* is mixt with *Awe*)
  She seeks to buy you for her *Son-in-Law.*

17

In you, out of their Blissful Bow'rs *Above*
Your *Grandsires* souls (both famous in their way,
The *one* in golden *peace,* which *Angels* love,
T'other in bloody *War*) themselves survay.
In you they hope their *glories* shall improve,
Their *Vertues* be recoynd with less *Allay*:
  And wide they sit, to keep for *you* a roome
  In *Heav'n's* eternal *Temple* 'gainst you come.

18

But now, because your time creeps slowly an
To rule your People, who much wish it so;
Play with the new Attempt of a bold man,
That up with *you* this Infant-*muse* may grow;
And you shall spye ploughing the *Ocean*
Your ARGONAUTS, that they may also know
  You see them tost upon the angry *Brine*:
  And use your self to be invok'd betime.

19

They now went sayling in the OCEAN vast,
Parting the snarling Waves with crooked Bills:
The whispring *Zephyre* breath'd a gentle Blast,
Which stealingly the spreading *Canvas* fills:
With a white foam the *Seas* were overcast,
The dancing *Vessels* cutting with their *Keels*
  The Waters of the *Consecrated* DEEP,
  Where PROTHEUS's Flocks their *Rendezvouses* keep,

20

When in the HEAV'N OF HEAV'NS the *Deities*,
That have of humane things the Government,
Convene in glorious *Councel*, to advise
One future matters of the ORIENT.
Treading in Clusters the *Diaphane* skyes
Thorough the *Milky way* their course they bent,
    Assembled at the THUNDERER'S command
    By *Him* That bears the *Caduceian Wand*.

21

They leave the *patronage* of the *Seav'n spheres*
Which by the HIGHEST POW'R to *them* was giv'n:
The HIGHEST POW'R, who with an eye-brow steers
The *Earth*, the raging *Ocean*, and the *Heav'n*.
There, in a moment, every one appears;
Those, where BOOTES'S *waine* is slowly driv'n,
    Those, who inhabit *South*, and where the *Sun*
    Is born, and where his golden *Race* is *don*.

22

With an austere and high *Majestick* grace
Upon a *Christal* Throne, with *stars* imbost,
Sublime THE FATHER sate (worthy that place)
By whom the Bolts, dire VULCAN forg'd, are tost.
An Oderiferous Ayre blew from his face,
Able to breathe new life in a pale *Ghost:*
    A scepter in his *Hand*, and his *Head* crown'd
    With one stone, brighter then a *Diamownd*.

23

On glitt'ring *chairs* (imbroyd'red richly o're
With infinite of *Pearles* and finest *Gould*)
The other *Deities* were placed low'r,
As *reason* and the Herald *order* would:
The *Seniours* first, to honor them the more,
And after *them* those who were not so ould:
    When thus the most high JOVE the silence brake,
    With such a voice as made OLYMPUS shake.

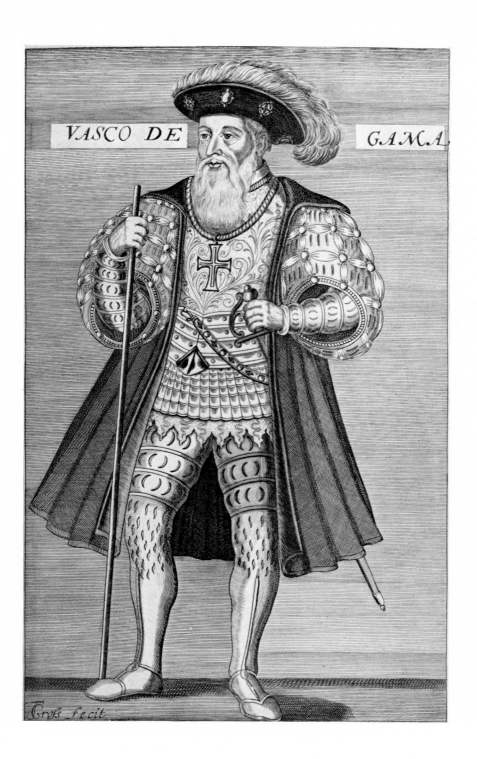

VASCO DE GAMA

Cro\ß fecit

24

"*Eternal dwellers* of the *Tow'r divine,*
"And *Impirean*-Hall with *starred* Vault;
"If the much *Vertue* of the valiant Line,
"Of Lusus be not worn out of your Thought;
"You needs must know what the *great* Fates design
"To crown the former Wonders *Those* have wrought,
  "That they shall darken with their *evening-Glory*
  "Th'*Assyrian, Persian, Greek,* and *Roman* story.

25

"*Your selves* were witnesses, with what a poor
"And naked Army it was giv'n to *Them*
"To take from the well-fix't, and num'rous Moor
"All that sweet Tagus waters with his stream.
"Then 'gainst the stout *Castilian-Warriour*
"Heav'n still beheld them with a fav'ring beam:
  "And still in fine with glory and Renown
  "The *hanging Trophies* did *their Churches* crown.

26

"I speak not (*Gods*) of that more ancient name
"Which with the *Queen of Nations* they did get
"When (led by Viriatus) so great fame
"They wan, whilst They and *hostile* Rome were met.
"I pass their other *Clash* with that proud *Dame*
"(Which 'tis impossible you should forget)
  "When a *Bandito* did their *Truncheon* bear,
  "Who feign'd himself *inspir'd* by a tame *Deare:*

27

"See *now,* how trusting to uncertain Waves
"In a fraile Barke, through ways untrod before
"(Fearless of horrid *Boreas,* and the Braves
"Of the fierce *Southern wind*) they throw at more!
"How (having yoak't before that *Sea* which laves
"Affrick's *North*-side, and yoakt her *Southern-shore*)
  "They bend their purpose and their forces turn
  "To win the *Cradle* of the budding Morn.

28

"To *Them* is promis'd by eternal FATE
"(Whose high *decrees* no *Power* can ere revoke)
"To be perpetual *Porters* of that *Gate*
"Through which the *Sun* first guides his silver spoke.
"They've spent at Sea the bitter Winter's date;
"The men are harast, and with Travaile broke.
  "'Tis now high time (as it appears to *me*)
  "To shew them that new Land where they would be.

29

"And therefore, since they have (as you have seen)
"So many *dangers* in this Voyage past;
"Tost through so many *Seas* and *Clymates* been;
"Of so sharp adverse *Winds* felt many a Blast;
"I purpose now they shall as friends be in
"The AFFRICK-*Land* refresh't with some Repast;
  "And, having victual'd there their wearied *Fleet,*
  "Proceed in their long course as it is meet.

30

Thus JOVE: when in their course of *Parliament*
The *Gods* reply'd in order as they Sate,
And to and fro by way of Argument
Upon the matter calmly did debate.
Then FATHER BACCHUS stiffly did dissent
From what great JOVE propos'd; As knowing, that
  His Fame ith' EAST must suffer an eclipse
  Should *there* arive the *Lusitanian*-ships.

31

He of the FATES had understood, from SPAIN
How that a *warlike People* was to come
Thorough the middle of the OCEAN,
Which all the *Indian-Coast* should overcome,
And which, with *modern* Victories, should stain
All *old* ones, whether *forraign,* or their *own.*
  It griev'd him sore, those *Actions* should be drown'd
  Which still in NYSA made his name resound.

32

He looks on INDIA as his old *Acquest*,
From whom nor *Time,* nor *deeds* by *others* don,
Had rob'd the stile of CONQ'ROUR OF THE EAST,
By ALL THAT taste the streams of *Helicon.*
But now he fears *that* Glorie's neer it's *West,*
In the black Water of *Oblivion*
    To set, should their desired Port obtain
    The valiant PORTINGALLS That Plough the *Main.*

33

Fair VENUS holds up the contrary Theam
Affected to the *Lusitanian-Nation,*
For the much likeness she observed in Them
To her old ROME, for which she had such passion,
In their great hearts, in the propitious beam
Of their to-AFFRICK-fatal constellation,
    And in the charming musick of their *Tongue,*
    Which *she* thinks *Latine* with small *dross* among.

34

These things did CYTHEREA move: But more
Because from FATE of truth she heard it sed
That all those Lands her *Altars* should adore
Where this Victorious *People* should be spred.
So *one,* to keep what was *his* own *before,*
T'other, to gain *new* honors to her head,
    Contest and stickle for their *sev'ral* ends,
    And *Both* are backt and favour'd by their Frends.

35

As when the fierce *South-wind,* and fiercer *North,*
Have got into the thickest of a WOOD,
Breaking the Boughs to force a passage forth
Through matted shades, impetuous and wood;
The Air, *that* yells; and all the *mountain* roar'th,
The *Leaves* are scattred, and the strong *Rocks* mov'd:
    Such was the tumult which amongst the GODS
    Was raised then in the *Supream Aboads.*

36

But MARS, who with more cordialness did take
Then any of the rest, the GODDESS' part;
Whether it were for old *Affection*-sake
Or for this valiant *People's own* desart
(His look confest him vext before he spake)
Amongst the GODS upon his feet did start.
  His heavy *Target,* at his shoulder hung,
  (Displeas'd, and dreadful) he behind him flung.

37

Lifting a little up his Helmet-sight
('Twas Adamant) with confidence enough,
To give his Vote himself he placed right
Before the Throne of JOVE, arm'd, valiant, tough:
And (giving with the butt end of his Pyke
A great thump on the floor of purest stuffe)
  The *Heav'ns* did tremble, and APOLLO's light
  It went, and came, like colour in a fright.

38

And thus he said; "O *sire,* whose will (whate're)
"All which thou hast created must obay:
"If *These,* who seek another *Hemisphere,*
"Thou wouldst not have to perish in the way,
"Whose deeds and Valour once thou heldst so deare,
"And did'st of old ordain what they assay:
  "Then hear no more (since thou'rt a *Judge* upright)
  "Reasons, from one who sees by a false light.

39

"For if sound *Reason* did not plainly show
"It self here vanquisht by excess of *Feare,*
"'Twere prop'rer BACCHUS should *his* pains bestow
"For LUSUS's Race, who was his *Minion* deare.
"But let this spleen of his at present goe;
"'Tis an *ill stomach* rising at *good cheare:*
  "And *envy* never found the way in fine
  "To do *Man* right, or what the GODS designe.

40

"And *Thou* (the Father of great *Constancy*)
"From the determination thou hast tooke
"Recoyle not. It is imbecility
"When once a Thing's begun, then back to looke.
"But since in speed the winged Mercury
"Outstrips the *Winds*, a *Shaft*, the swiftest *Brooke;*
    "Let *Him* now shew them to some *Countrey*, where
    "They may refresh, and news of India heare.

41

The pow'rful *Father* having said the same,
Gave with a nod the Soveraign *Assent*
To that which Mars said here with greater flame,
And over *All* his holy Nectar sprent.
Streight through *the milky way*, by which they came,
The Gods to their respective *Stations* went,
    Making a low obeysance to the *Throne*
    As they past by in Order one by one.

42

Whilst this in the High-Court is passing now
And beautiful Of Heav'n Omnipotent;
The *warlike People* the salt *Ocean* plough
Leaving the *South*, and face the *Orient*,
'Twixt Madagascar's Isle, where all things flow,
And Ethiopia's barren Continent.
    'Twas in that month, when Sol the *Fishes* fryes
    To which fear'd Brontes turn'd two Deities.

43

So pleasantly they went before a Wind
As those That now had got the *Heav'n* to frend.
Serene the Ayre was, and the Weather kind:
No Clowd, nor ought that danger might portend.
The Promontory Prassus left behind,
Which antient Ethiopia doth defend,
    Neptune disclos'd *new Isles* which he did play
    About, and with his billows danc't *the Hay*.

44

VASCO DE GAMA (a most valiant *Guide,*
Born and pick't out for that great *Enterprise,*
Of a high Soul, and strongly fortify'de,
Who FORTUNE to him by his *Boldness* tyes)
Stands *off,* to leave this *Land* upon one side,
Thinking, that uninhabited it lies;
      And *on* his course determines to proceed:
      But otherwise the matter did succeed.

45

For streight, out of that *Isle* which seem'd most neer
Unto the *Continent,* Behold a number
Of little *Boats* in companie appeer,
Which (clapping all wings on) the long Sea sunder!
The *men* are rapt with joy, and, with the meer
Excess of it, can onely *look,* and *wonder.*
      What Nation's this? (within themselves they say)
      What Rites? what Laws? what King do they obay?

46

Their coming, thus: in *Boats,* with finns; nor flat,
But apt t'o're-set (as being pincht and long)
And then they swim like Rats. The *Sayles,* of Mat
Made of *Palm-leaves,* wove curiously and strong.
The Mens *Complexion,* the self-same with *that*
HEE gave the *Earth's* burnt parts (from *Heaven* flung,)
      Who was more *brave,* then wise; That this is True
      The Po doth know, and LAMPETUSA rue.

47

The *Cloaths,* they came in, were a Cotton-*Plad*
With divers *Colours* strip'd, and *white* the ground;
Which *some* cast queintly under one *arm,* had;
Others, about their *Middles* streightly bound;
All else from the waste *up* remain'd unclad:
Their *weapons, Skeyns,* and crooked *Faulchions:* Round
      Terbants upon their heads; and, as they row'd,
      Resounded *Timbrels* in an *antick Mode.*

48

Waving their hands and kerchers, *These* made signe
To those of Lusitania to stay:
But the swift *Prows* already did incline
To come to Anchor in the *Island's* Bay.
Land-men, and *Sea-men* in this work *All* joyne,
As all their labours should have end that day.
  They haule the Roapes; *strike, strike,* the crew resounds:
  The salt Sea (stricken with the Anchor) bounds.

49

They were not Anchor'd, when the uncouth Folke
Already by the Cordage did ascend.
Their jovial countenances *wellcome* spoke,
To whom the Lordly *Chiefe* did (courteous) bend.
Bids streight the Boards be spread, the Bottles smoke,
With that rich juice which is the *Poet's* frend.
  Ours pow'r it into Bowles, and All *They* fill
  The burnt by Phaethon spare not to swill.

50

They ask (and still the cheerie Bowle goes round)
In the *Arabick-language,* "Whence The Fleet?
"*Who,* and of *whence,* the *men;* and Whither Bound,
"And through what Seas *It* came where now they see't?
Hereto the valiant Lusitanians found
Such answers as were proper, and discreet:
  "We are the Portugheses of the West,
  "We go to seek the Countreys of the East.

51

"All the great Ocean have we sail'd, and crost,
"To the *Antartick* from the *Artick* Strand
"Gone all the Round of Affrick's spacious Coast;
"We have felt many a *Clyme,* seen many a *Land.*
"We serve a potent *King,* who hath ingrost
"His *Peoples* loves so, that, at his command,
  "With cheerful faces, not vast *Seas* alone,
  But we would pass the Lake of Acheron.

52

"And 'tis by *that comand* we travel now
"To seek the *Eastern Land* which INDUS laves :
"By *that* this distant *Ocean-Sea* we plough,
"Where none but *Monsters* sayl'd the horrid Waves.
"But now 'tis reason, *We* should likewise know
"(If *Truth* have found a Harbour in your Caves)
　　"Who *you* are? what this *Land* in which you dwell?
　　"Or, if of INDIA you can Tydings tell?

53

"*We are* (one of the *Isle* replying said)
"Strangers unto this *People, Law,* and *Place;*
"The *Natives* being such, as *Heav'n* hath made
"Without the light of *Reason,* or of *Grace.*
"We have a *Law* of TRUTH, which was convay'd
"To *Us* from that *New-light* of ABRAM'S Race,
　　"Who houlds the *World* now in subjection due,
　　"By *Father,* GENTILE; and, by *Mother,* JEW.

54

"*This little Isle* (a barren healthless Nook)
"Of all these Parts is the most noted *Scale*
"For such as at QUILOA'S Traffick look,
"Or to MOMBASSA, and SOFALA, sayle.
"Which makes Us here some inconvenience brook,
"To gather, for a mortal life, and frayle :
　　"And (to inform you in one word of All)
　　"*This little Isle* Men MOZAMBIQUE call.

55

"And now (since you come seeking through long toyle
"INDIAN-HYDASPES, and the *Spicy Strand*)
"You shall have such a *Pilot* from this Isle,
"As through the waves the way doth understand.
"'Twere also good, you here repos'd a while,
"And took in *fresh provisions* from the Land;
　　"And that *our Governour* did come Aboard,
　　"To see what else may need for Him t'afford.

56

This the *Barbarian*, and retreated then
Into his Boates with all his companie,
Departing from the *Captaine*, and his Men,
With demonstrations of due Courtesie.
Mean time APOLLO in the Sea did pen
The golden *day*, and down to sleep doth lye,
  Leaving his *Sister* so much Torch to burn
  As may suffice the *World* till he return.

57

With unexpected joy their hearts on floate,
Blithely they pass the Night in the tyr'd *Fleet;*
To think that in a Country so remote
The news so long desired they should meet.
Within themselves they ruminate, and noate
The mens odd fashion, and admire to see't,
  Or how a People of their damned way
  Could take such root, and bear so vast a sway.

58

The silver *Moon's* reverberated Ray
Trembled upon the *Chrystal Element;*
Like *Flow'rs* in a great *Meade*, at middle *May,*
The *stars* were in the azure *Firmament.*
The furious *Winds* all husht and sleeping lay
In drowzy *Hyperborean* Caves dark-pent;
  Yet those of the Armada do not sleep,
  But in their turns accustom'd watches keep.

59

And when AURORA left her Spicy Bed,
Shaking her deawy locks the Earth upon;
And drawing, with a lilly-hand, the red
Transparent Curtains of the waking *Sun,*
To work go *All;* over the Decks to spred
The shadowing *Sailes,* and all their Streamers don,
  To entertain with feasting and with joy
  (Advancing in his Barge) the *Isle's* VICE-ROY.

60

Merrily sayling he advanc't, to see
The *Lusitanian-Frigates* in the Road,
With fresh provisions from the Land: For *Hee*
Still hopes, they are of that inhumane Brood,
Which, from their *mountains* neer the CASPIAN SEA,
The fruitful *Lands* of ASIA overflow'd;
    And, by permission of the POW'R DIVINE,
    Usurpt the *Empire* of GREAT CONSTANTINE.

61

The *Captaine*, with a meen benevolent,
Receives the MOORE, and all his company.
Things of great price he doth to *Him* present,
For such Occasions carryed purposely:
Gives him *Preserves,* and gives him of that queint
Unusual liquor which gives jollity.
    The MOORE receives it *all* in courteous part,
    But what he *Eats* and *Drinks* most glads his heart.

62

The nimble *Lusitanian* Mariners
Upon the shrowds in admiration hung,
To see a *mode* so different from theirs,
And barb'rous gibbrish of that *broken Tongue.*
No less confus'd the subtle MOORE appears,
Eying their *colour, habit,* and *ships* strong.
    Then, asking all things; This amongst the rest,
    If happily they came from TURKIE, prest.

63

Moreover, to behold desireth Hee
The *Books* of their *Religion, Law,* and *Faith:*
To see, if with his *own* the same agree
Or *that* of CHRIST (as he suspects) he saith.
And (that he *All* may note, and *All* may see)
He prays the *Captain,* shew him what he hath
    Of *Armes,* which by his *Nation* used are
    When with their Enemies they go to War.

64

To *whom* the valiant *Captaine* made reply
By one well versed in that *Bastard-Tongue*:
"*Illustrious Lord,* I shall to thee descry
"My *Self,* my *Faith,* and th'*Armes* I bring along.
"Neither of *Turkish-blood* nor *creed,* am I;
"Nor of a *Countrey* that delights in wrong.
    "In fair and warlike *EUROPE* was I born,
    "I seek the famous *Kingdoms* of the MORN.

65

"*We* worship HIM, who is by *every* Nature,
"(*Invisible, and visible*) obay'd,
"HIM, who the *Hemispheres,* and *every* Creature,
"(*Insensible, and sensible*) hath made:
Who gave Us *his,* and took on Him *our* feature:
"Whom to a shameful death *his own* betray'd:
    "And *who* from HEAV'N to *Earth* came down in fine,
    "That *Man, by* HIM from *Earth* to HEAV'N might climbe.

66

"Of this GOD-MAN sublime, and infinit,
"The *Books* which thou desir'st I have not brought,
"For that in *Books* we need not bring that Writ,
"Which (written in our *Hearts*) we have by rote.
"For th'*Arms,* whereof thou hast desir'd to git
"A sight, with all *my* heart I do allow't,
    "To see them as a *Friend;* For well I know,
    "Thou ne're wilt wish to see them as a *Foe.*

67

This having said, the ready-*Officers*
He doth command to shew the *Magazeen.*
Out come the *Backs,* and *Breasts,* glitt'ring and terse;
Fine *Mayles,* safe *Coats,* with quilted plates between;
Bucklers, where various Imagerie appeares;
Ball, Lead, and Iron; *Muskets* of Steel sheen;
    Strong *Bows,* and *Quivers* with barbd *Arrows* wedg'd;
    Sharp *Partesans;* and *Halberts* double edg'd.

68

The *morter-pieces* come; and with *them* came
(Confounding where they light) *Granadoes* dire;
Yet would he not permit the sons of Flame
Unto the dreadful *Cannon* to give fire.
For *valiant spirits* (which are still the same
With *generous*) to boast their utmost Ire,
　　To few, and timid *soules*, cannot indure.
　　"To be a Lyon among *Sheep,* 'tis poor.

69

But now the Moore from what he heard and view'd,
(All which he did observe attentively)
Conceiv'd within his Breast a certain *feud,*
A root of *Envy,* and *Malignity;*
Yet no such thing his outward gestures shew'd:
But, with a smiling hollow Courtesie,
　　He with himself resolves to treat them faire,
　　Till he his purpose may by deeds declare.

70

Pilots the *Captain* at his hands doth pray,
His *Ships* as far as India to guide:
Assuring him they shall with ample pay
For all their pains therein be satisfy'de.
The Moore consents; but still the poyson lay
Close, where it was, invenoming his side:
　　For, had he pow'r of blasting with his breath,
　　Instead of *Pilots,* he would give him death.

71

So great the *hate* was, and so great the *spight,*
Which to the *strangers* suddainly he took;
Knowing they follow that *unerring light,*
The Son Of David holds out in *his* Book.
"O the deep secrets of that Infinite
"Into the which no mortal eye can look!
　　"That *They,* whom Thou to be thy *friends* hast chose
　　"Should never be without perifidious *Foes.*

72

The trech'rous MOORE, when he his fill had seen,
Departeth from the *Frigates* with his *Crew*
(As false in heart, as flatt'ring in his meen)
And feign'd Regards on all the *Sea-men* threw.
Through the short Traverse of the *humid Green*
The Boats had quickly cut, when, wellcom'd to
    The shore, and met by an obsequious Train,
    To his known *House* they wait him back again.

73

The famous THEBAN, from th'*aethereal Hall*
(*He,* in his Thigh, whom JOVE his Father bore)
Seeing this meeting with the PORTINGALL
Is an abomination to the MORE*;*
Hath in his Brain a *Stratagem,* which shall
(He hopes) destroy him quite upon that score.
    Now whilst this plot is forging in his head,
    Unto himself these angry words he sed;

74

"Is it already then by FATE ordain'd,
"That so great *Victories,* and so renown'd,
"Shall by the men of PORTUGAL be gain'd
"On *warlike* People, and on *Indian* Ground?
"And I (son of the HIGHEST, unprofan'd
"With *carnal* mixture, and in whom are found
    "Such rare *Indowments*) must *I* suffer FATE
    "To a meer man *my* honors to translate?

75

"Unto the son of PHILIP it is true
"Such pow're the GODS did in those parts afford,
"Twas one with *Him,* to *See,* and to *subdue,*
"And MARS himself did homage to his *Sword.*
"But can it be indur'd, that to so *Few*
"FATE such stupendious puissance should accord,
    "That *that* of MACEDON, of ROME, and MINE,
    "The LUSITANIAN GLORY should *out-shine?*

76

"It must not, nor it shall not. For before
"This *Swabber* shall arrive the wished Land,
"I'l spin him such a Webb on yonder shore,
"That he shall never see the *Eastern*-strand.
"I'l down to *Earth,* and spur th'inraged MORE:
"The Iron cooles that suffer'd is to stand.
    "And who so means a business sure to make,
    "He by the foretop must occasion take.

77

Thus saying (vext, and little less then mad)
Upon the *Affrick*-shore he did descend,
Where, in a humane shape and visage clad,
To neighb'ring PRASSUS he his course doth bend.
The shape he took on him (thereby his bad
And false *designe* the better to commend)
    Was of a MOORE in MOZAMBIQUE known,
    Old, wise, and with the GOVERNOUR all one.

78

And (entring to his *Patron* when he spy'de
The fittest season to infuse his guile)
He tells him; "*These,* who in the Harbour ride,
"Are men That live by robberie and spoyle:
"That *Fame,* from *Nations* rang'd on the Sea side,
"With *hue and crye* pursu'd them to their *Isle,*
    "Of whom these *Vagabonds* a *Bootie* made
    "When they had anchor'd with pretence of *Trade.*

79

"Moreover I would have thee know (quoth Hee)
"These bloody CHRISTIANS (as I understand)
"With *Flames* and *Pyracies* have fill'd the *Sea,*
"As well as with their *Robberies* the *Land;*
"And that they have it in designe, how *Wee*
"May be reduc't too to their proud command:
    "How they may rob *us* of our *goods,* and *lives,*
    "And take for *Slaves* our *children,* and our *Wives.*

80

"And *this* I *know*, to morrow by day-breake
"To come on shore for water they intend,
"*Arm'd*, with their *Captaine:* Can Men plainer speake?
"They mischief mean, to feare it, who pretend.
"*Thou*, arm'd with *thine*, the same advantage take;
"Them in close *ambush* quietly attend:
  "Who, thinking to catch thee at unawares,
  "Will come with ease to fall into thy snares.

81

"And, should it so fall out, that by this feat
"They should not wholly be destroy'd, and slain;
"Another *Plot* (the which will give thee great
"Content, I'm sure) I have within this Brain.
"Send them a *Pilot*, skill'd so in deceit,
"And how to lay an undiscerned Train,
  "That he may lead them blinded, where they may
  "Be kill'd, wreckt, sever'd, or quite lose their way.

82

This said by *Him*, who plaid so well the Moore
Whom *years* and *Fraud* made wise to obviate Harmes;
Thanking him much for his advice mature,
About his Neck the Zeque throws his armes.
And from that instant bids his *Bands* be sure
To be all ready for the *Morn's* Allarmes.
  That so, when land the Lusitanian shou'd,
  He may convert their *water* into *blood*.

83

Farther (t'effect that other false device)
A *Moorish Pilot* he did ready git,
Subtle, dissembling, and in mischief wise,
To whom so great a Trust he might commit.
Him, through such *Seas*, where such and such *Coast* lyes,
He bids to guide the *Lusitanian Fleet*,
  That, should the danger in one place be past,
  It may be sure to perish at the last.

84

Now visited th' *Apollinean* Ray
The *Nabathêan* mountains with a smile,
When Gama and his *men* themselves aray
To go and fetch *fresh-water* from the *Isle.*
Plac't with good order in the Boates are They,
As he had known of the intended guile;
    And in a sort he did so: "For the *Wise*
    "Have a *divining* soul that never lyes.

85

Moreover for the *Pilot* he had sent
To land before, in need whereof he stood;
To which the sound of *Warlike Instrument*
Was all the answer he had understood.
For *this,* As likewise, to be confident
Of a false *Nation* being never good,
    He went as well provided as he could
    With no more people then three Boats could hold.

86

But the keen Moors (pickeering on the Strand
To keep them from the Fountain's thirsted draught,
With Buckler one on *Arm,* and dart in *hand,*
Another with bent *Bow,* and poyson'd *Shaft*)
Stay for the valiant Portingalls to land,
In secret Ambush others hid with craft:
    And send (to make them think the business sure)
    A small *Forlorn,* as *Faulkners* throw their *Lure.*

87

On the white Beaches the black *Warriours* prance,
Waving and vap'ring all the *Levell* o're;
And with heav'd *Target,* and with threat'ned *Lance,*
Dare the bold Portingalls to come on shore.
The noble people have not patience
To see the *doggs* grin at them any more:
    But spring in *Covey,* with such equal hast
    One could not say which landed first, or last.

88

So a brisk *Lover* in the bloody PLACE
(His beauteous Mistress *by* in a *Balcon*)
Seeks out the *Bull*, and (planted face to face)
Curvets, runs, whistles, waves, and toles him on;
But the stern *Bruite*, ev'n in a moment's space
(His horned Brow low'd to the Earth) doth run
    Bellowing about like mad; and (his eyes shut)
    Dismounts, strikes, kills, and tramples underfoot.

89

Loe, from the *ships* the Flames out of the hard
And furious *Cannon* roll'd, to Heaven rise!
The *Bullets* murther, whom the *Sound* but scar'd:
The hissing Aire, struck, bandies back the noise.
The MOORS hearts melt in them, they are so fear'd;
And the same passion chills their blood to Ice.
    Now *He*, That lay in hidden ambush, flyes:
    And *He*, That ventur'd the Incounter, dyes.

90

The *Lusitanian* People rest not here:
But, following their success, destroy and slay.
The *Wall-less-Town*, and *timber-Houses* there,
They waste with *fire*, and flat with *Cannon* lay.
His *sally* now the MOOR repents full deer,
For which he thought a cheaper price to pay.
    Now he blasphemes the *War*, curses *ill luck*,
    Th'old *devil*, and the dam that gave him suck.

91

The flying MOORS their Javelins backward threw
Faintly, through feare, and haste of their Retreat.
The Flint, the Stake, the Stone *in folio* flew.
"*Anger* makes all things weapons, when 'tis heat.
Now, to the *Victor* leaving the *Isle* too,
Unto the *Continent* they frighted get.
    The *Sea's* small Arm, that doth their *Isle* imbrace,
    They cut and traverse in a little space.

92

Some leap with their best goods into the Boats;
Some with their natural Oars swim to the shore;
This sinks into the crooked waves, then floats;
That puffs the Sea out, he new drank before.
The showred Bullets from the Cannon-Throats
The bruitish peoples brittle *Vessels* tore.
    Thus did the Portingalls in fine chastise
    The falshood of malicious Enemies.

93

To the *Armada* Victors they return
With the rich spoils and booty of the War.
Water they may have now to serve their turn
At their own time without controle, or bar.
The Moors (fresh smarting with their losses) burn
With greater malice then before by far:
    And, seeing so much unrevenged shame,
    Set their whole *Rest* upon the *After-game*.

94

The *Governour* of that infamous Land
To sue for Peace (as if repenting) sent.
Nor do the Lusitanians understand
That, under shew of peace, worse war is meant:
For the desired *Pilot* (underhand
Instructed in his trecherous intent)
    In token of the Peace which he did crave
    He sends to be their *Pilot* to the *Grave*.

95

The *Captaine* (who already understood
'Twas time to go his discontinued way,
And that the weather and the wind are good
To carry him for wished India)
Receives the *Pilot* with a cheerful mood:
And th'*Envoyé*, who did his answer stay,
    Dispatcht in haste (his minde is in the skye)
    To the large Wind lets all the Canvas flye.

96

Departed in this wise, the azure Waters
Of Amphitrite cuts the warlike Fleet,
Attended by a Troop of Nereus's daughters
(Sweet Friends, and no less constant, then th'are sweet)
The *Captain* (thought-less of those devilish matters
Which in his Brain the subtle Moor doth knit)
  Touching all India, and the Coasts they past,
  Informs himself by *Him* from first to last.

97

But the Moor well instructed in deceit
(To whom his lesson spightful Bacchus gave)
Prepares for Him, e're he to India get,
New Ills, either of *Thraldome,* or a *Grave.*
Giving accompt of *Indian* Harbours yet,
He shews him All that ever he did crave;
  That (judging Truth what he in *that* confest)
  The valiant People may not doubt the rest.

98

And then he tells him (with the same intent
With which false Synon witcht the men of Troy)
There is an *Isle,* not far from where they went,
Which ancient Christians from all times injoy.
The *Captain* (who to *all* he told him lent
Attentive Eare) at *this* so sprang with joy,
  That he conjur'd him with a golden spell
  To guide him speedy where those Christians dwell.

99

This very thing the trech'rous Moor design'd
Which the deluded Christian doth intreat,
Those, who possest this *Isle,* being the blind
Disciples of the filthy Mahomet.
Here death, and certain Ruine, he shall finde
(As he believes) for far more strong and great,
  Then Mozambique, is this *Isle;* by name
  Quiloa: frequent in the mouth of *Fame.*

100

To *It* the joyful *Fleet* he did incline.
But *Shee,* whose *Altars* in CYTHERA steam,
(Seeing him go astray from his right line,
To meet a death of which he doth not dream)
Permits not those in so remote a *Clyme*
To perish, whom *she* doth so much esteem:
      And puts them, with contrary winds, besides
      The *Place* to which the trayt'rous *Pilot* guides.

101

Then the base MOOR, when he did plainly finde
He could not work the Villany he meant;
Spawning another mischief in his minde,
And always constant to his black intent:
Tells him, that, since the waves are so unkinde
To put them *by* the *Port* to which they bent,
      There lyes another *Island* hard before,
      Where mixed live the CHRISTIAN, and the MORE.

102

Likewise in *this* the shameless Villain ly'de
(As his *Instructions* were in fine to do)
For not a *Christian-Soul* did there reside
But *All* of MAHOMET's detested Crew.
The *Captain* (who in all believ'd his Guide)
Made a short *tack* to bring his ships thereto:
      But (his *protecting Angel* saying, *nay*)
      Past not the *Bar,* and anchors in the *Bay.*

103

This *Isle* lay to the *Continent* so neer
That a small *Chanel* onely ran between:
In front thereof a *City* did appeer
Upon the Margent of the OCEAN green:
Fair and Majestical the *Buildings* were,
At a far distance plainly to be seen:
      Rul'd by an aged *King.* MOMBASSA, all
      The *Isle;* the *Town* too they MOMBASSA call.

104

And neer the same the *Captain* being come
Is much rejoyc't: *There* looking to behold
People, That had receiv'd their *Christendome,*
As the false *Pilot* promis'd him he should.
When loe, Boats coming from the *King,* with some
Provisions to the *ships*! For *He* was tould
    Of such a *Fleet* by Bacchus long before
    Taking the figure of another *More.*

105

Such the *Provisions* were, as *Friends* send *Friends,*
But there is poyson hidden in the Baite.
Of *Enemies* their *thoughts* are and their *ends,*
As will be too much manifested straight.
"O the perpetual danger which attends
"The lot of Mortals! O uncertain State!
    "That, where our trust seems to be anchor'd sure,
    "We are not *safe,* although we are *secure.*

106

"By *Sea;* how many *Storms,* how many *Harms,*
"*Death* in how many sev'ral fashions drest!
"By *Land;* how many *Frauds,* how many *Allarms,*
"Under how many *wants* sunk, and opprest!
"*Where* may a fraile *man* hide him? in what *Arms*
"May a short *life injoy* a little *Rest?*
    "Where *Sea,* and *Land,* where *Guile,* the *Sword,* and *Dearth,*
    "Will not *all* arm 'gainst the least *worm* o'th'*Earth?*

End of the first Canto.

Second Canto

STANZA 1

Now was the glorious *Guilder* of the *Pole,*
Who into *hours* distinguishes the DAY,
Come to his temp'rate and desired *Gole,*
From *Mortals* hiding his *celestial* Ray;
And GOD NOCTURNUS to descending SOL
Of THETYS's private Chamber turn'd the Kay:
    When to the *ships* the *faithless People* row'd
    Which were new-anchor'd in MOMBASSA'S Road.

2

Amongst them *one* (who had it in command
To Sugar o're the poyson) thus began.
"Undaunted *Captain,* That with *Keel* hast span'd
"The spaces of the briny Ocean;
"The noble *King* of this renowned *Land*
"At thy arrival is an o'rejoy'd Man:
    "The sum and heighth of whose Ambition is,
    "But to behold and serve thee with what's his.

3

"And, for he longs indeed thy Face to see,
"As *One's,* whose name *Fame* glories to repeat;
"Within the *Barr,* without suspition, *Thee*
"With all thy *ships* to come; he doth intreat.
"Also, because thy Men must wearied bee
"Through so long Toyle, and so excessive great,
    "He says, thou maist refresh them on the shore
    "Which *humane Nature* doth delight in more.

4

"Moreover, if thou seek for *Merchandize*
"Produc't by the Auriferous LEVANT;
"*Cloves, Cinnamon,* and other burning *Spyce;*
"Or any good and salutiferous *Plant;*
"Or, if thou seek bright *Stones* of endless price,
"The flaming *Ruby,* and hard *Adamant:*
  "Hence thou may'st *All* in such abundance beare,
  "That thou may'st bound thy *wish* and *Voyage* Here.

5

The *Captaine* by the Bearer did return
His humble thanks unto the *King,* and said;
Because the Sun already did adjourn
His Royal pleasure was not streight obayd:
But at the first disclosing of the *Morn,*
Whereby the *Anchors* might be safely weigh'd,
  With all assurance he would Enter, since
  He was oblig'd to more for such a *Prince.*

6

He asks him afterward, "if in the *Isle*
"Are CHRISTIANS, as the *Pilot* certify'de;
The subtle *Messenger,* (who smelt the Wile)
"Most of the *Isle* believe in CHRIST, reply'de.
With this, all jealousie he did exile,
And wise suggestion of the soul decride
  In the strange *Captaine;* Resting now secure,
  In a false *Nation,* and a *Sect* impure.

7

Yet, out of such as (having been condemn'd
For faults and horrid mischiefs done at home)
Had their lives giv'n them onely to the end
For desp'rate services with *Him* to come,
Two of the prime and craftiest Heads, to send
With the deceiptful MOORES, he pick't: By whom
  To spye the Town, and what their strength might be,
  And note those CHRISTIANS, whom he yearns to see.

8

And *He* by *them* sent presents to the *King,*
Through which the Friendship to himself pretended
Might be soft, pure, and without wavering,
Nothing of which was by the *King* intended.
Now was the wicked and perfidious *Ging*
Gone from the ships, and through the waves contended.
    The two of the *Armada,* with a faign'd
    Alacrity, on shore were entertain'd.

9

And when they had delivered to the *King*
The *Presents,* with the *message,* which they brought,
They walkt the *Town:* But no discovering
The half of what to have observ'd they thought.
For the suspitious *Moors,* not every thing
Would shew to them, which They to see besought.
    "Where *malice* reigns, there *Jealousie* doth nest,
    "Which doth suppose it in Anothers Brest.

10

But *He,* who hath perpetual *Youth,* and *Mirth*
In his plump Cheeks, ruddy with *blood* and *wine,*
And from two *mothers* took his wond'rous birth;
Who for the *ships* spun all this snare so fine;
Disguis'd into a Creature of the *Earth,*
Was in a House within the *City's line,*
    Feigning himself a man of *Christian* lore,
    And deckt an *Altar* where he did adore.

11

On *It,* the picture of that *Shape* he plac't
In which the HOLY SPIRIT did alight:
The picture of the *Dove* (so white, so chast)
On the BLEST VIRGIN'S head, so chaste, so white.
The SACRED TWELVE sate figur'd all aghast,
More wondring at *themselves,* then at the *sight;*
    As *Those,* who knew, what onely did inspire
    Their various *Tongues,* was those *faln* TONGUES OF FIRE.

12

The two *Companions* (carried by design
Where BACCHUS was in this deceitful guize)
Their knees devoutly to the *Earth* incline,
And raise their hearts to *Him* That's in the skyes.
Gums of the oderiferous and divine
PANCHAYA; Gums, in which the PHENIX dyes,
   LYEUS burnt: from whence it doth insue,
  That the *false* God came to adore the *true*.

13

Here entertained and carest that night,
With all good Treatment, and Reception fair,
Were the two *Christians:* heedless of the slight
By which with *holy shew* deceiv'd they were.
But when the *Sun* displayed his glorious light
(Having dispacht before him through the Ayre
   Old TYTHON's youthful Consort, to proclame
  With Blushes to the world her *Gallant* came)

14

The MOORS return, who to the *City* went,
With Orders from the *King* for entring There:
With them, the Couple whom the *Captain* sent,
To whom the *King* appear'd a Friend sincere.
So that (assur'd there is no Evil meant
To PORTINGALLS, which he should need to feare,
   And that CHRIST hath some *Sheep* amongst those *Wolves*)
  To enter the salt River he resolves.

15

His own ENVOYEES say, "they saw on shore
"Religious *Altars,* and a holy *Priest;*
"That they were nobly treated, and did snore
"Till fair AURORA left her rosie nest,
"Nor ought but joy, and wellcome more, and more,
"By *King,* or *People,* could they see exprest:
   "So that to doubt a thing so fair, and cleer,
   "No ground of reason did to them appeer.

16

Therefore the noble GAMA did receive
With open arms the MOORS That came aboard:
For wariest minds 'tis easie to deceive
When words and deeds so seemingly accord.
His *Ship* is cram'd with faithless folk, who leave
The Boats which brought them, ty'de to't with long Cord.
      Blithe they are *all,* as Those that understand
      They have the *Prey* as sure as in their hand.

17

Weapons, and Ammunition of the War,
They have on Land prepared secretly;
That, when the *Ships* are anchor'd past the *Bar,*
They may invade them, bold, and suddainly,
And, by this treachery, resolv'd they are
To ruine Those of LUSUS totally;
      Making them (unexpected) to pay, so,
      The score which they in MOZAMBIQUE owe.

18

Hoysting the holding *Anchors,* the ships Men
In the accustom'd *Nautick* clamour joyn'd.
To thrid the *Barr's Land-marke* they *bord* it then,
Giving the *fore-sails* onely to the Wind.
But fair DIONE (never absent, when
The gallant Folk need her in any kind)
      Seeing so neer so cruel a surprize,
      From HEAV'N to th'OCEAN like an Arrow flyes.

19

She calls together NEREUS's snowy daughters,
With all the azure Flock That haunts the *deeps;*
(For, being born from the salt-Sea, the Waters
In her obedience as their *Queen* she keeps)
And, telling them the Cause that thither brought her,
With all in Squadrons to that part she sweeps
      Where the *ships* are, to warn them come, *no nigh,*
      Or they shall perish fundamentally.

20

Now through the *Ocean* in great haste they flunder,
Raising the white foam with their silver Tayles.
Cloto with bosom breaks the waves in sunder,
And, with more fury then of custom, sayles;
Nise runs up an end, Nerine (younger)
Leaps o're them, frizled with her touching Scales:
 The crooked *Billows* (yielding) make a lane
 For the feard Nymphs to post it through the *Maine*.

21

Upon a Triton's back, with kindled Face,
The beauteous Ericyna furious rode.
He, to whose fortune fell so great a grace,
Feels not the Rider, proud of his fair load.
Now were they almost come upon the place
Where a stiff gale the *warlike Navy* blow'd.
 Here they devide, and in an instant cast
 Themselves about the *Ships* advancing fast.

22

The *Goddess,* with a party of the rest,
Lays her self plum against the *Am'ral's Prow,*
Stopping her progress with such main contest
That the swoln sayl the Wind in vain doth blow.
To the hard Oak she rivets her soft Brest,
Forcing the strong *ship* back again to go.
 Others (beleagu'ring) lift it from the Wave,
 It from the *Bar* of *Enemies* to save.

23

As to their *Store-House* when the Houswife *Ants,*
Carrying th'unequal Burthens plac't with slight
To their small shoulders (lest cold *Winter's* wants
Surprize them helpless) excercise their might;
This tugs *that* shoves, *one* runs, *another* pants;
Strength far above their size, they *All* unite:
 So toyl the *Nymphs,* to snatch and to defend
 The men of Lusus from a dismal end.

24

The *ship* (inforced *contre*) goes back, back,
In spight of those she carries, who with *Cries*
Handle the Sayls. They fume, their wits they lack;
From side to side the shifted *Rudder* flyes.
The skillful *Master* from the *Poop* doth crack
His Lungs in vain, for in the Sea he spyes
  A horrid Rock just just before the *Ship*,
  Threatning a Wreck should she advance a step.

25

Here the rude saylors raise a *Cry* indeed,
As they are busie at their work. The More
This hideous clamour strikes with such a dread,
As when in horrid fight the *Cannons* rore.
From *them* the cause of all this fury's hid:
Nor whom t'approach know *They*, or what t'implore.
  They think their *treacherie* is made appeer,
  And that for *it* they must be punisht heer.

26

Loe! in the twinckling of an Eye some dart
Themselves into their speedy Boats agin:
Others betake them to their swimming Art,
Making the Sea leap up as they plump in.
They vault o're the ship-sides from ev'ry part,
So mainly are they frightend with the din:
  Advent'ring rather to the Ocean, so,
  Then to the hands of a provoked *Fo*.

27

As *Froggs* (in ancient Ages *Lycian-Folkes*,
Confin'd to live in *Water* they deny'de)
If, basking heedles on the Banks, or Rocks,
Some *Person* on the suddain they have spy'de,
Skip back again, and fill the *Pond* with croakes,
Flying the danger which they have describe;
  And (scaping to their *Sanctuary* known)
  Shew above Water their black heads alone;

28

So fly the Moors.   And so the *Pilot* (who
To this great peril had misled the *Ships*)
Thinking *his* Treason was discovered too,
Into the briny water, flying, skips.
But that fixt *Rock* to scape and to exchue,
Which the sweet life might drive out of their lipps,
    The *Admiral* threw streight an anchor out;
    And close to her the others likewise do't.

29

Th'observing Gama, seeing the great fright
And unexpected of the Moors; withal
The *Pilot's* suddain and accusing flight,
Found what the bruitish Folke hatcht in their gall:
And seeing, how in spight of *wind,* in spight
Of *Tyde* (both with him) and in spight of all
    Their *Art,* the *Ship* would not advance a *head*
    (Holding it for a miracle) thus sed;

30

"O great, undreamt of, strange *deliverance!*
"O *Miracle* most cleer and evident!
"O *fraud* discover'd by blind *Ignorance!*
"O faithless *Foes,* and *Men* dev'lishly bent!
"What *Care,* what *Wisdom,* suffisance
"The stroake of *Secret* mischief to prevent,
    "Unless the Sov'raign Guardian from on *high*
    "Supply the strength of frail *Humanity?*

31

"Well into Us hath Providence infus'd
"What little safety in *these* Ports is known:
"Well have we found how much we were abus'd
"With *shows* of *Friendship,* and *Religion.*
"But since to *humane Prudence* is refus'd
"To pierce *intents,* and where such *masks* are on;
    "O thou (Guardian Divine) to guard *Him* daigne,
    "Who without *Thee* doth guard *himselfe* in vain.

32

"And since *thy* heart is toucht with so great Ruth
"For a poor People wandring on the Seas,
"As of thy goodness (whence alone it doth
"Proceed) to save us from such *Wolves* as these;
"Unto some *Haven* now, where there is *Truth,*
"Resolve to lead us for a little Ease;
    "Or shew us to the long desired *Coast,*
    "If for thy honour we desire it most.

33

These *pious* words the fair Dione heard
And (to compassion being mov'd thereby)
Goes from among the Nymphs, who sad appear'd
That they must lose so soon her company.
Now doth she pierce the *Stars;* now in the *therd*
Sphere, she is entertain'd : whence by and by
    (Having repos'd her) she doth forward move
    Towards the *Sixt,* where is her Father Jove.

34

And (ruffled with her motion) *now* so fair,
So fresh, so gay, so lovely is her *look;*
That *Starrs,* and *Heav'n,* and circumfused *Ayre,*
And *All* That see her, are with passion took.
Her *Eyes* (the Nests of Cupid whom she bare)
Breath'd such quick *Spirits,* and such *fire* they strook;
    They burn the *World* again like Phaeton,
    And to the *torrid* turn the *frigid Zone.*

35

And (to bewitch her *Sov'raign Sire* the more,
Whose *dearling* she was always, and his *joy,*)
She comes to Jove, as she had done of yore
In the *Idean* Grove to *Him* of Troy.
The *Huntsman,* who the Horns (transformed) wore,
For seeing thus that other Goddess coy;
    Had he seen *this,* had ne're been torn asunder
    By his own *doggs:* But di'de of *love,* and *wonder.*

36

The golden *Tresses* on her *shoulders* fell,
Whose whiteness smuts the Fleece of unfaln Snow:
Her *Breasts* (and those ev'n their own milk excel)
Playd with by unseen Cupid, trembling go:
Her *Cestos* white doth mounting flames expel,
Which, that *Boy* kindling, those white *bellows* blow:
    Of this fair *Pyle* the *Pillars* smooth, and round,
    Desires, like *Ivy*, have about them wound.

37

Those parts, of which *Shame* is the natural Screen,
In a thin Veile of Sarcenet she doth fold;
Not wholly *shewd*, nor wholly left *unseen*,
Not *Prodigal*, nor *niggard*, of *that* Gold.
But this transparent Curtain draws between,
To double the desire, by being control'd.
    Now Heav'n is fill'd with *jealousie*, and *love*:
    This mov'd in Mars, in Vulcan that did move.

38

And then, discov'ring in her Angels face
A *Sadness* temper'd with a little smile,
Like some nice *Dame*, who by the rude embrace
Of heedless *Lover* got a bruise, or soyl;
She's *pleas'd* and *angry* in one instant space,
And one while *chides*, and *laughs* another while:
    So spake the Goddess who admits no *Peer*,
    Less *sad* then *Minion*, to her *Father* deer.

39

"O *pow'rful Father*, I had always thought
"That, for such things on which my heart were set,
"Kinde I should finde thee, affable, and soft,
"Though some *Opposer* should the same regret.
"But since I see, without neglect, or fault
"Of mine, thy love is sounding a retreat;
    "What remedy? let Bacchus have his will:
    "In fine, *his* luck was *good*, and *mine* is *ill*.

40

"This *People* (who are *mine,* for whom I pore
"These tears out, which I see in vain distill)
"The more I *love,* I seem to *hate* the more;
"*Thou* being resolv'd to break me of my will.
"For *Them* I weep to thee, for *them* implore.
"And 'gainst my *Fate* in fine am fighting still.
  "Well then, because I *love* them they're misus'd,
  "I'l *hate* them, then they will be better us'd.

41

"But let them dye by bruitish Peoples hands;
"For since *I* was — and heer with pearly drops
(As when the *morning's-dew* on Roses stands)
Making a salt *Parenthesis,* she stops:
As if her words obey'd not her commands,
Through melting pity of the mens mishaps.
  "Then (going to proceed where she gave o're)
  "The mighty Thund'rer lets her say no more.

42

And, mov'd by that dumb *Rhet'rick* (which would move
A *Tygers* flinty Breast) with the same *Face*
Of cheerfulness, with which he doth remove
The Clowds from *that* of Heav'n, and Tempests chace,
He wipes her Tears, and (kindling with new love)
Kisses her *Cheek,* her white *Neck* doth embrace.
  Who, had he hated Portugal before,
  Would now have lov'd it meerly on *her* score.

43

And (pressing her *lov'd* face with *his*) She burst
Into fresh Tears, and faster then before:
As when, a child being beat by mother curst,
The more one moans it, it will sob the more.
Now, to allay this Passion, He is forc't
To tell her much which he till then forbore:
  And, with these words, out of the secret womb
  Of pregnant Fate, rips many things to come.

44

"Fair *daughter* mine, fear no adversitie
"Which to thy Lusitanians may betide;
"Nor *Any,* to have greater pow're with *me*
"Then the sweet Tears which from these cleer *Springs* glide
"For, let me tell thee (*daughter*) thou shalt see
"Both Greeks and Romans (so much magnify'de)
        "Forfeit their *ancient Honours* by the *New*
        "*Acts,* which this *People* in the *East* shall do.

45

"For if the *Eloquent* Ulysses fled,
"The Sirens Song, and dire Calypso's spell;
"And if Antenor with his ship did thred
"Th'*Illyrian-Sleeve,* and reacht Timavus's *Well;*
"And if 'twixt Scylla, and Charibdis dread,
"*Pious* Eneas with his *Navy* fell:
        "How much worse dangers pass *Thine* dayly over,
        "Who, sayling round the *world,* new *worlds* discover?

46

"Thou shalt see (*daughter*) *Cities,* and strong *Ports,*
"And lofty *Walls,* which *These* shall build, and found;
"Thou shalt see warlike Turks, and *their* proud *Forts,*
"By *These* destroy'd and level'd with the ground:
"The Indian Kings (secure in their free *Courts*)
"By a more potent King Thou shalt see bound.
        "*He,* in conclusion holding *All* in awe,
        "Unto that Land shall give a *better* Law.

47

"This very *Man,* who *now,* through so much fright
"And misty Errour, stumbles to the Ynd,
"Thou shalt see Neptune tremble at his sight,
"Curling his waves without a breath of wind.
"O wonderful, nor seen by mortal Wight,
"The *Winds* lockt up, and yet a *Storm* to find!
        "O valiant *People,* and for great things made,
        "Who make the Elements themselves afraide!

48

"That LAND, which *water* late to *Him* deny'de,
"Thou shalt behold it a commodious *Port*,
"Where in their way to rest them shall abide
"The *Ships* that (weary) from the WEST resort.
"All this wyl'd *Coast* in fine (which *now* hath try'de
"By wicked trechery to cut him short)
 "Shall pay him *Tribute;* knowing they must down,
 "If they withstand the LUSITANIAN CROWN.

49

"And Thou shalt see the ERYTHREAN lose
"It's native *red,* and *pale* with Terrour look:
"And see the potent *Kingdom* of ORMUSE
"*Twice* taken, *twice* subdu'de unto their yoak:
"And see the furious MOOR stands in a Muze
"With his *reverberated* Arrows strook:
 "That he may learn, if against *Thine* he fight,
 "His Treacherie on his *own* pate shall light.

50

"The famous *Fort* of DIO Thou shalt see,
"Being twice besieg'd, thy People *twice* defend.
"*There* will their prowess manifested be,
"*There* will their name in *Arms* to HEAV'N extend,
"*There* will they bring great MARS under their *Lee*
"With deeds which, told, would set the Hayr on end.
 "*There* will the falling MOOR blaspheming ban,
 "And dam with his last breath the ALCORAN.

51

"Thou shalt see GOA taken from the MORE,
"GOA, That by her loss at last shall gain;
"When, on the wings of Conquest made to soare,
"*Shee,* as the QUEEN OF ALL THE EAST shall raign.
"The stubborn GENTILES (who the *Sun* adore)
"High and triumphant *then,* she shall restrain
 "With a rough *Bitt,* and *All* who in that LAND
 "Against *thy* People dare to lift a Hand.

52

"Slenderly mann'd, and in poor order put;
"Thou shalt see held the *Fort* of CANANOWR;
"And shalt see won the *City* CALICUT,
"In *People* infinite, boundless in pow'r;
"And in COCHIN shalt see such honor got
"By *one*, shall stand in battail like a Tow'r,
  "That never *Lyre a Victor* did resound,
  "Who so deserv'd to be with Lawrel crown'd.

53

"Never was so LEUCATE of a flame
"With shocking *Fleets* when (gilding with their Trim
"The *Actian* waves) *hence* young OCTAVIUS came,
"Bringing *Italian* pow'rs along with *Him*;
"*Thence* ANTHONY (with a fresh *Victor's* name)
"*Barbarians* from the ORIENT, from NYLE's brim,
  "And from the farthest BACTRIA; and (the bane
  "Of *All!*) th'*Egyptian Mistress* in the Traine:

54

"As thou shalt see the *Sea*, and neighb'ring *Shores*,
"Fire with *thy* Peoples Battails. Who, in bands
"Shall *coupled* lead IDOLATERS with *Mores*
"(Triumphing over many *Tongues* and *Lands*)
"And (GOLDEN CHERSONESUS's pretious stores
"To farthest CHINA conquer'd by their hands
  "With the EAST's outmost Islands) in the end
  "Make all the OCEAN to their TAGUS bend.

55

"In so much (daughter *mine*) that, at the rate
"This *Nation's* valour passes humane bound,
"The WORLD hath not to match them in debate,
"From silver GANGES, to th'HERCULEAN SOUND;
"Nor from the *Northern Ocean*, to that *straight*
"Which the *affronted* LUSITANIAN found;
  "Though all the ancient HEROES (defide)
  "Should rise again to have the *mastry* try'de.

56

This having said, his *consecrated Poast*
(The son of MAY) down to the *Earth* he sends,
To finde some peaceful *Port* upon that *Coast*
Where the *Armada* may repose with Frends.
And (lest the valiant *Captain* should be lost,
If longer time he at MOMBASSA spends)
  He gives his *Legate* farther in command
  To shew him in his sleep that friendly *Land.*

57

Now swift CYLLENIUS cuts it through the *Ayre:*
Now to the *Earth* his winged feet declin'd.
Badge of his office, *the black Rod* he bare:
This HELL's sad Pris'ners doth release, and *bind:*
This lays asleep the Eye opprest with *Care:*
Whisking with *this* he doth outstrip the *Wind:*
  His *Hat of maintenance* upon his Crown:
  And thus he comes into MELINDE's Town.

58

With him he carries FAME, that *she* may tell
The *Lusitanian* prowess, and rare parts:
"For an illustrious *Name* is a strange *Spell*
"To attract *Love,* and *good Report* hath darts.
Thus he prepares their way with a sweet smell,
And takes up *lodgings* in the Peoples *hearts.*
  Now all MELINDE is on fire, to see
  What kind of men these valiant souls should bee.

59

From *thence* he parteth to MOMBASSA straight,
Where, what to do, the *Ships* uncertain stand;
To bid them, without question or debate,
Leave that Foes Harbour, and suspected *Land.*
"For, wicked plottings of infernal hate
"In vain are Force and Courage to withstand:
  "In vain, to extricate our selves, is *Wit,*
  "If HEAV'N do not both prompt, and second, *it.*

60

Now sable N<small>IGHT</small> had finisht half her Race,
And in the *Heav'n* the *Stars* with borrow'd light
Supply'd the *Moon's,* as *she* her *Brother's,* place;
And sleeping now was *Mortals* whole delight.
Th'illustrious *Captain* (who had all that space
Been kept awake about the last day's fright)
    Gave then to his tyr'd Eys a little sleep:
    The rest by *Quarters* did their *Watches* keep:

61

When in a *Vision* he did H<small>ERMES</small> see.
"And fly (*he bid him*) L<small>USITANIAN</small> fly
"The Ambush of a *wicked* King, which Hee
"Hath laid, to make thee yet obscurely dye:
"Fly, for the wind and Heav'n *Both* favour Thee.
"Thou hast the *ocean* calm, serene the *skye,*
    "And not far of another *King,* to frend,
    "On whose reality thou mayst depend.

62

"Look for no better entertainment *here,*
"Then what was giv'n by T<small>HRACIAN</small> D<small>IOMED</small>*;*
"Whose Horses (us'd to bloody Provendere)
" He with the Bodies of his *strangers* fed.
"Th'infamous Altars of B<small>USIRIS</small> (where
"*His* Guests inhumane *humane offrings* bled)
    "Unless thou quit it, look for in this place:
    "Fly a perfidious and a cruel Race.

63

"Steer straight alongst the *Coast,* and thou shalt light
"Upon a Countrey where more *Truth* resides;
"Close there, where burning S<small>OL</small> at constant hight
"The *night* and *day* with equal *line* divides:
"Then shall a *King* receive with much delight
"*Thee,* and thy *men;* and give to you (besides
    "Safety, and Treatment worthy of a *King)*
    "One, who the *Fleet* shall unto I<small>NDIA</small> bring.

64

Thus Hermes; who the *Captain* (parting) woke.
He, rowz'd out of his Nest in a great fright,
Perceives the circumfused darkness broke
With a shot *Ray* and *stream* of *divine light:*
And (seeing it imports *Him,* and his *Folke,*
From that infamous Land to take their flight)
      Commands the *Master,* with a spirit new,
      To hoyse the sayles unto the Wind that blew.

65

"*Set sayl* (he cride) set *saile* to the large Wind:
"*Heav'n* is our Guide, and God our course directs.
"These Eys saw the *Express,* he was so kind
"To send from his high *Court* to guard our steps:
At this, the *Mariners* before, behind,
As with one motion spring upon the Decks.
      They towe the Anchors in the ship-side
      With that rude strength which is the *Sea-mans* pride.

66

The self-same time they did their Anchors weigh,
(Hid in the mask of night) the trech'rous More
Sawing their Cables husht and silent lay,
So to destroy them being run ashore.
The Christians (though there shone not the least Ray,
Yet) in their heads the Eyes of *Lynces* wore.
      The *other,* finding how they were awake,
      With *Wings,* and not with *oares,* away did make.

67

But now did the sharp *Keels* go cutting through
The liquid *Element* of silver pure:
The *Wind* ('twas a *side-wind*) gently it blew
With motion calm, and steddy, and secure.
Discoursing, on their dangers past they chew
As they sayl on: for 'tis not easie sure
      To pass in silence a *deliverance*
      So great, and brought about as 'twere by chance.

68

The burning *Sun* had finisht *one* Career,
Began *another,* of his *annual* Race;
When, as far off as they could *ken,* appeer
Two *Vessels* creeping on the Water's face.
Knowing they must be Moors, who coast it there,
Forthwith ours *veer* their *Sayles* to give *those* chace.
    One (as more nimble, or as frightened more)
    To save her *People* ran *herself* ashore.

69

Her *Fellow* (not so light to make away)
Into the hands of those of Lusus falls,
Without or Mars to board her; or, to play
On her bruiz'd sides, black Vulcans horrid Balls:
For (she being weakly man'd, nor built for Fray)
At sight of his own Men the *Master* falls
    His *courage,* and his *sayles* (his wisest course).
    Had he resisted, he had far'd the worse.

70

Then Gama (who did this but to procure
A *Pilot* for the Indies so long sought)
Amongst those Moors thought to have found one sure,
But found he was deceived in that thought.
There's not a man of *them,* That can assure
Under what part 'tis of the *heav'nly* Vault.
    This *All* can tell him; That Melinde's nigh,
    Where he may finde a *Pilot* certainly.

71

The *goodness* of that King the Moors extol,
His *bounteous* nature, and his Breast *sincere,*
The *greatness* like the *goodness* of his *Soule,*
With other *parts,* which win him *love,* and feare.
The *Captain* easily believes the whole,
Concurring with that very *Charactere*
    Hermes had given in his sleep before:
    So goes, bid by the *dream,* and by the More.

72

That gladsome season 'twas, in which returns
Into EUROPA's *Ravisher* the *Sun;*
Putting new lights in *both* his gilded Horns
Whilst FLORA pours out AMALTHEA's *one.*
And now that glorious *Planet* turn'd the *Morn's*
Red finger, to that *moving Feast;* whereon
       He, who was *dead* the soul-sick *world* to heal,
       To it's *Redemption* rose to put the *Seal:*

73

When, to that distance from the which their Eys
Might reach MELINDE, the *Armada* came;
Adorn'd with *Tapistrie* triumphant-wise,
As that *day's holiness* it well became.
The *Standart* trembles, and the *Streamer* flyes,
The Scarlet-*W*ast-cloaths at a distance flame,
       The *Drums* and *Timbrels* sound. Thus they that BAR,
       Like CHRISTIANS enter, and like MEN OF WAR.

74

With *People* hid is the *Melindian* shore,
That come to see the joyful *Fleet.* More kind
Are *These,* more *humane,* and of *truth* have more,
Then *Those* of *all* the *Countreys* left behind.
The *Lusitanian Navy* drops, before,
The heavy *Anchors,* which fast rooting find.
       One, of the MOORS they took, is sent on *Land:*
       To let the KING their coming understand.

75

The KING (who was already by report
Of those of LUSUS's gallantry possest)
The *Captain's* so frank entrie in his *Port*
Takes as a favour from so brave a Guest:
And with *true* heart, and in most *courteous* sort
(*Both* individual from a *noble* Brest)
       Bids the man pray them much to come on *Land,*
       Where they shall have his *Realms* at their command.

76

The *offer* as real *is*, as it appears,
The *words* full of unfeign'd *Sinceritie*,
Which the KING sent the noble *Cavaleers*,
Who had past so much *Land*, and so much *Sea*.
He sends them more, *Live-sheep* aboard, fat *Steers*,
And *Poultry* cram'd by Houswifes industrie,
      With all such *Fruit* as then in season was:
      And the *good will* the *Present* did surpass.

77

The well-pleas'd *Moor,* who with this *Errand* went,
The *Captain* pleas'd receiv'd, with what he brought;
And instantly another *Present sent*
Unto the KING, far fetcht, and dearly bought:
Illustrious *Scarlet* (colour of content),
Brancht *Coral* fine, for *Nobles* greatly sought:
      Of double nature, under water soft
      And *velvet-horn'd, hard-pen'd* when 'tis aloft.

78

Sends more, one dext'rous in th'*Arabick-Tongue,*
To treat a firm *League* with the ROYAL MORE,
Excusing him he did not leave his strong
And lofty *Ships,* to kiss his hand on shore.
Unto the noble KING, led through a Throng
Presents himself the fit *Ambassadore;*
      And with these words (which PALLAS herself dips
      In her own *Nectar*) disunites his lips.

79

"*Most high and mighty King,* to *whom* the pure
"And incorrupted JUSTICE from Above
"Gave, to restrain the rough and haughty MOOR;
"Nor more to *force* his *Feare,* then *win* his love:
"As to the strongest *Port,* and most secure
"Of all the EAST, Hither we flye; to prove
      "What FAME reports, and find in *It* and *Thee,*
      "A *certain* Port in our nesessitie.

80

"*We* are not Men, who spying a weak *Town*
"Or careless, as we pass along the shore,
"Murther the *Folks,* and burn the *Houses* down,
"To make a *booty* of their thirsted store:
"But (by a KING we have, of high renown,
"Sent from fair EUROPE, never to give o're
    "Our compassing the *World,* till we have found
    "The wealthy INDIA) thither are we bound.

81

"How *stony* yet some Race of People was!
"What *barb'rous* guize! what stile of a *Man-Hater*!
"To bar not their *Ports* onely (let that pass)
"But the cold *Hospitalitie* of *Water*!
"To whom have *we* done wrong? wherein (alas!)
"Have *we* discover'd such a *savage* nature,
    "To make so *many* of so *few* afraid?
    "That *Traps* and *Pitfals* should for *us* be made?

82

"But *Thou* (O gracious KING from whom, to have
"*True dealing* we are *sure;* and *hope,* we may
"That certain help too, which ALCINOUS gave
"Unto the wandring *Prince* of ITHACA:
"*To Thee* secure we come, as boldly crave
"*Of Thee,* conducted by the *Son* of MAY:
    "For, since JOVES Harbinger was *ours,* 'tis cleare
    "Thy *Heart* is *large,* is *humane,* is *sincere.*

83

"Nor think (O King) our noble *Chiefe* declin'd
"To come, to see and serve thee pers'nally,
"For any thing he scrupled of unkind;
"Or hollow dealing possible in *Thee:*
"But the true reason, why he stayd behind,
"Was, that in *all* he might obedient be
    "Unto *his* KING; who gave him in command
    "In *Port,* or *Roade,* never to go on Land.

84

"And, because *subjects* are the self-same Thing
"With *Members* governed by the *Head,* or *Crown;*
"Thou, bearing here the *Office* of a KING,
"Wouldst not that *Any* disobey'd his own.
"But, he doth promise an *acknowledging*
"Of thy great *Grace* and *favours* now bestown,
    "With *all* That can by *Him* and *His* be done,
    "So long as *Rivers* to the *Sea* shall run.

85

Thus He *harangu'd:* And, with one Voice, the whole
Presence (comparing notes there where they stand)
The matchless courage of the *men* extol,
Who traverse so much *Sea* and so much *Land.*
But the wise KING (revolving in *his* Soul
The PORTINGALLS's obedience to command)
    In Scales of *wonder* and of *rev'rence* weigh'd
    A KING, who so far off could be obey'd.

86

Then answers (gracious) with a Brow serene
Th'*Ambassadour,* to whom inclin'd he seem'd.
"Wipe all suspition from your Bosoms cleane;
"Let no cold Fear be harbour'd there, or teem'd:
"For such your *worths* are, and your *deeds* have been,
"To make you over all the *world* esteem'd.
    "And *They* who injur'd *you,* We will be bold,
    "Know not what price *Vertue* and *Honor* hold.

87

"That all your People do not come on shore
"Observing the respect due to our *Port,*
"Though in our *own* regard it grieve us sore,
"Yet our esteem of *them* is greater for't.
"For if *your Rules* permit it not, no more
"Shall *we* permit, that (onely to comport
    "With *our desires*) such *loyal* excellence
    "Should lose it self, or suffer Violence.

88

"But when tomorrows light shall come, to *greet*
"And *shew,* the WORLD, with our own Barges, *Wee*
"Shall go in person to the warlike *Fleet,*
"Which we so many days have long'd to see.
"And, if it need any convenience meet,
"Through shatt'ring storms, and keeping long at Sea,
  "A *Pilot* it may have, and *Victuals* here,
  "And *Ammunition,* with intention cleere.

89

This was his language, and LATONA'S Boy
Into the *Ocean* div'd. The *Messenger*
(Returning with this *Embassie* of joy)
To the *Armada* rows with merry cheer.
Out of all Breasts is banisht black Annoy,
Seeing the proper remedie is heer
  To find the *Land* whereof they sayl in quest:
  So all that night they keep a double *Feast*.

90

There wants not *there* the *artificial star*
Like trembling *Comet* (nor less cause of wonder).
The *Gunners* do *their* Part, making the *Ayre,*
Water, and *Earth,* resound with *Mortalls's* Thunder.
The CYCLOPPS (practising for t'other War
On JOVE) with *Bullets* rend the *Clowds* in sunder.
  Others on lofty *Cornets* (singing) playd:
  And *These* with *Musick* did the SPHEARES invade.

91

They answer from the *shore* at the same time
With *Squibs* that crack amongst the Rout: In gyres
The whizzing *Vapours* up to HEAVEN climbe:
Th'imprison'd Powder with a bounce expires:
Heaven's brazen Vault ecchoes the Voyces's chyme:
The *Sea's* cleer Glass reflects the joyful fires:
  The *Earth* is not behind them. In this sort
  Both sport in earnest, and *Both* fight in sport.

92

But *now* the restless *Heav'n,* wheeling about,
To their day-labours mortals doth incite;
And Memnon's mother (fair Appollo's scout)
Sets bounds to sleep by her arriving light;
With her approach dull shadows, put to rout,
In a cold sweat upon the Flowers light;
  When the Melindian King (embarqued) plide
  To see the *Ships* That in his Harbour *ride.*

93

The shores are crown'd with people (of a fire
To be *Spectators onely* of the *show*):
The *Scarlet* Coates flame with the *dye* of Tyre:
The glossie *Silks* with all *May's* flow'rs do blow.
Instead of *Arrows* (part of *Warr's* Attire)
And of the horn'd *Moon*-imitating *Bow,*
  Palm in their *hands,* in sign of *Peace,* they bear:
  Which on their *Heads* victorious Heroes wear.

94

In a *Canoe* (which was both long and broad,
And glissend in the Sun with *Cov'rings,* made
Of mixed *Silks*) Melinde's King is row'd,
Wayted by *Princes'* mongst their own obay'd.
In rich *Attire* (according to the *mode*
And custom of that Land) he comes arayd.
  Upon his Head he weares a *Terbant,* roll'd,
  Of *silk* and *Cotton,* with a Crown of *gold.*

95

A *Roabe,* of *Scarlet-damask,* (high-extold
By Them, and worth the wearing of a King)
About his *Neck* a Collar of pure *gold:*
The *work* worth twice the substance of the Thing.
A *Velvet* sheath a *dagger* keen did hold,
With *Diamond*-hilt, hang'd by a *golden* string.
  Sandals of *Velvet* on his *Feet* he wore,
  With *gold* and *pearl* imbroydred richly o're.

96

O're *Him* a round Silk-*Canopy* he had
Advanc't aloft upon a *gilded* Pole;
With which a *Boy* behind to *burn* forbad
Or *trouble* the Great KING, the beams of SOL.
Musick ith'Prow, so *merry* that 'twas *mad*,
Grating the Eare with a harsh noise. The whole
    Consort, is onely crooked Horns, wreath'd round,
    Which keep no time, but make a dismal sound.

97

No less adorn'd, the LUSITANIAN
From the *Armada* in his *Boats* doth dance,
To meet *Him* of MELINDE with a Train
Whom *much* their *cloaths*, but *more* their *deeds* advance:
GAMA comes clad after the use of SPAIN,
But wears a Cassock *ala mode de France:*
    The *Stuff*, a *Florence-Satin;* and the *dye*,
    A perfect *Crimson*, glorious in *their* Eye.

98

The *Sleeves* have *golden* Loops, which the Sun-shine
Makes too too bright and slippry for the Eyes:
His close *Camp-Trowzes* lac't with the *same myne*,
Which *Fortune* to so many men denyes:
Poynts likewise of the *same*, and *Tagging* fine,
With which his *Doublet* to his *Hose* he tyes.
    A *Sword* of massive *Gold*, in *Hanger* tyde:
    A *Cap* and *Plume;* the *Cap* set *at one side.*

99

Mong'st his *Camrades*, the noble *Tyrian dye*
(Not *liv'ry-wise*, but) sparcled here, and there,
The sev'ral *Colours* recreate the Eye:
So do the diff'rent *Fashions* which they weare.
Such their inamel'd *Cloathes* Varietie
(Compriz'd in one survey) as doth appear
    The painted *Bow*, in *water-colours* laid,
    Of JUNO's Minion, the *Thaumantian* Mayd.

100

The ratling *Trumpets, now,* their joy augment
As, *other times,* they had their courage done.
The *Moorish* Boats cover'd the Sea, and went
Sweeping the Water with their silks Anon.
The *Clowds* of HEAV'N the thund'ring *Cannon* rent,
And with new *Clowds* of *Smoak* put out the *Sun.*
     Before the *Blow* the winged lightning flies:
     The MOORS's *hands* stop their *Eares,* the *lids* their *Eyes.*

101

Into the *Captain's* Boate the KING doth come
(Folding him in his Arms) And He agin
With such respect and rev'rence, as become,
Doth both receive, and speak unto, the KING.
A while with wonder and Amazement, dumb,
The MOOR on GAMA stands considering,
     As He That highly doth esteem the Man
     Who came so far to seek the *Indian* Stran.

102

Then makes him a large proffer, of whate're
To do him good his *Kingdom* can afford;
And that he freely would demand it *there*
As his own goods, if ought he lackt aboard.
Adds, though till now he saw the LUSIANS ne're
Yet he from FAME had heard much of their Sword;
     And how, in other *Parts* of AFFRICA,
     They have had wars with People of *his* way.

103

And how through all that spacious LAND resown
The glorious *Actions* of that NATION,
When they therein did gain that *Kingdom's Crown,*
Where the HESPERIDES of old did won.
And *most* of That, which to the KING was known
(Although the least the PORTINGALLS had done)
     He spread out thin in words, and magnifide:
     But to the KING de GAMA thus reply'de.

104

"O great and gracious KING, who dost (alone)
"The *Lusitanian* People's sad estate,
"(By NEPTUNE'S rage, and *adverse Fortune,* thrown
"Into so many streights) Commiserate:
"The KING OF KINGS (who, from th'eternal *Throne,*
"Turning HEAV'N round, did the round *Earth* create,
 "Since *Mercy* is his chiefest Attribute)
 "Reward thee for it, for *We* cannot do't.

105

"*Thou* onely, of all Those APOLLO blacks,
"In peace receiv'st us from the Ocean vast:
"In *Thee,* from peril of *Eolian* Wracks,
"We find a *Refuge* kind, syncere, and fast.
"Whilst the *Sun* lights, whilst *Night* his presence lacks,
"In HEAV'N's blew *Meade* whilst *Stars* take their repast,
 "Where're *I* go, in either *Hemisphere,*
 "Thy *Name,* and *Praises,* shall be sounded there.

106

This humbly said, towards the *Fleet* they row
(The KING requesting that he *now* may see't).
Ship after *Ship* about it round they go:
That he of *All* may note *all* he thinks meet.
Lame VULCAN walks on *Lynstocks* to and fro,
With which the *Guns* salute him from the *Fleet.*
 The *Trumpets* play unto him in shril notes:
 The MOORS with *Cornets* answer from the *Boates.*

107

But when the gen'rous King had ceast to Noate
All That he would, nor heard with little wonder
Th'unusual *Instrument* with the wide Throate
That speaks so big, and tears the Clowds in sunder;
He bids them (in the *Sea* anch'ring the *Boate*)
Suspend their *Oars,* as they had done their *thunder:*
 That he may know *at large* of brave DE GAME
 Those things, which *lightly* he had heard from FAME.

108

The Moor doth into sev'ral questions run,
With *gust* inquiring, sometimes of the great
And famous *Wars* between our Nation,
And *Those* who do believe in Mahomet.
Now of the Land we dwell in, which the *Sun*
Bids last *good night*, when he makes hast to set;
    Now, of the Nations which therewith confine;
    Now of *his* ploughing through the *Gulphs* of *Brine*.

109

"But rather, valiant *Captain* (quoth the King)
"Make us a full and orderly *narration*
"Under what *Part* of the Celestial Ring,
"Under what *Clyme* ye have your Habitation;
"Also your ancient *Generation's* spring,
"And, of a Realm so potent the Foundation;
    "With the successes of your *Warrs:* For (though
    "I know them not) that they were vast I know.

110

"Tell us besides, of all that tedious *maze*
"Through which thou hast been tost with angry flaws
"On the salt *Seas,* observing the strange ways
"Of our rude Affrick, and the *barb'rous* Laws.
"*Tell;* For the *Horse* of the new *Sun,* the Day's
"Imbroydered *Coach* with golden *traces* draws,
    "Postilion'd by the Morn: The *Wind's* asleep,
    "And the curst *Billowes* couch upon the Deep.

111

"And if the *Winds* and *Seas* are husht, to hear
"The *story* thou shalt tell: no less are *Wee*.
"*Who* would not lend *your* Acts a *greedy* Eare?
"*Who* hath not heard of Lusus's Progenie?
"Sol (who the Brain of *man* doth purge and cleer)
"Drives not his *Coach* thus nigh us as you see,
    "To have Melindians thought so dull a *Breed,*
    "As not to value an *Heroick* deed.

112

"A daring War the haughty Gyants made
"Upon Olympus permanent and pure:
"Rash Theseus, and Perithous, did invade
"Grim Pluto's Kingdom horrid and obscure.
"If such *high Boys* as these the world hath had,
" 'Tis not less *hard*, nor will less *Fame* procure,
    "Then the attempting Heav'n and *Hell* by *Them*,
    "That *others* should attempt the *Watry Ream*.

113

"Diana's Temple built by Tesiphon
"(Rare *Architect!*) Horostratus burnt down,
"To be talkt of, though for a Thing ill done,
"And *dye defam'd*, rather then *live unknown*.
"If on so false, and vile Foundation,
"The sweet desire deceives us of *Renown*,
    "How much more lawful is't to seek a name
    "By deeds deserving everlasting Fame!

***End of the second* Canto.**

Third Canto

STANZA 1

Now what illustrious Gama, neer the *Line*,
Inform'd that King, report Caliope:
Breathe an immortal *Song*, and *voice* divine,
Into this mortal *Breast*, that's big with *Thee:*
So, never the great God of *Medicine*,
(To whom thou Orpheus bar'st) love Clycie,
    Court Daphne more, or call Leucothoe Frend,
    Since *Thou* in Beauty doest them *All* transcend.

2

Thou, *Nymph,* promote my pious just desire
To pay my Country what to *It* I owe;
That the whole *world* may listen, and admire
To see from TAGUS AGANIPPE flowe.
Leave PINDUS's flow'rs: For (Loe!) the MUSES's Sire
Bathes me in *Sacred* dew from top to toe.
>   If not, I swear thou hast some jealousie
>   ORPHEUS (thy joy) should be eclyps'd by *me.*

3

To hear the noble GAMA, In a *Ring*
Gather'd was all th'attentive Companie;
When (having sat a while considering)
Raising his manly Visage, thus said *He.*
Thou doest command me to unfold (O KING)
My noble NATION's *genealogie:*
>   Thou bid'st me not to tell a *forraign story,*
>   But of my *Own* thou bid'st me tell the glory.

4

Upon *Another's* Prayses to dilate
Is usual, and that which Friends doth raise:
But of One's *Own* the Prayses to relate,
Will prove (I fear me) a suspected praise.
Besides, to praise *ours* to the worth, the date
Would first expire of six the longest days.
>   But (to serve *Thee*) a double fault I'l do:
>   I'l praise my own, and crop their praises too.

5

Yet what in fine doth animate me, is,
I'm sure of *Lying* I shall run no danger:
For of such *deeds* say what I can, I wis
I shall leave more to th'utterance of a stranger.
But (to pursue that *method* in all this
Thy self prescrib'd, nor seem in all a Ranger)
>   First, of the *Territory* large I'l tell;
>   Then, of the bloody *Battailes* that befell.

6

Between the Zone where *Cancer* bends his clutch
(To the bright *Sun* a Bound *Septentrionall*)
And *that* which for the *Cold* is shun'd as much,
As for the *Heate* the middle *Zone* of all,
Prowd EUROPE lyes: whose *North*, and parts which touch
Upon the *Occident*, have for their Wall
        The OCEAN; and, with unreturning Waves,
        Her *South* the SEA-MEDITERRANEAN laves.

7

Upon the *East* the neighbours ASIA:
But that *cold River* with the *doubling* stream
(Which from *Riphean Mountains* ploughs his way
To the *Meötick Lake*) divideth Them:
So doth that furious and that horrid *Sea*
Which with their *Fleet* th'incensed GREEKS did steme;
        From whence the Sayler *now* with his *mind's* eye
        Sees the name onely of once glorious TROY.

8

There, in the confines of the *Artick Pole*
The *Hyperborean Mountains* she doth see;
And *those*, where EOL raigns without controle,
Owing to blustring their *Nobility*.
The *Sun*, That spreads his lustre through the *Whole*,
His rays have *here* such imbecility,
        That a deep snow is *still* upon the Mountains,
        The Sea *still* frozen, frozen *still* the Fountains.

9

Here SCYTHS, and TARTARS, in great numbers, live;
Who were ingag'd in a sharp *war* of old,
About their *Pedigrees* prerogative,
With those who *then* th'EGYPTIANE-LAND did hold.
But, where the justice of the *Cause* to give
Being hard by erring *Mortals* to be told,
        To get more certain information, look
        In the *Clay-Office* from which *Man* was took.

10

In that far *Nook* (to name of many some)
Are the cold LAPLAND; NORWAY comfortless;
SCANDIA that triumpht o're triumphant ROME
(Which her proud ruines to this day confess).
Here, whilst the waters are not stiffe, and numb,
With *Winters* Ice glazing the BALTICK-SEAS,
    That *Arm* of the SARMATICK OCEANE
    Sayles the brave *Swede,* the *Prussian,* and the *Dane.*

11

Betwixt *this* Sea, and TANAIS, live strange *Nations:*
RUTHENI, frozen MUSCOVITES, LIVONIANS,
That were in former Ages the SARMATIANS,
And, in th'HERCINIAN FOREST, the POLONIANS.
Held of the GERMAN EMPIRE are ALSATIANS,
SAXONS, BOHEMIANS, HUNGARS, or PANNONIANS:
    With divers *other,* whom the RHINE's cold waves,
    The ELVE, the MOZELL, and the DANOW laves.

12

'Twixt wandring ISTER, and that NARROW-SEA
Where, with her life, fair HELLE left her *name,*
The warlike THRACIANS dwell: who lay a plea
To MARS his Sword, as from whose loyns they came.
Here HAEMUS, and ORPHEAN RHODOPE,
Obey the OTTOMAN; and (to the shame
    Of Christendom) BYSANTIUM's noble Seat,
    A proud affront to CONSTANTINE THE GREAT.

13

The next in order MACEDONIA stands,
Bath'd with the *Actian* (now LEPANTO's) Sea:
And likewise *you,* O admirable LANDS,
Where *Wit,* and *Manners,* were in high degree;
Which bred those solid *Heads,* and valiant *Hands,*
Those streams of *Eloquence,* and *Poetrie,*
    With which *Thou* (famous GREECE) unto the skies
    As well by *Letters,* as by *Arms* didst rise.

14

DALMATIANS follow *Them:* and, in that Bay
ANTENOR chose for his new *City's* Syte,
VENICE (Like VENUS) rises from the *Sea;*
From low beginnings swoln to that proud hight.
That *Sea,* an Arm of *Land* doth overlay,
Which the whole WORLD subjected by its might.
    That *Arm* (no less then GREECE) to HEAVEN soar'd
    With the two *wings* of LEARNING, and THE SWORD.

15

'Tis wall'd by *nature,* part, where it doth joyn
Unto the ALPS thick shoulders: NEPTUNE barrs
The rest with his salt waves: The APPENINE
Cuts ith' middle: where your LYBIAN MARS
Wan him such Fame. But *now,* since the *divine*
Porter hath got it (impotent in *Wars*)
    'Tis stript of the vast pow'r it had before:
    "So much is GOD delighted with the *pore.*

16

Pass we from thence to FRANCE, so much of old
With CAESAR's triumphs through the World renowned.
'Tis water'd with the ROYAL SEYN, the *cold*
GAROON, the pleasant LOYRE, the RHINE *profound.*
Now those high *Mountains* in the clowds behold
Which still the lost PYRENE's name resound:
    From which, being fir'd (as ancient Books have told)
    Rivers ran down of *Silver,* and of *Gold.*

17

Loe! here displays it self illustrious SPAIN,
As *Head* there of all EUROPE: In whose strange
Successes of their *Wars,* and ways of *raign,*
FATE's wheel gave many a *turn,* wrought many a *change.*
But never *Force,* or *Fraud,* shall fix a stain
(Through *Fortune's* humor always giv'n to range)
    But SPAIN will finde a time to wipe it out,
    And make her blasted *honors* freshly sprout.

18

She faces TINGITANIA: and There
(As if to make the *Mid-land Sea* an *Isle*)
The well-known STREIGHTS to close their jaws appeare
Innobled with the THEBAN's latest *Toyle*.
With diff'rent *Nations* she her head doth reare
(*Sea-girt* three sides, the fourth with *Hilly* Pyle)
     Of such Nobility and Valour *All*,
     That *each* pretends to be the *principal*.

19

She has the ARRAGONIAN, so renown'd
For conqu'ring twice stubborn PARTHENOPE:
Those of NAVAR: ASTURIANS, who did bound
The MOORS, broke in upon us like a Sea.
She has the shrewd GALLEGO, many-crownd
CASTILIAN, whom his *Star* reserv'd to be
     SPAIN's great *Restorer* and her *Lord:* SEVILIA,
     GRANADA, LEON, MURCIA, with CASTILIA.

20

The LUSITANIAN KINGDOM here survay,
Plac't as the *Crown* upon fair EUROPE's Head:
Where (the *Land* finishing) begins the *Sea*,
And whence the *Sun* steps to his watry Bed.
This, first in *Arms* (by gracious HEAV'N's decree)
Against the filthy MAURITANIAN sped:
     Throwing him out of *Her* to his old Nest
     In burning AFFRICK; nor *there* let him rest.

21

That, That, the loved EARTH where I was born!
To which if kinder HEAV'N do so dispose
That I (this *Task* perform'd) alive return,
With *It*, my dying Eyes *there* let me close.
From LYSUS (which the *Latines* LUSUS turn),
Old BACCHUS's *Camrade*, or (as some suppose)
     His *Son*, was LUSITANIA's name deriv'd,
     When in that Countrey his *Plantation* thriv'd.

22

Here was that *Shepherd* born, who in his *Name*
(As well as in his *Actions*) did write MAN:
Whom none must hope to equal in his *Fame*
Since that of ROME he to eclipse began.
This *Spot*, through shuffling of light *Fortune's* Game,
TIME (who devours his *children*) saw, anan,
    On the WORLD's *Theater* a great *Part* play
    Rays'd to a *Kingdom:* and it was this way.

23

There was in SPAIN a *King* (ALPHONSO hight)
Who made so close a *War* upon the MORE,
That (what with *policy,* and what with *might*)
Many he slew, and many a Town he bore.
This KING's sublime *Renown* taking her flight
From *Streights Herculean* to the *Caspian Shore,*
    Diverse (affecting an *immortal name*)
    To *Him* and *Death* to offer themselves came.

24

Others (more fir'd with an *intrinsick* love
Of *Christian Faith* then Honour *popular*)
Flock from all Corners: willing to remove
Both from sweet *Countrey,* and from private *Lar.*
But, when their names, by *Actions* rais'd above
The vulgar pitch, they *All* advanc't in War;
    The fam'd ALPHONSO, for such gallant deeds,
    Would have them reap proportionable meeds.

25

Amongst These HENRY (saith the History),
A younger son of FRANCE, and a brave *Prince,*
Had PORTUGAL in lot, in the *World's* eye
Not *then* so glorious, nor so large, as *since.*
And the same KING did his own *daughter* tye
To *Him* in Wedlock, to infer from thence
    His firmer love: as giving, in her hand,
    The *Livery and Seisin* of that LAND.

26

He (when against the *Off-spring* of the *Hand-*
Maid HAGAR mighty Conquests he had won,
Gaining in much of the adjacent LAND,
And doing what was comely to be done)
Obtains from *Him,* who doth high *Heav'n* command
In a short time (to guerdon All) a *Son* :
     Who (adding to his *Father's* worth, his *owne*)
     Shall first erect the LUSITANIAN THRONE.

27

HENRY was now come from the HOLY LAND,
And Conquest of enslav'd JERUSALEM;
Having seen consecrated JORDAN's Strand,
That saw the flesh of God bath'd in his stream;
For, GODFREY finding nothing could withstand
After JUDEA was subdu'd by Him,
     Many, who in that *War* had giv'n him Ayd,
     Their wisht return to their *Dominions* made :

28

When, come to the last *Exit* of his Age
The famous FRENCH-MAN (to a wonder brave)
Pull'd by DEATH's hand down from this mortal Stage,
His *Spirit,* unto *Him,* that gave it, gave.
His *Son* remain'd in tender *Pupillage,*
True Copy of his *Sire* that's in the Grave :
     Then whom more excellent the world had none,
     For such a *Father* must have such a *Son.*

29

But *old* Report (how *true* I cannot say :
For things so distant with much night are spred)
Tells, how the *Mother,* taking all the sway,
Scorn'd not to stoop unto a second Bed :
And, for herself an *After-Game* to play,
Her *Fatherless-Son* disinherited :
     Claiming for *Hers* the *Land,* and *Princely Pow're,*
     As giv'n her by *her Father* for a *dow're.*

30

Then young ALPHONSO (so the *Prince* they call,
Inheriting his *Grandsire* in his Name),
Despairing by fair means of PORTUGALL,
For that the *Mother,* and her *Groom,* the same
Usurp, and mean from *Him* to give it All:
(His bosom boyling with a *Martial* flame)
  By force to seize it in his mind revolves,
  As briskly executes what he resolves.

31

The blushing Plains of ARADUCA groan,
With *one-same* blood of *War intestine* dide;
In which the *Mother* (whose *deeds* spake her *none*)
The *Son* her *love,* and his own LAND deny'de:
Now stands against him in *battalion,*
And cannot see (being blinded with her pride)
  How much she sins 'gainst HEAV'N, and *natural Love*:
  But in her Breast the *sensual* swims above.

32

O Witch MEDEA! PROGNE, with blood-stain!
If for their *Fathers,* not their *own* misdeeds,
By *you* your *children* in Revenge were slain,
Behold, TERESA's *Sin* ev'n *yours* exceeds!
Incontinence, the sacred Thirst of *Raign,*
These are the Causes whence *her* Crime proceeds.
  SCYLLA her aged *Father* slew through *one:*
  Through *Both* TERESA goes against her *Son.*

33

But the brave *Prince* a perfect conquest had
O're an *ill mother,* and a *Father-in-Law.*
Forthwith, the *Victor* all the LAND obay'd
That did before their swords against him draw.
Then (by his *Wrath* his *judgement* oversway'd)
Fast laid in *Irons* he his *Mother* saw:
  Which GOD's avenging Hand did soon pursue.
  "Such *Reverence* is to *all Parents* due.

34

Loe! proud CASTEEL unites her Forces all
(To be reveng'd for sad TERESA's wrong)
Against the few-in-People PORTINGALL:
But, though his *Troops* be *weake*, his *Heart* is strong.
His mortal Head with Shield *Angelical*
Hid in the day of Battail from a throng
    Of falling darts, not onely firm he stands
    Their shock, but routs the formidable Bands.

35

Yet, not long after, was this valiant *Prince*
In the same ARADUCA (his chief Nest)
Blockt up with a vast Army, to which, since
Their late defeat, the angred *Foes* increast.
But by his faithful *Tutor* EGAS, thence
(Offring himself to death) he was releast.
    Else (of all needful matters ill bested)
    He in that streight had surely perished.

36

But the best *Servant* ever *Master* found,
Seeing his *Prince* can no resistance make,
That he should hold of *Him* the Countrey round
To the CASTILIAN KING did undertake.
He (having honestes EGAS MONIZ bound)
The dreadful siege did presently forsake.
    But the *Illustrious youth* cannot afford
    To pay low *Homage* to another *Lord*.

37

The time prefixed was arrived now
When the CASTILIAN MONARCH made account
To do him homage that *the Prince* would bow
As to his *Founder*, and *Lord Paramount*.
EGAS (who knew *that* would not be, and how
Because of Him CASTEEL rely'de upon't)
    Resolves his broken promise, at the rate
    Of his sweet life's expence to expiate.

38

And, with his *children,* and dear *Wife,* he went
T'unpawn and to redeem his morgag'd Faith,
Barefoot and bareleg'd, and with eyes so bent
To th'Earth, as would move pity more then wrath.
"If my rash *confidence* thou have intent
"To scourge as it deserves (O KING), he saith;
  "Loe, here I bring thee of mine own accord
  "A *life,* in lieu of ill-accomplished *word*!

39

"Loe here (to piece out *mine*) the innocent
"Lives, of my *Wife* and *Babes,* before thy Eyes!
"If *Bosoms* generous and excellent
"Accept so frail and dire a *Sacrifice.*
"Loe here the guilty *Hands,* and *Tongue*! invent
"All sorts of *pains* and *deaths* to exercise
  "On *These:* such as may prove fierce SCINIS dull
  "In mischief; and out-roare PERILLUS's *Bull.*

40

Just as before the *Heads-man* one condemn'd,
Who doth in *life* his *death* anticipate,
And now upon the *Block* his Neck extend,
For the fear'd stroak which must dispatch him straight:
So EGAS look't, expecting the worst end
Could be pronounc't by KING's deserved Hate.
  But the KING seeing such stupendious *Faith,*
  Mercy at length could more with him, then *Wrath.*

41

O *great,* and *Portingal-Fidelitie,*
Payd by a *Subject* to his *Prince*! What more
Perform'd the PERSIAN in that *Project* high,
When *Nose* and *Face* he carbonado'd o're;
Which made the great Darius (sighing) cry
A thousand times (it greiv'd his hart so sore)
  His brave ZOPYRUS, such as he was once,
  H'had rather have, then twenty BABILONS?

42

But *now* the Prince ALFONSO did provide
The *happy Hoast* of LUSITANIA
Againsrt the MOORS, who, on the other side
Of TAGUS's delectable River lay.
Now in the fam'd ORIQUE's Champion wide
The proud and warlike *Troops* he doth aray,
 Just in the beard of the confronted MOOR:
 As rich in *courage,* as in *numbers* poor.

43

His *Trust* is not in *Flesh,* but placed all
In the eternal GOD, That *Heav'n* doth steer:
For the *baptized* Army was so small,
To his one man an hundred MOORS there were.
Those, who consider things by *Reason,* call
It *madness* rather, then th'effect of cleer
 And sober *heate,* on such vast *Heapes* to run,
 Where there's an *hundred Horsemen* to his *one.*

44

Five MOORISH KINGS he hath that day defy'de
Of whom the *Chief* hath ISMAR to his name:
All with the style of SOLDIER dignify'de,
By which is purchased immortal *Fame.*
Each had his *Mistress* fighting by his side,
Like *that,* as beautiful, as warlike, DAME
 Who helpt so long to prop up falling TROY,
 And *Those* who streams of THERMODONT injoy.

45

Now did AURORA, beautiful and cleer,
Out of the *Welkin* chase the *golden Fry:*
When MARYS son, ALPHONSO's heart to cheer,
Appear'd to him upon *the Cross* on high.
Whom worshipping, That thus vouchsaf't t'appeer,
(All of a fire with *Faith*) the *Prince* doth cry,
 Not to *me* LORD, but to the INFIDEL:
 Not unto *me,* who know thy pow'r so well.

46

This *miracle* of mercy so inflam'd
The PORTINGALLS, and did their minds erect,
That they the gallant *Prince* their KING acclam'd,
Whom with such cordial love they did affect;
And (*drawing up* before the *Foe*) proclam'd
To HEAV'N, and to the *World*, their new *Elect*:
       Crying alowd: THE ARMY, CROWN AND ALL,
       FOR GREAT ALPHONSO KING OF PORTUGALL.

47

As a fierce *Mastiffe* in the woody CHACE
(Whom *Shouts,* and *Hunters Instruments* incite)
Attacks a *Bull,* the which his Trust doth place
In his sharp *Horns's* irrefragable might;
Now fastning on his flank, now on his Face,
More nimble at the turn, then strong in fight;
       Till, tearing out his Throat, down falls the *Beast,*
       The groaning *Mountain* with his weight opprest:

48

So the *new* KING (with courage no less *new*
Inflam'd by GOD, and by *the People,* Both)
Upon the *barb'rous Hoast,* before him, flew
With his bold Troops, impetuous, and wroth.
With this, the *doggs* take up a Howle and rue-
Full Cry, the *people* rowze, th'*Alarum* goeth:
       They snatch their *Spears,* and Bowes, the *Trumpets* sound;
       Lowd Instruments of *war* go bellowing round.

49

As when a fire in Stubble dry begun
(The whistling *Boreas* hapning then to blow)
Fann'd by the *Bellows* of the *Wind,* doth run
To the next *Field* which *Furzes* overgrow;
And *there* a knot of *Sheepherds* (who upon
The grassie ground sweet slumbers undergo)
       Wak't by the crackling flames in the thick Brake,
       Snatch up their *Hooks,* and to the *Village* make:

50

So the surprized MOORS, and thunder-strook,
Catch up their *weapons,* which lye round about.
Yet fled not, *these*; but to their *Arms* they took,
And spur'd their warlike *Barbs,* resolv'd and stout.
The PORTINGALL incounters them unshook,
He makes his *Lances* at their *backs* come out.
    Some drop half-dead, some tumble dead outright,
    Others invoke the ALCORAN, and fight.

51

Most terrible Incounters, *there,* resound;
Enough to shake in its firm seat a Rock:
When those fierce *Beasts,* the *Trident*-strooken ground
Produc't (with their more furious *Burthens*) shock.
No *Nook* exempt, the *war* is kindled round,
Vast *wounds* are giv'n, *Neither* hath cause to mock:
    But those of LUSUS, Armours, Males, and all,
    Break, cut, hack, batter, penetrate, and maule.

52

Heads from the *shoulders* leap about the *Field;*
Arms, Leggs, without or *Sence,* or *Master,* flye.
Others (their panting entrails trailing) wheel'd;
Earth in their bloodless *cheek, death* in their *Eye.*
Th'*impious Army* now the *day* doth yield:
Rivers of Blood flow from their wounds, whereby
    The *Field* it self doth lose *its* colour too,
    And into *Crimson* turns the *verdant* hew.

53

The PORTINGALL victorious doth remain,
Reaping the *Trophies* and the wealthy *Prey.*
Having discomfited the MOOR of SPAIN,
Three days the GREAT KING on the *place* doth stay.
In his broad *Shield* (which he till then bore plain)
A *Badge* eternal of this glorious *day,*
    Five small *Shields azure* he doth now include,
    In sign of these *five Kings* by *Him* subdu'de.

54

In these *five Shields* he paints the *Recompence*
For which THE LORD was sold, in various Ink
Writing *his* history, who did dispence
Such favour to him, more then *Heart* could think.
In every of the *Five* he paints *Five-pence,*
So sums the *Thirty* by a *Cinque-fold Cinque;*
     Accounting that which is the *Center,* twise,
       Of the *five Cinques,* which he doth place *Cross-wise.*

55

Some time after *he* gave this grand *defeat*
Th'illustrious KING (whose Thoughts to *Heaven* soare)
To take in LEYRIA marcht; which Those, *He* beat,
Had took from *Him* a little while before.
To boot, the strong ARRONCHEZ he doth get:
And, with her pleasant *Vale,* the evermore
     Glorious SCABELICASTRO (Santarene)
       Which *Thou,* sweet TAGUS, waterst so serene.

56

Unto these noble *Towns* reduc't, he soon
Adds MAFRA, dar'd by his victorious *Wings;*
Then, in the famous *Mountains of the Moon*
Cold SYNTRA (forc'd) to his obedience brings:
Syntra, in which the NAYADES do run
From the sweet *Snare,* hiding themselves in Springs.
     But Love hath *Nets* will *there* too serve their turn:
       And in the *water* will his *wild-fire* burn.

57

And *Thou,* fair LISBON (worthy to be crown'd
Of all the *Cities* of the WORLD the *Queen*)
Which that great *Prince of Eloquence* did found,
Who by *his wit* TROY-TOWN had ruin'd seen;
Thou (whom obeys the *Ocean-Sea* profound)
By the brave PORTINGALLS wert taken in,
     Helpt by a potent *Fleet,* which at that time
       Happen'd to come out of the *Northern Clime:*

58

Thence, from the *German* ELVE, and from the RHENE,
And from the *Brittish-Sea-commanding* THEAMES,
Sent to destroy th'usurping SARACEN,
And free their sister JORDAN's captive streames.
These, entring TAGUS's pleasant mouth, and then
With great ALPHONSO joyn'd (whose *Glory's* beames
    Attract *all* Hearts, but *those* his name appalls)
    A *Seige* is laid to th'ULYSSEAN WALLS.

59

Five times the *Moon* had hid her horned head,
And other five her face at full displayd;
When by main force the *City* entered
The will of the *Beleaguerer* obayd.
Fierce was the *Battail*, much the *blood* there shed,
As needs they must be (circumstances waigh'd)
    Between rough *Conquerours*, That all things dare,
    And *conquer'd People* driven to despaire.

60

Thus *Shee* was after some few Months expence
Compell'd to stoop to this *new Victor's* law;
Whom in *old time* to *their* obedience,
With all their might, cold *Vandals* could not draw:
Whose *pow'r* (which own'd no *bound*, stuck at no *Fence*)
EBRE, and GOLDEN TAGUS, trembling saw:
    And BETIS *they* did so entirely tame,
    They did *that Land* VANDALUSIA name.

61

If noble LISBON could not stand it out,
Where is that *City* so resolv'd, and strong,
That can resistance make to such a stout
And warlike people (FAME's immortall song)?
Now all ESTREMADURA's at his Foot,
OBIDOS fair, ALENQUER proud (among
    Whose pleasant *Groves* runs many a River sweet,
    Murm'ring, as if too good to wash their Feet)
And TORRESUEDRAS.

62

You likewise, O ye fair Trans-Tagan Lands
(Which golden Ceres with her Bounty crowns)
Hee, who brings more then *Mortall* strength, commands
Out of your *Forts,* and Arms. And you (the *Clowns*
Of Affrica) who plough'd them with *your* hands,
Hope not to reap the *Fruits*: For the good *Towns*
     Of Moura, Serpa, Yelves, by assault
     Are taken, and Alcacer Of The Salt.

63

Lo! now that noble *City* (certain *Seat*
Of the brave Rebell in old time, Sertorius;
Where still his far-fetcht Water pure and neat,
To serve the place b'an act so meritorious
Through *Arches* on Two hundred *Pillars* set
Doth pass, with *Royall restauration* glorious)
     Ev'n *Her,* the bold Gerardo's prowess brings
     To own, and serve, the Lusitanian Kings.

64

Against the *City* now of Beya,
To take revenge for spoyl'd Trancoso's Town,
Alphonso goes; who cannot rest a Day
For ymping a *short life* with *long Renown.*
Before this *City* long he doth not stay;
And (storming it b' a part that's beaten down)
     Enraged enters: where, of all that breathes,
     His hungry *Steel* he in the Bowels sheathes.

65

Jointly with *these,* Palmela doth he *win;*
Fishy Cizimbra too: nor *wins* alone,
But (his good *star* assisting him therein)
A potent *Army* there hath overthrowne.
The *Town* saw his intent, so did her *King:*
Nor was he backward to relieve the *Towne.*
     Careless he marcht along the Mountain-side,
     Little imagining what did betide.

66

'Twas *He* of Badachoz (a haughty More),
Four thousand furious *Spirits* were his Horse,
Of Infantry innumerable store,
With gilded Arms (*Gallants,* and *Warriors*).
But, as in *May* a jealous *Bull* (before
He is perceiv'd) rushes with all his force
    Upon a *Travailer,* and runs him over,
    (Twice mad, both as a *Beast,* and as a *Lover*):

67

Just so Alphonso, from an *Ambush* close,
Assaults the people that securely past;
Strikes, overturns, and kills; The Field he mows;
The Moorish King flyes for his life in hast.
Struck with a *Pannick* fear, the *Remnant* throws
Away their *Arms;* and follows him as fast:
    They That made all this Havock, being a *Force*
    (*Good God!*) consisting but of sixty *Horse.*

68

The *Victory* without delay, the great
And indefatigable King pursues,
Causing his Drums through all the *Realm* to beat
(Conqu'ring of Lands he as his *Trade* doth use),
Besiegeth Badachoz, and soon doth get
The end of his desire: For *there* he shews
    So much of *Souldier,* and a *Soul* so high,
    That keep *It* must the *others* company.

69

But the great GOD (who keeps his *Rods* in store,
For such as merit them, till his own time;
Whether, for *Sinners* to amend, before
They fall: or Causes, *Man* can not divine)
If he, *till now,* the valiant King forbore,
And (through all dangers leading) gave him *line:*
    Yet *now,* he will *no longer* let him be,
    From his imprison'd Mother's curses, free.

70

For lying in this *City* weakly man'd,
The Leon-Men besiege th'ill-guarded Walls,
'Cause he that *Conquest* took out of *their* Hand,
Being of Leon, and not Portugal's.
Here, dear did *Him* his Pertinacy stand,
As in the *World* out oftentimes it falls:
 For in a furious *Sally* (his leg burst
 Against an Iron) he to yield was forc't.

71

"O famous Pompey! Be not *Thou* in pain
"To see thy *Glorie's* sad *Catastrophie;*
"Or that just Nemesis should pre-ordain
"Thy *Father-in-Law* to triumph over *Thee;*
"Though frozen Phasis, and Bootes's *Wayn;*
"The *Land* under the Burning Axle-Tree;
 "And strange Syene, where no *oblique Sun*
 "A *Shadow* casts, and all the *day* is *Noon;*

72

"And Eniochians fierce; and Arabs rich;
"And Colchos, famous for the *Golden Sheep;*
"And Cappadoceans; and Judeans, which
"Abolisht *Rites* so obstinately keep;
"And soft Sophena, scurft with pleasures Itch;
"And (with Silician-Robbers on the Deep)
 "Armenia, That *two Rivers* boasts, which came
 "From Paradise; All trembled at thy name:

73

"And though, in fine, from the Atlantick-Sea
"To Scythian-Taurus with erected Crown,
"*Victorious*: Wonder not, that thou shouldst be
"In the Pharsalian-Battail overthrown.
"For *high* and *great* Alphonso thou shalt see
"Bear *All* before him, and at last burn down.
 "By a *Cross-match* of Fate were *Both* undon,
 "*Thou* by a Father-In-Law, *He* by a Son.

74

The noble KING, thus scourg'd by HEAV'N, at length
Restor'd was to his PORTUGAL again.
There (after he had been, by a vast strength
Of MOORS, in SANTAREN besieg'd in vain;
And, after that the *Corps* of St. VINCENTH
The *Martyr*, from that *Head of Land* in SPAIN
    Which by his name to all the world is known,
    Translated was to th'ULYSSEAN TOWN)

75

To carry on the Work by *Him* begun,
The *old man* (weary) doth his *Son* command
With men and warlike preparation
To march into the ALENTEIAN-LAND.
SANCHO (to prove himself his *Father's Son*)
Like a strong stream let loose, passes beyand;
    And makes the *River* of GUADALQUIVEER
    Run *Moorish blood*, That wont to run so cleer.

76

Flesht with his *winnings*, the young *Gamester* grows
Now Covetous; and cannot rest, before
He in a second Battail overthrows
(In sight of BEIA) the beleagu'ring MORE.
Nor long with this *design* in labour goes
E're he the *Bays* by *Him* desired Wore.
    The MOOR (on both sides justled to the Wall)
    Resolves at once to be reveng'd for all.

77

Now, from the *Mountain* which MEDUSA star'd
Out of *that* Body which the HEAV'N sustayn'd,
From AMPELUSA's *Promontory*, hard
They march; from TANGER, where ANTEUS raign'd.
Of AVILA the *dwellers* are not spar'd:
Doth likewise march (well-*arm'd*, and choicely *train'd*)
    At the harsh *Mauritanian* Trumpet's sound
    Of noble JUBA all the *Kingdom* round.

78

With this huge mass of men his inroad made
The great MIRAMOLIN in PORTUGAL.
Twelve *Moorish Kings* he carryed in his Ayd,
'Mongst whom *He* wears the *Crown Imperial.*
These, having in their march by *Parties* prey'd,
And, where they could, destroy'd the Countrey all,
    In SANTAREN Don SANCHO close impound:
    But a sad Seige it will for *them* be found.

79

Furious *assaults* th'incensed MOOR doth make:
A thousand *Stratagems* in practice puts.
In vain huge *Stones* from horrid *Engins* brake:
In vain the *Mine* is hid, and the *Ram* buts.
ALPHONSO'S *Son* is everywhere awake,
Here his Care *Shields,* and *there* his courage *cuts.*
    So what with *these,* and what with *martial Art,*
    Stopt is each *Meuse,* and guarded is each *part.*

80

But the *old man* (whose burthen'd *Lims,* and *Head,*
With *years,* and *Cares,* oblig'd him to repose)
Retir'd into that *City,* whose fair Mead
To sweet MONDEGO'S streams its verdure ows;
Hearing his *Son* is close beleaguered
In SANTAREN by blind and barb'rous Foes,
    Flyes from that *City* to his Ayd: For *Age*
    Cramps not his wonted *speed,* nor cools his *rage.*

81

He, with his *Troops* inur'd to warlike Feats,
Thund'ring the *Reare,* and his *Son* salying out;
The PORTINGAL (who *now* of custom beats)
In a short space the MOORS doth wholly rout.
With *Terbants, Cassacks, Faulchions, Coverlets,*
Cloaks with wrought *Capes,* the Field is strew'd about:
    Horses, and their *Caparisons* (rich Prey)
    And by the *Horses* their dead *Masters* lay.

82

The *Lusitanian* Bounds the rest forego,
Put to a hasty and disordred flight.
The great MIRAMOLIN, he flyes not though:
For before *he* could flye, he fled the light.
To HIM, who did this Victory bestow
Are rendred thanks and Praises infinite:
    "For in so great, and so apparent odds,
    "The part *man* acts is the dumb shew to GOD's.

83

This was the great ALPHONSO's latest wreath
Of *Victory* (a *Prince* of vast Renown)
When *He* who forg'd it with his *Sword* (his breath
Deserting him) exchang'd his MORTAL CROWN.
The *hand* of *sickness* ush'ring *that* of *death*,
Toucht his weak Body, and so pusht it down.
    Thus, whom so many had paid Tribute to,
    Paid the last tribute unto *Nature* due.

84

Him did the lofty *Promontories* moan:
With all their streams the widow'd *Rivers* wept,
And (overflowing the Fields, newly sown,
With rueful Tears) the next years Harvest swept.
But through the world his living FAME is blown:
And, where he raign'd, his *name* so fresh is kept,
    That *there* each *Hill,* and ev'ry ecchoing *Plain,*
    ALFONSO calls, ALPHONSO — But in vain.

85

SANCHO succeeds (*valiant,* and in his *Spring*)
True Copy of his *Sire,* examin'd *well*
By the *Original,* alive yet being
When he with barb'rous blood made BETIS swell;
And overturn'd the *Andalusian King*
Of the accursed Race of ISHMAEL:
    But *better,* when at BEJA's siege he made
    Them feel the weight of his *Victorious* Blade.

86

After he ware the Lusitanian Crown
(Some years elaps'd since he to reign began)
Before the City Silves he sat down
Then in possession of the Affrican.
Assisted was he to take in this *Town*
By *Strangers* from the *Northern Ocean,*
  With *Men,* and *Arms,* for ASIA bound: to joyne
  In rescue of distressed Palestine.

87

They sayld to second in the *Holy Cause*
Red Frederick; who with a potent Hoast
To the defence of that plagu'd *City* draws,
By which the Lord Of Life his own life lost:
When Guido with his *Troops* (having their jaws
Parcht up with drowth) to the Great Soldan, forst
  Were to surrender, where the *Miscreants*
  Have prepossest the *Springs* which Guido wants.

88

But the fair *Navie* (forc't upon our shore
By adverse *Winds,* though Sancho's prosperous *Star)*
Assists him willingly against the More,
Since *one* and t'*other* is a *Holy War.*
As thy great *Father* Lisbon took before,
Just *so,* and with the same *Auxiliar,*
  From the fierce *dwellers* tak'st *Thou* Silves: This
  Also, a noble *Realm's* Metropolis.

89

And, if from the Mahumetans thou hast
So many *trophies,* neither didst thou let
The men of Leon (though in *Mountains* plac't,
And nurst in bloody *Battail*) quiet set:
Till thou a *Yoke* upon the Neck hadst cast
Of their proud Tui, adding a *Coronet*
  Of *Towns* her Neighbours, on which Thou didst put
  (Renowned Sancho) thy triumphant Foot.

90

But *death* (like a bold *Thiefe*) did *Him* assault
In his Career of *glory*. He was heyr'd
B'a *Son* whom many Vertues did exalt:
Second ALPHONSO, of our *Kings* the *Therd*.
In his *Raign* was ALCACER OF THE SALT
Subdu'de again in spight of the MOOR's Beard;
    By whom late took, 'tis now re-took, with great
      Destruction of them, and four *Kings'* defeat.

91

ALFONSO dead, The *Second* SANCHO came
To hold the *Scepter;* Tame, and negligent:
To that degree both negligent, and tame,
That for the shadow of Himself he went.
Then did *Another* (fitter for the same)
Wrest from his hands that pow'r, he was content
    To delegate. And why? He having none
      Himself, his *Minion's* Crimes were call'd his *owne*.

92

No, no, our SANCHO was not of that mood
Lewd NERO was, who married with a *Boy;*
And after (with less guilt he shed her blood)
His mother AGRIPPINA did injoy:
Nor (like the self-same NERO) piping stood,
Then clapt his hands to see his burning TROY:
    Nor did his *daughter*, like one *King*, devour:
      Nor change his *Sex* like t'other *Emperour*.

93

He did not o're his People tyrannize,
Like *Those* who Tyrants in SYCILIA were:
Nor hyr'd he men, strange Tortures to devise,
Like PHALARIS, one of the *cruellst* there.
But the proud *Realm*, which too indulgent *skyes*
Had us'd to *Kings*, who would indure no *Peere;*
    That likewise to such niceness did arrive
      T'indure no *King*, who had his *Peer* alive.

94

Therefore BOLONIA's *Earl* the Helm did guide:
Which he did after in his own right hold,
When his still-sloathful Brother (SANCHO) dy'de.
He (nam'd ALPHONSO, and surnam'd *the Bold*)
After he had the *Kingdom* pacify'de;
And all sharp humors setled, or controll'd;
    Thinks, how he may enlarge it by his merit:
    Too *small* a *Circle* for so *great* a spirit.

95

Of the ALGARVES's land (the conquering
Whereof was giv'n him with his *Queen* in dow'r)
He gains in much, outing the *Moorish King;*
On all whose *Actions* now curst MARS did low'r.
But out of PORTUGAL did wholly fling
(By *Prudence* part, and part by *martial* pow'r)
    That pertinacious People, and did chace
    From that *good Land* which LUSUS left his Race.

96

Now, DENIS! worthy his own *Parentage:*
And for whom *such* a *Father* should make room.
DENIS! Who strikes (in way of *Patronage*)
The fame of ALEXANDER's bounty dumbe.
The *Land* got breath, and flourisht in that *Age*
(Mild *Peace,* and with peace, *Justice* from *Heav'n* come)
    With *Constitutions, Laws,* and *Customes* right:
    Of a calm *Kingdome* LUMINARIES bright.

97

He was the first That made COYMBRA shine
With *Lib'ral Sciences* which PALLAS taught;
By *Him,* from HELICON the *Muses Nine*
To bruize MONDEGO's grassie brink were brought;
Hither transferr'd APOLLO that rich *Mine,*
Which the old GREEKS in learned ATHENS wrought;
    Here Ivy-Wreaths with *Gold* he interweaves,
    And the coy DAPHNE's never-fading leaves.

98

Now noble *Cities* from the ground ascend,
Castles, and warlike *Fortresses* secure;
Scarce any Corner but this *Prince* doth mend :
Convents he builds, and *Towns* he doth immure.
But Atropos (the Best must have an End)
Shearing his golden *Thrid* in years mature,
  His *Son* succeeds; not *dutiful* (the *Fourth*
  Alphonse) but of high *courage,* and much *worth.*

99

On proud Casteel he still with *Scorn* did look :
Yet free from *malice* as 'twas free from *feares,*
Onely men have a custom, in that *Nook,*
To dread no *pow'r* for being more then *theirs.*
For when the Mauritanian undertook
Hesperia's second Conquest; and appeares
  Just ready now Castilians to invade :
  The brave Alphonso pow'rs in to their Ayd :

100

Never Semiramis with such an *Hoast*
Did swarm Hydaspes's banks, his Sands out-number;
Nor Attila (He who *Himself* did boast
The *Scourge* of GOD, and was the *fright,* and *wonder*
Of Italy) so many Goths ingrost
And *Northern People* : As of Moors were under
  The Affrick-Moor (with Those Granada yields)
  At that time mustred in *Tartessian* Fields.

101

Then the Castilian King (who saw so great
And vast a pow'r, against his Countrey bend;
Nor weigh'd his *life,* but the intire *defeat*
Of Spain it self (once lost) did apprehend)
Help from the valiant Portingall t'intreat,
His dearest *Consort* to that *Court* did send :
  His *Wife* from whom the *Embassie* is sent,
  And his dear *daughter* unto whom it went.

102

Vertuous MARIA, and as *fair* as *good*,
Enters her Father's *Palace* (glorious dame!)
Lovely in *Grief*; nor, though the water stood
In her sweet eyes, did *that* suspend their flame.
Her *Angel's* Tresses with a *golden* flood
Covered her *Ivory* shoulders. When she came
    Before her *Sire* (*He* overjoyd and kind)
    It rain'd down right, and thus she brake her mind.

103

"As many *Nations* as all AFFRICK bred
"(A People *barbarous* and *inhumane*)
"Hath the great *King* of the MOROCCO's led
"To take possession of illustrious SPAIN.
"So vast a pow'r ne're marcht under one *Head*
"Since the dry *Earth* was compast by the *Main*.
    "It terrifies the *living* where it rolls,
    "And ev'n alarums their dead *Fathers'* Souls.

104

"His frighted subjects to protect and skreen,
"*He,* whom *thou* hast my *Lord* and *Husband* made,
"Stands with small strength exposed to the keen
"And thirsty edges of the *Moorish* Blade;
"And *I* shall soon depriv'd of *all* be seen,
"If thou afford him not thy present ayd:
    "A *sad* and *private* Woman, *Husbandless*,
    "Without a *Crown*, or *Him*, or *Happiness*.

105

"Therefore (O *King*) for very fear of whom
"The streams of hot MALUCO do congeale;
"Succour, O! quickly to the succour come
"Of miserable and despis'd CASTELE.
"If that deare *smile* be an assenting dumb,
"If *that* thy fatherly affection seal;
    "*Run* Father; if thou do not, by the MORE
    "I fear thou'lt find it *over-run* before.

106

This with the self-same tone Maria said
To *King* Alphonso on her trembling knees,
With which sad Venus once *her* Father pray'd
For her Eneas tost on *Lybian Seas;*
At which, with sense of the deep moan she made,
Such tender pitty did Jove's bowels seize,
  (Indulgent Sire!) he let his *Thunder* fall,
  And (griev'd she askt no *more*) granted her *all.*

107

Streight armed *Squadrons,* glitt'ring in the Sun,
Are mustred in the Fields of Ebora :
Scowr'd is the *Sword,* the *Lance,* the *Murrion:*
In rich *Caparisons* the *Horses* neigh.
The *Trumpet* shrill, with pendant *Banner* done,
Rowzes from *peaces* down (where long they lay)
  Their tickled Hearts to disaccustomed *Arms;*
  And concave *Drums* go thund'ring fresh *Alarms.*

108

Amongst them and *above* them *All* appeers
Higher by head and shoulders then the rest
(And where *He* goes the *Royal Standart* veers)
Valiant Alphonso with erected Crest.
His very *look,* it animates and cheers
(If *there* are any) ev'n the *Coward's* Brest.
  Into Casteel thus marching is he seen
  With his fair *daughter,* the *Castilian Queen.*

109

The two Alphonsos, in conclusion joynd,
In wide Taryfa's Fields confronting stood
The endless numbers of the people blind
For whom too narrow are both *Plain* and *Wood.*
Of *ours* not one so hardy, but did find
Somewhat of cold and shiv'ring in his blood,
  Save onely such as cleerly understands
  Christ fights the battail with his *People's* hands.

110

Derided are the thin-spread *Christian-Bands*
By Bond-Mayd Hagar's Progeny unclean;
Who, by anticipation, all *their* lands
Divide amongst the Army *Hagarene,*
Which by false Title in possession stands
Of the illustrious Name of *Saracene:*
  Just as *Another's* noble Land they boast
  Now for their *own;* reck'ning without their Host.

111

As that big-bon'd and barbrous *Gyant* (whom
King Saul so fear'd, and all his *Army* worse),
Seeing a simple *Swain* against him come,
Onely with *Peebles* arm'd, and a *clean* force,
With haughty language (arrogant and grum)
Scorns the poor Boy, and sends him to his Nurse;
  Whom rounding with his sling, *He* taught at length
  The diff'rence betwixt *Faith,* and *humane strength.*

112

So the perfidious Moor (advancing) cracks
Over the *Christian Hoast;* nor understands
What Pow'r it is that their weak *Powers* backs,
Which *Hell* with all its *Fiends* in vain withstands.
Helpt by that Pow'r, *He* of Casteel attacks
Morocco's *King,* who *there* in *Chief* commands:
  The Portingal (who sleights their whole *Armada*)
  He takes to Task the *Kingdom* of Granada.

113

Now crack the *Lances,* and the *Swords* cry clink
Upon the *Armours,* Pow'rs incountring Pow'rs;
Invoking (when they stand on danger's brink)
Theirs Mahomet, and St. Iago *ours.*
The strook strike *Heav'n* with Cries, making a sink
And standing Pool with thick Vermilion show'rs:
  Where some (half dead) lye drowning where they stood,
  In too much *now,* who fell for want of blood.

114

With so great blood-shed did the Portingal
Make Spoyl and Havock of the Granadine,
That in small space he kills, or routs, them *All*,
'Spight of their *Mayles* and *breast-plates* of steel fine.
His hungry *Blade* (which will to supper fall
In Fez, if in th'Alhambra it did dine)
    The brave Castilian helps to end the Fray:
    Who hath the Mauritanian at a Bay.

115

The burning Sun was making his retreat
To Thetys's grotts, and the bright *Ev'ning Star*
Drawing that glorious day to it's red *Set,*
Whose memory no time shall ever bar:
When the two *Kings* consummate the defeat
Of the Moors's Powers assembled in this War,
    With so much Tragick slaughter, as no *Age*
    Beheld before, or since, on the World's Stage.

116

Not a fourth part rough Marius slew, of Those
That lost their lives in this day's Victory,
When water dasht with blood of their dead Foes
He made his *Army* drink, which then was dry:
Nor *He* of Carthage (sworn, a child, t'oppose
With Fire and Sword the Pride of Italy)
    When he so many *Knights* kill'd famous Rome,
    That their *Rings* tane did to three Bushels come.

117

And if *Thou* (noble Titus) couldst alone
So many souls to black Cocytus send,
When thou the *Holy City* didst unstone
Of that stiff *People,* never to be wean'd
From their abolisht *Rytes*: This GOD did owne,
And christned it *his* Act, that what was pen'd
    By the Old Prophets might be verify'de,
    And JESUS said too, whom *they* Crucify'de.

118

After this great and prosperous event
(ALFONSO come to PORTUGALL again,
There to injoy in *peace* and sweet content
The spreading Glories he in *War* did gain)
A black and lamentable accident
(Worthy in Fame's *Memorials* to remain)
    Was on a miserable *Lady* seen,
    Who, after she was dead, was made a *Queen.*

119

Thou, onely *Thou* (pure LOVE) with bended bow,
Against whose Force no brest whate're can hold,
As if thy *perjur'd Subject,* or *Sworn Foe,*
Did'st cause her death whom all the World condol'd.
If *Tears* (which from a troubled Fountain flow)
Quench not thy Thirst, as hath been said of old;
    It is, that such is thy *tyrannick* mood,
    Thou lov'st thy *Altars* should be bath'd in *blood.*

120

Thou wer't (fair YNES) in Repose, of LOVE's
Reflected Fires fost'ring the sweet heat, young;
In that sweet *Error,* that worse *Fates* removes,
Which *Fortune* never suffers to last long:
In sweet MONDEGO's solitary *Groves,*
Whose streams no day but thou didst weep among:
    Teaching the lofty *Trees,* and humble *Grass,*
    That *Name* which printed in thy bosom was.

121

Thy pensive *Prince,* with *thine* did sympathize
Remembrances, which in his Soul did swim,
Bringing thee always fresh before his Eyes,
When, from thy fair ones, bus'ness banisht *Him:*
By night, in *dreams*; that cheat him with sweet lyes:
By day, in thoughts; that pencil *thy* each *lim:*
    And *all* he mus'd, and *all* he saw, in fine,
    Were dear IDEAS of thy *Form* divine.

122

Of other *Ladies* fair, and *Princesses*
The tend'red Matches he did vilifie;
For, of a *Heart* 'tis hard to dispossess
True *Love*, that hath had time to fortifie.
Upon these highly am'rous passages
The *Father* looking with an old man's Eye
    (Enrag'd with what the common-people sed
    And his *Son's* resolution not to wed),

123

YNES determines from the *World* to take,
His *Son* from *Her* to take, and to remove:
Believing, with her *blood's* ill let-out Lake,
To quench the kindled flames of constant love.
O! that sure *Sword* (which had the pow'r to make
The *Moorish* Rage strike saile) what Rage could move
    Thee, from the honor'd *Sheath*, where thou did'st rest,
    To be new sheath'd in *Lady's* gentle Brest?

124

The horrid *blood-hounds* dragg'd her to the *King*:
Whose bowels *now* to mercy stood inclin'd.
But *ill-Advisers* with false reasoning
To her destruction re-inflam'd his mind.
Shee (with Heart-breaking language which did spring
Onely from sense of *Those* she left behind
    In solitude, her Prince, and children deare,
    Whose *Griefe* she more, then her *death* did feare;

125

Lifting unto the azure *Firmament*
Her *Eyes*, which in a Sea of Tears were drown'd;
Her *Eyes*, for one of those malevolent
And bloody *Instruments* her *hands* had bound;
And then, the same on her dear *Infants* bent,
Who *Them* with smiling innocence surround
    By whom poor *Orphans* they will streight be made)
    Unto their cruel *Grand-Father* thus said.

126

If *Beasts* themselves (*wild Beasts*) whose use, and way,
By *Nature's* dire instinct, is not to spare;
And vagrant *Birds*, whose bus'ness 'tis, to prey,
And chace their *Quarrey* through the yielding Ayre;
The world hath seen take *Babes* expos'd, and play
The tender *Nurses* to them with their care,
       As Ninus's mother once it did befall,
       And the *Twinn-Founders* of the *Roman* Wall :

127

O *Thou*, whose *Superscription* speaks thee, *Man*
(That the *Contents* were suited to the Cover!
A feeble Maid thou wouldst not murther than
Onely for loving *Him*, who first did love her)
Pitty these *Babes* (*the babes about him ran*)
In thy hard doom since *I* am spot all over.
       Spare, for *their* sakes, *their* lives, and *mine* : And see
       Whiteness in *Them*, though thou wilt not in *Me*.

128

And if subduing the presumptuous Moor,
How to give *death* with fire and sword thou know'st,
Know, to give *life* too, to a *damsel* poore,
Who hath done nothing why it should be lost.
Let my hid *Innocence* thus much procure :
Exile me to some sad *intemperate Coast*,
       Cold Scythia, or burn't Lybia, to remain
       A weeping Tomb, and never more see Spain.

129

Plant me where nothing grows but *Cruelty*,
'Mongst *Lyons*, *Bears*, and other *Savage* Beasts :
To see, if *They* that mercy will deny
Which I in vain implore from *humane* Breasts.
There, in firm love to *Him* for whom I dye,
I'l breed his *Pieces*, thou here seest, *their guests*
       And *my Companions*; to slide off with *Those*
       Part of the burthen of their *mother's* woes.

130

Fain would have pardon'd her the gracious *King,*
Mov'd with these words, which made his Bowels yearn:
But *Fate,* and *whisp'rers* (That fresh Fewel bring)
They would not pardon. 'Tis those mens concern
(Having begun) to perpetrate the Thing.
They strip their steel out of the Scabbard (stern).
     Out Villains! Butchers! What? imploy your spights,
     Your swords, against a *Lady,* and call'd *Knights?*

131

As at the breast of fair Polixena,
Condemn'd to death by dire Achilles's shade
(The last dear stake of Aged Hecuba)
Revenged Pyrrhus bent his cruel *Blade;*
But with a *look* that drives ill Ayrs away
(Patient, as any *Lamb*) The *Royal Maid,*
     On her mad *Mother* casting up her Eys,
     Presents her self a *Sacrifice,* and dyes:

132

So gentle Ynes's bruitish Murtherers,
Ev'n in that *Neck* (white Atlas of that *Head*
Whose stars, though set, had influence o're the pow'rs
Of *Him,* That crown'd her after she was dead)
Bathing their thirsty *Swords,* and all the *flow'rs*
Which her fair Eyes had newly watered
     (Mindless of the insuing Vengeance) stood
     Like crimson'd *Hunters* reeking with her blood.

133

Well mightst Thou Phebus from an Act so dire
(Pyrous starting) have reverst thy look;
As from Thyestes's Table, when the *Sire*
Din'd on the *Son,* the *Uncle* being the Cook.
You, hollow Vales (which, when she did expire,
From her cold lips the dying accents took)
     Hearing her Pedro nam'd with her last breath,
     Form'd Pedro, Pedro, after Ynes's death.

134

Like a sweet *Rose* (with party-colours fair)
By *Virgin's* hand beheaded in the Bud
To play withal, or prick into her Hair,
When (sever'd from the stalk on which it stood)
Both *Scent* and *beauty* vanish into Ayre:
So lies the *Damzel* without *breath*, or *Blood*,
     Her *Cheeks* fresh *Roses* ravisht from the Root
     Both red and white, and the sweet life to boot.

135

This Act of horror, and black night obscure,
MONDEGO's daughters long resented deep;
And, for a lasting Tomb, into a pure
Fountain transformd the *Teares* which they did weep.
The name they gave it (which doth still indure)
Was YNES's loves, whom PEDRO there did keep.
     No wonder, such sweet *Streams* water those *Flowers*:
     TEARES, are the substance; and the *Name*, AMOURS.

136

It was not long ere PEDRO found the way
To that *Revenge* which in his breast did boyle;
For, taking in his hands the *Kingdom's* sway
Hee takes it on the Murd'rers (who chang'd soyle)
With licence of another PEDRO, They
(Partners in mischief) having made that vile
     And bloody pact AUGUSTUS did with those
     He was new *Friends* with, of exchanging *Foes*.

137

A rigorous *Chastizer* was this King
Of *Thefts*, of *Murthers*, and *Adultries* blind,
The Ill to condigne punishment to bring
Was the delight and banquet of his mind.
Restraining *Cities* with rough *disciplin*,
From *Vice* and *Insolence* of every kind,
     He gave more *Robbers* their deserved meed
     Then wandring THESEUS, or ALCIDES, did.

138

From the just PEDRO, and severe (Behold
How *Nature* sometimes can prevaricate!)
Sprang the remisse, the Carelesse, the sheep-fold
FERNANDO: who set all of a Flame straight.
Whence the CASTILIAN entring uncomptrold,
Went wasting so the weake disnerved *State,*
  That at last gaspe it lay: For it's seen oft,
  "A soft KING makes a valiant *People* soft.

139

Whether it were GOD's Judgement, for his sin
Of taking from her Husband LEONORE,
And marrying Her; besotten with her *win-*
Ning looks, and by his Flattring *Casuists* more;
Or that faynt *Vice* (through custom soaking in
Into his Breast, thence breathing through each pore)
  Made him all *Pap* within: For, tis as true,
  "*Unlawfull* fires make Valiant Kings soft too.

140

"*Lust* oft hath brought *great men* to great mishap:
"God that permitting, and ordaining *thus.*
"Witness th'ABETTORS of fair HELEN's Rape:
"*King*-TARQUIN, and *Triumvir*-APPIUS.
"Why could not holy DAVID judgement scape?
"Why was destroy'd the TRIBE illustrious
  "Of BENJAMIN? DINAH cost SICHEM deer:
  "Nor (SARAH onely wisht) went PHAROAH cleer.

141

"Then, whether *manly* Bosoms *melt,* or not,
"With *fires* that are not kindled from *Above;*
"ALCMENA's *Son* (who ware a *Petticot*
"To please OMPHALE) well may serve to prove:
"And ANTHONY, who lost the fame he got,
"And the *World's Crown* for CLEOPATRA's love.
  "And *Thou* of CARTHAGE, in full conquest stayd,
  "By stumbling on a mean *Appulian* mayd.

142

"But *who* is priviledg'd from the sweet snare
"Which *Love* so subt'ly weaves, and hides it (oh!)
"In *Damask* Roses, in bright *auburn* haire,
"*Transparent* alabaster, and *warm* Snow?
Who, from the poyson'd Arrows of the *Faire?*
"From a MEDUSA's *head* (I term it so)
    "That turns the hearts of them whom she doth tame,
    "Not into *Stone* (then it were well) but flame?

143

"*Who* sees a *crystal* Brow, a *piercing* look,
"A *lushious* and *Seraphick* excellence,
"(Transforming *Soules* into it) That can brook
"The *object,* or pretend the least defence?
"*All* That have swallow'd LOVE's bewitching Hook,
"With poor FERNANDO's frailty will dispence:
    "And some (as when MARS seen in courser snares,
    "The *Gods* did once) ev'n wish *his* crime were *Theirs.*

End of the third Canto.

Fourth Canto

STANZA 1

After a pitchie, and a dripping *night,*
Poor *Travailers* confounding in their way,
A glorious *Morn* (succeeding) glads the sight;
And, with the long'd-for *Sun,* returns the *day:*
After the whistling winds have spent their spight,
On the calm'd Sea the wanton *Dolphins* play:
    So the afflicted *Kingdom* it befell
    When soft FERNANDO bade the world farewel.

2

And if ours wisht a *Champion,* to fullfil
Their Vengeance upon *Those,* from whom alone
(Using remiss Fernando's favours *ill*)
They make account that all their *ills* are grown,
Now they'l have one according to their will,
Putting illustrious John into the *Throne,*
    As Pedro's onely Son they could come at:
    And his *true* Son, though *Illegitimat.*

3

That this was *Heaven's* Ordinance divine
By most cleer Tokens evident became,
When a young girl, speaking before her time,
In Ebora distinctly form'd his name.
And as a *Herald-Angel* sent in fine
The *Portingall Successour* to proclaime,
    Lifting i'th'Cradle *Body, Hand,* and *Tone,*
    "Cry'd Portugal For The New King Don John.

4

Such, at this time, was the confus'd Estate
Of the poor *Realm,* and the mad *Peaple's* spleen;
That (to disburthen their conceived Hate)
Flat *Cruelties* in ev'ry part were seen:
Killing the Kin, and all that did relate
To the adult'rous *Earl,* and to the *Queen,*
    With whom her lewdness (they affirm'd) was more
    In widowhood, then it had been before.

5

But true, or false, the scandal which they gave
Forfeits his *Head* (and rightly) to the *Axe.*
He dyes for't in her presence: Others have
The self-same sawce.   It catches like fir'd flax.
One, whom religious *Orders* could not save,
Thrown from a *Steeple* like Astianax:
    A *Second, Orders, Sex,* nor th'*Altar's* Horn:
    A third dragg'd naked, and to mamocks torn.

6

In long forgetfullness may now be laid
Those horrid *Massacres,* which ROME beheld,
By bloody SYLLA, and fierce Marius, made,
When one another they by turns expel'd.
Then LEONÓRE (whom th'unrevenged shade
Of her dear *Count* with open fury swell'd)
     Invites CASTEEL, who did her *daughter* wed;
     Saying, the CROWN belongeth to *her* head.

7

Her daughter BEATRICE was *she,* as due
To whom *he* of CASTEEL that *Crown* might clame:
Reputed daughter of FERNANDO too,
With the permission of her *mother's Fame.*
Into the *Field* CASTILIA therefore drew,
To seize the *Kingdom* in his *Consort's* name,
     Amassing men (our *Spot* to overwhelm)
     From every Province of his spacious Relm.

8

Troops came (on this occasion) from that LAND
To which one BRIGUS gave his name of yore:
From *Lands* recover'd (by their GREAT FERNAND,
And greater CID) from the usurping MORE.
Nor *those,* who high in MARS his favour stand,
Who with their Ploughs (laborious) travaile o're
     The Hills of LEON, slowly did advance:
     The ancient Terror of the *Moorish* Lance.

9

The VANDALS came, who to this day confide
In *Valour* which of old they made appeer.
SEVILIA came (ANDALUZIA's Pride)
So sweetly water'd by GUADALQUIVEER.
The noble ISLAND, which was *colonied*
Sometimes by TYRIANS, was not wanting here,
     Who, on their *Banners* in those days of yore
     The famous *Pillars* of ALCIDES bore.

10

Came likewise Troops from old TOLEDO's Reame,
Whose nimble *Tongue* the neatest *Spanish* trolls:
And TAGUS clasps her with his amorous streame,
Which from the *Hills* of CUENCA sweetly rolls.
Nor *fear* kept *you* from being joyn'd to *Them*,
Sordid GALLEGOS (refractory Souls!)
      That arm your selves again, those swords t'oppose,
      Of which already ye have felt the blows.

11

Likewise black Furies of the *war* drive an
The BISKAYNER, A mortal enemy
To *Complement;* nor of a Heart, that can
From any stranger brook an injury:
He of GUIPUSCUA, and th'ASTURIAN,
Fam'd for their *Yron-Indies* far and nigh:
      These (arm'd with their own *Mines*) conducted are
      To serve their LORD in the denounced War.

12

JOHN, from whose manly Bosom's bristles, grew
That courage, SAMPSON borrow'd of *his* hairs,
Though all his men amount but to a Few,
To play the best of a bad Game prepares.
Nor, that he's unresolved what to do,
Calls the chief Counsellors in his Affairs;
      But, to observe how every one inclines:
      "For among many there are many minds.

13

There want not such, as, ev'n against that *Cause*
They follow, Reasons do insinuate:
Whose sence with a *Castilian* Byas draws
From all that's *Portingal* degenerate:
Whom *Fear* so freezes, and so overaws,
That *natural love* it doth exterminate.
      Their *King,* and *Countrey,* they deny: and wou'd
      With PETER, too for fear deny their GOD.

14

Don NUNIO (to be sure) was none of *Those*:
But though his *Brothers* (whom he deerly lov'd)
Take t'other side, and big the danger grows,
Them whose *Faith* staggers sharply he reprov'd;
And at these People, with their *I's*, and *No's*,
Laying his Hand upon his *Hilt* (more *mov'd*
       Then *Eloquent*) these words abruptly hurl'd:
       Threatning the *Earth,* the *Ocean,* and the *world*.

15

"What? 'Mongst the *Portingal*-Nobility
"Shall there by any less then *Sons* of MARS?
"What? in *this* Realm (victorious far and nigh)
"Shall there be born, That shun *defensive* wars?
"That will their *Hearts*, their *Hands*, their *Heads* deny,
"At such a pinch, their *Fortunes*, and their *Stars*?
       "Or who, for any cause that can be thought,
       "Will see their *Countrey* in subjection brought.

16

"What?   Are not *you* then of those *worthies* bred,
"Who (fierce and valiant as the *Swords* they wore),
"Under the great HENRIQUEZ Standart led,
"O'rethrew this *warlike* Nation once before?
"When *Them* so many routed *Squadrons* fled,
"So many *Flaggs,* that (besides thousands more
       "Of lesser Rank, amongst the opulent *Prey*)
       "Sev'n potent *Earles* our Pris'ners were that day?

17

"With *whom,* perpetually were trodden down
"*These,* That are now so dreadful in your view,
"By DENIS and his *Son,* of *high* Renown,
"But with your *Sires,* and *Grandsires*? and if *you*
"*Were* (by the *Sins,* or *weakness,* of the CROWN)
"Kept under, in FERNANDO's days, Renew
       "Your strength with the *new* King: "For 'tis not strange
       "(You see) for *People* with their *Kings* to change.

18

"Ye have one *now,* that, if your courage rose
"Equal with his *You* lifted to the *Throne,*
"Ye might o'rethrow the *World*; how much more *Those,*
"Whom ye have oft already overthrown?
"And if, in short, with *Him* ye cannot lose
"Those fears that seem t'have turn'd you into *stone*;
    "Stand but like stones (I ask you not one stroke)
    "Whilst I *alone* resist a *forraign* yoak.

19

"*I* onely, with *my* Tenants, and with *this* —
(And at that word he pull'd out half his *Blade*)
"Will save from *force,* and all that shameful is,
"This *Land,* which hitherto hath liv'd a Maid.
"By the *King's fire,* and *mine* (lighted at *his*),
"Our *Countrey's Tears,* By *Faith* (by you not waigh'd).
    "Not onely *These* upon their knees I'l bring,
    "But *All* that ever shall oppose *my* King.

20

As when, despairing now, the *Flowr* of Rome
(All that survived CANNAE's fatal Field)
Stood ready (rallyed in CANUSIUM)
Themselves unto the *Conquerour* to yield,
But young CORNELIUS doth amongst them come,
And swears them *All* upon his sword, compel'd;
    That they the *Roman wars* shall never leave,
    Till *life* leave *them,* or *Those* their *lives* bereave:

21

So NUNIO animates, whom he did force.
Whose boyst'rous *Rhet'rick* such quick flame imparts,
Chiefly the Tail and sting of his discourse,
As thaws those fears that had congeal'd their hearts.
And presently they call *to Horse, to Horse,*
Tossing about their heads their brandisht darts.
    They run: and "*live* (with open mouth they cry)
    "*The famous King that gives us Liberty!*

22

Amongst the fiercer *Commons, some* up-cry
This war, by which their Countrey is assoyl'd:
Others scowr up their *Armours,* and supply
What with the rust of *peace* was eate, and spoyl'd:
These, stuff old *Murrions; Those,* new breast-plates try:
Each takes those *Arms,* he hath most skill to wield.
    With sev'ral colour'd *Garments, others* flaunt:
    Others, Love-*Mottos,* and *devices* paint.

23

With all this well-appointed Company,
Doth valiant JOHN from fresh ABRANTES go:
Abrantes, which injoys abundantly
The streams from CUENCA's frozen Caves that flow.
The well-arm'd *Vanguard* is commanded by
One who was fit t'have led against a Foe
    Those *Oriental* Forces without Compt,
    With which *King* XERXES past the HELLESPONT.

24

Don NUNIO ALVAREZ I mean: the true
And fatal scourge of proud CASTILIANS,
No less, then once the valiant HUN was to
The ancient GAULLS, and the ITALIANS.
Another *Knight* (to whom much praise is due)
Leads the *right wing* of LUSITANIANS:
    As skilfull to conduct, as bold in fight,
    Of VASCONCELOS MEM RODRIGUEZ hight.

25

The *other wing,* that corresponds with *this,*
ANTONIO VASQUEZ of ALMAAD commands,
Who after *Conde* of Abranchez is:
And *Hee* comes up with the *Sinestre* Bands.
In the *Reer-Gard* the *Standart* none can miss,
Where (Circling PORTUGAL) CASTILIA Stands,
    With JOHN, accomplished in every part,
    Who makes a *dunce* of MARS in his own Art.

26

Trembling upon the Battlements, and een
Cold (betwixt *hope* and *feare* suspended now)
Wives, Mothers, Sisters, Mistresses, are seen.
Prayers they preferr: *Fasts, Pilgrimages,* vow.
Our *Troops* (advancing with undaunted meen)
Down by the *Foe* they sit them, brow to brow;
     Receiv'd with shouts, which rock the *Firmament*:
     Yet *one,* & *t'other,* doubted the event.

27

The vocall *Trumpets* challenge, and accept:
The *Drumms,* and whistling *Fifes* in consort joyne.
The dusty *Field* the flourisht *Ensigns* swept,
Where all the Colours of the *Rainbow* shine.
It was the time, when, CERES's fruits being reapt,
She lends her *Lab'rers* to the God of *Wine,*
     When (into *Libra* entred *August's Sun*)
     Plump BACCHUS puts sweet *Must* into the Tun.

28

Castilian Trumpets did the On-set sound,
Loud, furious, dismall, terrible, and hoarce;
Heard it ARTABOR's *Mount,* and underground
Her way did frighted GUADIANA force:
Heard it the DWERE, and ALENTECHO round:
TAGUS looks back, then hastens on his course:
     And *Mothers* (who that baylefull noyse did heare)
     Claspe to their *Breasts* their tender *Babes* for feare.

29

How many *Cheeks* were *there* discolourd seen,
Whilst to the *Heart* the frendlie blood repaird?
"In great *Incounters* greater is I ween
"The feare of danger, then the danger feard:
"But, when the first *brunt's* over, *Rage,* and *Teen,*
"Desire of *honour,* and to *Plume* the *Beard*
     "Of a proud Foe; *These* take away the sence
     "Of losing *limbs,* or dearest *life's* expence.

30

On *either* side the first *Battalions* move:
The doubtfull war on either side began:
These fighting for their *Country,* which they love;
Those, to possess *another's* if they can.
The great Pereyra first his force did prove:
Summing an *Armie's* valour in one *Man.*
      Hee shocks, strikes down, in fine he makes their *Grave,*
      And with their *Corpses* sows the *Land* they crave.

31

Now through the darkned Ayre barbd Arrows fleet,
Javelins, with other shott, fly whizzing round;
Under the fiery *Coursers's* yron Feet
The *Earth* doth tremble, and the Vales resound:
Lances are crackt, and (dropping thick as Sleet)
The Horsemen armd come thundring to the ground.
      Upon feirce Nunio's Few, fresh Foes are pact:
      Their Art, to *multiply; his,* to *abstract.*

32

Loe now his *Brother's* swords against him bent
(Cruell, and ougly)! But *Hee* wonders not.
For they, who 'gainst their *King,* and *Country* went,
Would never stick to cut a *Brother's* Throat.
Of these *Revolters* many did present
Themselves in the first Ranks: And *who* so hot
      To kill their *Friends,* as *They?* So kindred Hoasts
      Of yore incountred in *Pharsalian* Coasts.

33

O Cataline, and Thou *Sertorius* bould,
Noble Coriolanus, with the rest,
Who 'gaynst your *Countrey* drew your swords of ould
From an *Impious,* though *provoked,* Brest!
If in the darke *Abysse* of Pluto's Hould
Ye find your selves with Furies's whipps opprest,
      Tell them (to cloake the horrour of your sin)
      Some *Portingalls* sometimes have *Traytors* bin.

34

Ore-whelmed with growing *Foes's* impetuous flood,
Now were the formost of our *Squadrons* burst;
There Nunio, like a *rampant Lyon,* stood,
Whom in her neighb'ring Mountains Ceuta nurst;
But now he is invirond with a wood
Of Hunters speares, ore *Tetuan* plains that courst;
  Those All are bent at *Him,* His Brows Hee draws,
  Nor is it *Feare,* but *Anger* makes him pause;

35

Musty he looks, nought pleased with the sight,
Yet (his wild Nature, and undaunted heart
Incompetible with ignoble flight)
Himself amongst the thickest he doth dart:
So with the blood of *Aliens* dyes our Knight
The *Lusitanian* Grass. Some fall, some start
  Ev'n of his *own.* "For, where there is such *odds,*
  "*Strength* often fails, and firmest *Vertue* nods.

36

John saw how hard brave Nunio was put to't:
(For, as a wise and careful *General,*
His *Eye* was in *all* parts, in *all* his *Foot,*
His *Presence,* and his *words,* gave life to *All*).
As a *She-Lyon,* and a *Nurse* to boot,
That finds, whilst Hunger *Her* from home did call,
  (Leaving her whelps unto themselves) a bold
  Massylian shepherd lurcht them from her Hold;

37

Raving she runs, and grinds her Teeth, and rends
The Seaven Brother Mountains with her Voice:
So John, so runs he (to assist his Frends)
To the *Head Squadrons* with some soldiers choice.
"O brave *Camrades,* noble as are your Ends,
"(How in your matchless *Valour* I rejoyce!)
  "Defend your *Country,* and defend your *Lands:*
  "The Hope of *Freedom* in your *Lances* stands.

38

"See *me,* your *King,* your *Fellow,* and your *Head,*
"'Mongst *Darts,* 'mongst *Arrows,* and thick *Pikes* among,
"Rush on the Foe! Nor are you sent, but led.
"Shew, fighting, to what Countrey ye belong.
This the irrefragable *Warriour* sed;
Who, four times poysing a sharp Lance, and strong;
    Throws it with force: and through this *Throw* alone
    Many a *Soule* out of her House is throwne.

39

For (loe!) his men with honorable shame
Are kindled new and with a noble Ire.
Who shall bet most at MARS his bloody Game,
Is th'onely Thing to which they *All* aspire.
They *Vye, revye,* and dip their steel in flame,
Break stubborn *Mayles,* nor leave thick *Plates* intire.
    Thus wounds they give, and wounds they take again,
    Nor doth it grieve them, slaying, to be slain.

40

Many are posted to the *Stygian* Wave,
Into whose Bodies entred *Steel,* and death.
Of St. IAGO there the MASTER brave
Dyes fighting stoutly to his last of breath.
Another MASTER dire of CALATRAVE
Pulls *Troops* down with him to the shades beneath.
    The *Renegade* PEREYRAS likewise dye
    Reneaguing HEAVEN and their *Destiny.*

41

Went thousands of the *Vulgar* without noat,
And *nobles* too, unenter'd in FAME's rolls,
Where that lean dog still gapes with triple throat,
Which never can be fill'd with humane souls.
And (more to humble *them,* who, when on float,
Thought the whole World must stoop to their controlls)
    The high *Castilian Standart* now doth fall,
    And kiss the foot of that of PORTUGALL.

42

With deaths, with groans, with blood, with gashes dire,
The battail cruel above measure grows.
The multitude of men, that here expire,
Makes *all* the *Flow'rs* in colour like the *Rose*.
All *fly,* or *dye* : Now out of breath was *Ire* :
Now *Valour* lost an *Arm* for want of Foes :
  Now routed sees himself CASTILIA's *King,*
  And quits the purpose he from home did bring.

43

The *Field* he leaves unto the *Conquerer,*
Glad that he did not leave him his life too.
The poor remainder follow : To whom Feare
Gave *wings,* not *Feet:* nor did they run, but flew.
The loss of so much men, and Treasure there,
Profoundly in their silent hearts they rue :
  Hiding the smart, the sorrow; and the soyle,
  To have *Another* triumph in *their* spoyle.

44

"Some *Him* with open mouth blaspheam'd, and curst,
"Who first invented *War* mankind to quell;
"In whose obdurate Breast *Ambition* first,
"And *Covetise* of others goods did dwell;
"Nor car'd for feeding his *hydropick* Thirst
"How many silly soules were pack't to *Hell*;
  "Who taught the way to shorten humane lives,
  "To orphan *Children,* and to widow *Wives.*

45

Victorious JOHN upon the place stays out
In martial glory the accustom'd days :
With *Offrings* then, and *Pilgrimage* devout,
To *Him,* That gave the *Conquest,* gives the Praise.
But NUNIO (minding what he was about,
As He That knows, a lasting Fame to raise,
  No way like *Arms,* which all the world command)
  Passes his *Troops* to the *Trans-Tagan* Land.

46

To *Him* his stars so favourable were,
That the success applauded the *designe:*
For he both conquers, and the spoyls doth weare
Of *Andalusian* Countreys That confine.
The *Betick Standard* of Sevilia there,
Under which divers neighb'ring *great ones* joyn,
  With small resistance at his feet soon falls,
   Quell'd by the *force,* and *name,* of Portingals.

47

With *these* and *other* Victories opprest
A tedious while were the Castilians brave,
When *Peace,* and *now* by both desired *Rest,*
The *vanquisht* People from the *Victors* have:
After the King Of Heav'n, for ever blest,
To the *Foe-Kings* in holy marriage gave
  Of English Sisters an unequall'd pair,
   Illustrious, lovely, beautiful, and Fair.

48

But long that Breast, inur'd to bloody Broile,
To live without a *Foe,* could not sustain;
So (having *none* upon the *Land* to foyle)
Goes to extend his Conquest o're the *Maine.*
This is our first of *Kings,* who doth exile
Himself from Spain, to make the Affricane
  By force of *Arms* perceive the diff'rence great
   Betwixt CHRIST's *Law,* and *that* of Mahomet.

49

Behold on curled Thetys's silver flood
Their wings a thousand *swimming Eagles* beat,
To catch the swelling wind (a moving *wood*)
Where the *World's* utmost bounds Alcides set.
Mount Avila he takes, and the Walls good
Of noble Ceuta, outing Mahomet
  With his blind Worship: and secures all Spaine
   From *Treason of* another Juliane.

50

Death envies so great Bliss to Portugall
As to injoy the Ages it desires
This worthy *Prince*; and takes him from *Earth's* Ball,
To add a new *Voice* to the *Angells's Quires*.
But that Good Pow'r, which *Him* to *Heav'n* did call,
Left his large *off-spring* to supply their *Sire's*
    Lamented want: Princes, who shall command,
    Augment, and with *new* Vertues deck the *Land*.

51

King Edward was not of the *happiest*, though,
The while that *He* the *Regal Throne* did fill:
"For moody Time goes blending *joy* with *woe*:
"And with *alternate* Hand gives *good* for *Ill*.
"Who ever *Happiness* did *constant* know?
"Or Fortune with *one* face continue still?
    Yet to this Kingdom *she*, and ev'n this King,
    More of her *honey* gave, then of her *sting*.

52

He saw his *Brother* Captive (good Fernand)
Who had a *Soul* so *publike*, and so *brave*,
That, for his *Troops*, distrest in Affrick-Land,
Himself a *Pawn* unto the Moors he gave.
Where, when his ransome was in his own Hand,
He (born a Prince) would rather dye a slave,
    Then that for *Him* we Ceuta should restore.
    Freedom he lov'd, but lov'd his *Countrey* more.

53

Codrus, because the Foe should not o'recome,
Deviz'd a noble *Stratagem* to dye:
To save the martial *discipline* of Rome
Did Regulus to *Death* with *Torments* flye:
Ours, distant fear to keep his *Countrey* from,
Invites himself to *endless slavery*.
    Codrus, nor Curtius (so much wonder'd at)
    Nor loyal Decii, did so much at *That*.

54

But Edward's onely *Son*, ALPHONSO hight,
(A lucky *Name* to our HESPERIA)
Who, the prowd threatnings of *Barbarian* might
In bord'ring *Lands*, low as the dust did lay;
Would have been doubtless an unconquer'd *Knight*,
Had he forborn t'invade IBERIA.
     AFFRICK will tell you, 'twas impossible
     To overcome a *King* so terrible.

55

To pull the *golden Apples* was *his* hap,
Which none before him but ALCIDES bit.
On the feirce MOOR he such a *Yoake* did clap
From which they cannot rest their Necks out yit.
The *Palme* and *Lawrell* green his Temples wrap,
Of *Victories*, he at the *Seige* did git
     Of *Popllous* TANGER, Strong ALCACER'S Towers,
     And tough ARZILA, o're the *Barb'rous* Powers.

56

Infine, the ever-conqu'ring PORTINGALLS
(The succours beaten) entring *These* by force,
Threw to the ground the *adamantine* walls,
And *All* that thwarted their Victorious course.
Wonders (deserving *Pens* whence liquor falls
Immortalizing with its *Nectar* source)
     Wrought *private Swords* in this *Exployt* of fame:
     Exalting more the *Lusitanian* name.

57

But *after* taynted with *ambition*,
And *Rule's* sweet Thirst (though soure to *Him* at last)
FERNANDO he invades of ARRAGON,
About the *Kingdom* of CASTILIA vast.
Of the proud NATIONS (which depend thereon)
A num'rous *Hoast*, t'oppose him, is amasst,
     From CADIZ to the lofty PERYNEE:
     All which the *King* FERNANDO did obey.

58

The young Prince John disdayns it should be said,
Hee is the only idle Man in SPAINE;
And therefore, his ambitious *Sire* to ayd
Resolves forth with: nor is his *Ayd* in vaine.
The *Battayle's* bloody period, undismayd,
Hee sees; and with a brow serene and plaine,
    The warlike *Father* put to totall Rout,
    Yet leaves the *Son* the *Victory* in doubt.

59

For the sublime and truly *Royall* son
(Gay *Knight* undaunted, confident, and high),
Having vast spoyle to th' *Adversary* done,
Stays one whole day the *Field* to justify.
Thus was OCTAVIUS CAESAR overthrowne,
And *Victor* his companion ANTHONY,
    When *They* on *Those*, who noble JULIUS kil'd,
    Revenged themselves in the *Philippick* Feild.

60

Now when on sable wings of endlesse Night
ALPHONSO mounted to high *Heav'n* serene;
The *Prince,* That then the *Scepter* swayd of right,
Was *Second* JOHN, who made of Kings fifteen.
Hee (to attain to *Glory's* utmost hight)
Began a *Taske,* exceeding strength terrene
    (Whose *weight* is *now* by *my* weake shoulders born),
    To seek the *Cradle* of the purple MORN.

61

He sends fit *Mesengers* from his owne *Court*
Through SPAINE, FRANCE, celebrated ITALY:
There to imbarque in that illustrious *Port*
Where was interr'd, of old, PARTHENOPE:
NAPLES; which *Fortune* made her *Tennis-Court,*
By several NATIONS held successively,
    To place it *glorious* (no more change to feel)
    In sov'raign SPANIARDS, who can fix *her* wheel.

62

Away they sayle through the CALABRIAN DEEP;
Passe by the RODIAN ISLAND's sandy Bay;
Along the Coast of ALEXANDRIA keep,
For POMPEY's death infamous to this day.
They travayle MEMPHIS, and those *Lands* which steep
Themselves in NYLE. To ETHIOPIA
  They mount, which EGYPTS upper part doth lock,
  Where CHRIST hath feeding an out-lying *Flock*.

63

The ERYTHREAN SEA they likewise crost,
Which, dry-foot, past the seed of ISRAEL.
The NABATHEAN MOUNTAINS' sight they lost,
So named from the *Son* of ISHMAEL.
The oderiferous SABEAN-COAST
(Inricht with *Teares* which from the *Mother* fell
  Of fayre ADONE) and BLEST ARABIA trac't
  Throughout (the STONY balking; and the WAST).

64

The PERSIAN GULPH they enter. To *This* neer,
Great BABEL's Ruines are *yet* visible.
Swift TIGRIS mingles with EUFRATES heer:
Brothers, That with their *Fountain's* glory swell.
Hence they proceed in quest of INDUS *cleer:*
From which great things *Posterite* shall tell,
  Of *Troops,* that through long *Seas* shall passe thereto:
  Which, even *by Land* nigh Trajan durst not doe.

65

Of INDIA, TARFE, and CARMANIAN HILLS,
The strange and uncoth *Nations* they beheld:
Noating the sev'rall *Customes,* sev'rall *Skills,*
Which sev'rall *Regions* doe produce, and yeild.
But from such *Distant* parts (joynd to the Ills
Of so *rough* journeys) Men return but seld.
  In fine, *there* did *These* dye; they stuck fast *there:*
  For back they came not to their *Countrey deare.*

66

Seems, gracious HEAV'N reserv'd for *Thee* alone,
EMANUEL, and for thy great desart
So *hard a worke*: For *Thee*, with thoughts *high-flown*
Inspir'd, and cut out fit to *act* this *part*.
MANUEL (succeeding JOHN, both in the *Throne*,
And in the haughty *purpose* of his Heart)
  When first he *took on Him* the *Kingdoms Charge*,
  The Conquest *undertook* oth'OCEAN large.

67

Hee, as a person whom the noble thought
Of th'obligation he inherited
From his *Fore Fathers* (who intirely sought
The *Realm's* advancement) hourly combated;
When PHEBUS, quitting the *supernal Vault,*
Unto the *low* ANTIPODES was fled,
  And setting *stars* (which in his place arose)
  With twinkling eyes invited to repose:

68

Extended now upon his *golden Nest*
(Such are the *Beds* where thoughts *tumultuous* brood)
And *there* revolving in his silent Brest
The *obligation* of his *place* and *blood*:
Slumber possest his *Eyes, nor dispossest*
His *Heart* of Cares, which made *that* station good:
  For his tyr'd *Lidds* whilst sleep (*resisted*) shutts,
  MORPHEUS a thousand *shapes* before him putts.

69

So high above ground seems he lifted heer,
That his proud *Crown* the *Firmament* doth peirce:
From whence *new worlds* before his eyes appeer,
Nations of num'rous people strange and fierce:
And *yonder* (to the springing MORNING neer)
As through the Ayre his *visual* Raies disperse,
  Hee sees, farr off, from high and antient *Mountains,*
  Melt down a payre of deep and crystall *Fountains.*

70

With *Birds* of monstrous Forms, *wild-beasts* and *Flocks,*
One of those *Mountains* was inhabited;
Where thousand savage Trees with leavie Locks
The intercourse of people hindered.
The shaggie *Forrest,* and the craggie *Rocks's*
Inextricable *Knots,* demonstrated
    That to those days of *ours* from ADAM'S sin
    No humane Foot had ever trod therein.

71

Out of these *Waters* (as to *Him* appeares),
Addressing *towards* him their hasty pace,
Two *Fathers* rise, *both* wondrous struck in yeares,
With *Rustick* both, yet *venerable,* Face.
Their *Snowy* Curles distill in *silver* Teares
Which bathe their Bodyes down in every place.
    Tan'd were their *Skins,* and rusty: Their *Beards* kept
    Rough and unshorn, with which the ground they swept.

72

The Temples of their heads were trimly bound
With health-restoring *Druggs,* and *Fruits* unknown.
The *one* lookt weather-beaten and half-drowned,
As if a longer voyage *Hee* had gone;
And (fierce, ev'n at his *Fountain*) underground
Seem'd to have stoln from a *remoter* one:
    As from *Arcadian* plains ALPHEO sly
    To ARETHUSA'S bed in SICILY.

73

This (as the more authoriz'd of the Twain)
"Spake thus (farr off) unto the *King. O Thou*
"For whose high *Crown,* and *Empire* soveraign,
"*Much* World is kept, that's hid from the *world* now.
"Wee (through the *Earth* so fam'd, whose *Necks* in vain,
"Strave *others* wholly to *their* yoaks to bow)
    "Are come to wish *thee* send some Men, That may
    "Receive large *tributes* we to *Thee* must pay.

74

"I am illustrious GANGES: born and nurst
"In Paradice: where is my *mother-Spring*.
"My *Mate* (That from the *Cliffes* thou seest, doth burst,
"Nor other *Cradle* knows) is INDUS KING.
"Yet a severe *Warr* shall we cost thee first:
"But *Thou* (persisting) in the end shalt bring,
        "By Victories *prodigious*, to the *Bitt*,
        "All these *viewd Nations* humbly to submit.

75

The *Holy* and *illustrious River* sed
No more: But in a moment vanisht *Both*.
EMANUELL wakes surpriz'd with a strange dread,
And earthquake in his Bosome. PHEBUS goeth
In the meane time his glittring *Cloke* to spred
Over the WORLD, buried in *downe*, and *sloath*.
        AURORA came: who, when *she* forth doth rush,
        Strikes *Lilies* pale, and makes the *Roses* blush.

76

The KING in hast to councell calls his *Lords*,
To *them* the figures of the *Vision* shows;
To *them* repeates the Holy *Elder's Words*:
Whence in them *all* great admiration grows.
A NAVY is resolv'd on by the BOARD'S
Unanimous *Voate*: In which (magnanimous) *Those*,
        Whom *hee* shall send to plough the OCEAN blew,
        Must seek new *Nations* out, and *Clymates* new.

77

I, who despayr'd to see put in effect
What had so long been tumbling in my mind:
(For my presaging *Soule* could nere be checkt
From prompting great things to mee of this kind)
Comprize not for what *cause*, for what *respect*,
Or for what *merit*, he in *mee* could find;
        But the good *King* was pleas'd to pick out *mee*
        To be this weightie *enterprize's* Key.

78

And with *Intreaties,* and with *sugard* phrase
(Which are the pow'rfullest *commands* of KINGS)
He sayd to me: "Through *deep* and *rugged* ways,
"VERTUE attains the *best* and *noblest* things.
"A *Life* well *lost,* or *hazarded,* to *Bays*
"Of everlasting *Honour* persons brings:
    "For (if to sordid *Feare* it never bends)
    "The *shorter* 'tis, the *Farther* it extends.

79

"*You* have I chose (and all the rest set by)
"To a *Taske* fit for *you* to undergoe:
"A Taske Heroick, difficult and high,
"Which (for my sake) you will think light, I know.
I could not suffer more: but *thus* reply,
"O my dread LEIGE! through *swords,* through *fire,* through *snow,*
    "For *Thee* to venture, only is *Annoy*
    "When I consider *life* is such a *Toy.*

80

"Put me on *Tasks* as great as *those* of yore
"Suborn'd EURISTEUS to ALCIDES gave;
"The fruitful HYDRA, ERIMANTHIAN BORE,
"The HARPIES dire, NEMEAN LYON brave;
"In short, to visit the *infernal shore*
"Where *Styx* moats PLUTO's House with its black Wave:
    "For *Thee* (O KING) worse *dangers,* and worse *Toyls,*
    "My *Spirit* leaps at, nor my *Flesh* recoyles.

81

With sumptuous *Boons,* and *words* that *those* exceed,
My good will *He* doth praise, and gratifie:
"For *Vertue,* spurr'd with praise, doubles her speed;
"And is inflam'd to *Enterprises* high.
To second me in this Exployt, agreed
(Oblig'd by *Nature's,* and by *Frendship's* Tye,
    Thirsty alike of *Honour,* and of *Fame*)
    My dear and loving Brother, PAUL DE GAME.

82

Nich'las Coellio makes a *Third* : for pains
Most indefatigable. And *These* are
My *two Supporters*, strong of *Hand*, and *Brains* :
Experienc't *both, both* no less bold in warr.
I get me a young *Crew* of sturdy *Swains*,
Whose budding *Valour* itcht for *martial jarr* :
    All metled *Lads*; and so, it well appeers,
    That came to such a business *Volunteers*.

83

These too have *gifts* from Manuel's hand, t'equip
Themselves, and make the love they bear him, more :
And with the *praising* bounty of his *Lip*,
Are arm'd 'gainst *All*, hard *Fates* can have in store.
Thus man'd King Pelias that *prophetick* ship
In which (through *Euxine* Seas, unsayl'd before)
    With AEson's Heyre the vent'rous *youth* of Greece
    He sent to Colcos for the *Golden Fleece*.

84

Now in the famous *Port* of Lisbon-Town
(Where golden Tagus mingles his *sweet* Flood
With the Salt Ocean, and his *Sands* doth drown),
With noble *longings*, and *transported* mood,
The Ships lye ready. *There* no sullen *frown*,
No frosty *Fear*, benumms the *youthful* blood :
    For both the *Sea*-men, and the *Land*-men *there*,
    Will go with *me* about the World, they sweare.

85

Upon the *shore* the strutting *souldiers* sayle
In cloathes of sev'rall *colour*, sev'rall *cutt*,
Their *minds* more brave : bent to extend our *pale*,
And plant in *lands unknown* their daring foot.
The gentle *wind* breathing a tempting Gale,
On the tall *Shipps* the *Standarts* ope and shutt.
    The *Shipps* expect, for this new *Navigation*,
    To bee (like Argo) made a *Constellation*.

86

Wee (fitted and provided thus with All
That such a *Voyage* doth require and crave)
To fit our *soules* for *death* devoutly fall:
Which *Saylers* see in ev'ry rounding Wave.
From *Him*, whose presence *Beatificall*
Is all the Food that *Saints* and *Angels* have,
    Favour we beg, for to prepare our way,
    And to conduct us with his *heavenly* Ray.

87

Thus of *that Temple* took we a long leave,
Which (on the Margent of our Ocean plac't)
From the *blest City* did it's name receave
Where GOD was born (a *Gem* in *Clay* enchac't).
I promise thee (O KING) how wee did heave
Our *Anchors* from that shore, when I recast;
    With doubt of ever seeing it again,
    Scarce can my *bridled* eyes from Tears repair.

88

The'Inhabitants of LISBON, that sad day
(For *Frendship* some, and some for *Kindreds* Tyes)
Others, as meer *spectators*, flockt: *dismay*
And *solitarinesse* writt in their *Eyes*.
And *wee* (whom thousand *Priests* upon our way
Did bring with *Psalms*, and all solemnities
    Of grave *procession*), praying to our GOD,
    Went to take shipping in the Noble Road.

89

In so *long Voyage*, and so doubtfull ways,
The gazing people give us All for lost;
This, by their *Teares* the softer *sex* bewrays:
The *Men* by *Sighs*, as they would yeild the Ghost;
Sisters, and *Mothers*; And poor *Wives* (always
Where there is most of *love*, there *feare* reigns *most*)
    Increase the doubt upon the *gen'rall* score,
    That they shall never see our *Faces* more.

90

"*One*, following, Cryes: O *Son*! (the only gage,
"The prop, the stay, the comfort and the joy,
"Of this my weake unprofitable *Age*,
"Which *Floods* of bitter *Tears* drown in Annoy)
"*Why* leav'st thou mee in this sad equipage?
"*Why* wilt thou goe, and leave mee (my deare Boy!)
  "To make the greedy *Seas* thy *Sepulchere*,
  "And *Fishes* feed That take their pastime *there*?

91

"*Another* (with loose Hayr) O my deer *Mate*,
"Without whom *Love* tells mee my roote must pine!
"Why wilt thou goe, and venture at this rate
"That *life* to GULPHS, which is not thine but *mine*?
"How canst thou change, for so uncertain Fate,
"The chaste embraces of thy constant *Vine*?
  "Our *loves*, our *joyes* (in vain how sweet!) must *They*
  "To *Sea*, and with this *wind* be *blown* away?

92

In *these* and other speeches of this kind
(Which from deer *love*, and soft *compassion* rose)
Old men and *children* (to *like Ruth* inclin'd
By diff'rent *Ages*) imitated *Those*.
The neigb'ring *mountayns* in dull *consort* joyne:
And, melting, *bare* the *burthen* of *their* woes.
  The *golden Sands* the *Silver Tears* bedow'd:
  Which seemd to strive with *them* in multitude.

93

Wee (not so much as lifting once our Eyes
On *Wife*, or *Mother*: though our *Soules* it grinds,
Whereby in vain laments to *Sympathize*,
Or change the purpose of our *fixed* minds)
T'embarque our selves conceiv'd it was most wise,
Without those *Farewells* to which custom binds:
  Which (though it bee *Love's* most indeering way)
  Galls more, both *Those* That *goe*, and *Those* that *stay*.

94

But an *Ould man* of *Venerable* look
(Standing upon the shore amongst the Crowds)
His Eyes fixt upon *us* (on ship-board) shook
His head three times ore-cast with sorrows clowds:
And (streining his *Voyce* more then well could brook
His aged *lungs*: It rattled in our shrowds)
    Out of a *science practise* did *Attest*,
    Let fly these words from an *oraculous* Brest:

95

"O *Glory* of *commanding*! O *vain* Thirst
"Of that same empty *nothing*, we call *Fame*!
"O *Ignis fatuus*, kindled and nurst
"With *vulgar* breath (and *this* we *Honour* name)!
"What *Plagues*, what *stings*, what secret *scourges* curst,
"Torment those *Bosomes* which *thou* doest inflame!
    "What *deaths*! what *dangers*! what impetuous *storms*!
    "What *cruelties* on *them* thy Hand performs!

96

"Fell *Tyrant* of the *soule*! *life's* swallowing *Wave*!
"*Mother* of *Plunders,* and black *Rapes* unchast!
"The *secret miner,* and the *open Grave,*
"Of *Patrimonies, Kingdoms, Empires* vast!
"They call thee *noble,* and they call thee *Brave*:
"(Worthy t'have other names upon thee cast!)
    "They call thee *Fame,* and *Glory soveraign*:
    "Titles, with which the foolish *Rout* is tane.

97

"What new *disaster* dire intendest *Thou*
"To lead these *Kingdoms,* and these *Folk* into?
"What *deaths,* what *Horrours* must they swallow now,
"Under pretence to spread *Religion* true?
"What *holdings forth* of *golden Mines,* and how
"Great *Kingdoms* shall ge conquer'd by a Few?
    "What *Fames* dost thou advance? what *Histories*?
    "What *Palms*? what *Triumphs*? and what *Victories*?

98

"But *Thou* (the *lignage* of that *Foole*, who *twice*
"Undid thee by his *disobedience* :
"Not only when he lost thee PARADICE,
"Into this *Vale* of *Teares* exild from thence;
"But when by growth of his *infectious* Vice
"He forfeited thy *second Innocence*,
 "And *Thee*, out of a *golden exile* hurld
 "Into an *Iron* and *contentious world*)

99

"Since in this sweet and pleasing vanity
"Thy giddie *Brain* is so bewitcht, and drownd;
"Since bloody *Rage* and *Inhumanity*,
"*Valour*, and *Brav'rie*, in *thy* language sound;
"Since thou doest valew, and esteem so high,
"The disesteem of *life*, which we are bound
 "To cherish, and in great accompt to have it :
 "('Cause so much fear'd to *loose* it, *Hee* who *gave it*)

100

"Hast thou not, close at hand, the ISHMAELITE
"To cut thee work out, more then thou canst doe?
"If for the *sacred Law* of CHRIST thou fight,
"The'ARABIAN's *false one* does not *He* pursue?
"Hath *Hee* not thousand *Citties*, Infinite
"Of *Land*, if *Power's* a baite, if *Wealth's* one too?
 "Hath not *Hee* got in *Arms* a mighty *Name*,
 "If *Honour*, and not *Bootie*, be *thy* Ayme?

101

"Leav'st thou a *growing Foe* just at thy *dore*,
"To goe and seek *another* Foe so farr,
"Dispeopling an *ould Realm*, wasting *her* store,
"Quitting thy *Countrey*, and thy private LAR?
"That flatt'ring *Fame* to *Heav'n* may make thee soare,
"Through *waves uncertain* seekst thou *certain warr*?
 "In thy swoln *Style* in words at length to find,
 "ARABIA, PERSIA, ETHIOPIA, YND?

102

"Accurst be *Hee*, who first forsook the Ground,
"And fastned *canvas wings* to a *dry Tree*!
"Worthy, in endlesse darkness to be bound;
"If that, which I was taught, Religion bee.
"May never *Judgment*, solid and profound,
"May never *Happy Veyn* in *Poetrie*,
    "Retrive his *memory*, adorn his *Fame*:
    "But dye, with *Him*, his *Glory*, and his *Name*.

103

"The son of Japet stole from Phebus's Carr
"*Fire*, which in *humane* Breast he did infuse;
"*Fire*, which the *world* did kindle into Warr,
"*Plagues*, and *debaucheries* (a great abuse!).
"Prometheus, had it not been better farr
"For *Us*, and for the *world* (which *wee* misuse)
    'Thy noble *Statue* had excus'd that *fire*,
    "Which made it with *Ambition's* wings aspire?

104

"Then had not the much pittied *youth* been driving
"His *Sire's* gilt charet; nor that great *contriver*
"Through the'empty Ayre sayld with his Son (*This* giving
"The *sea* a *name*, Hee *Fame* unto a River).
"Nothing so *high*, nothing so barrd the living,
"Through *Fire, Sword, Water, Calm,* and *Cold,* what ever:
    "Which Man projecteth, and attempteth not,
    "A strange *Condition*! an unquiet *Lot*!

End of the fourth Canto.

Fifth Canto

STANZA 1

The rev'rend *Father* stood inculcating
These *Sentences;* when *Wee* to a serene
And gentle Gale expand our Canvas wing;
When from the loved Port our selves we weane:
And sayles unfurling make the *Welkin* ring
(After the manner of *Sea-faring* Men)
      With Boon Voyage.   Immediatly the *Wind*
      Does on the *Trunks* his Office and his kind.

2

The ever burning *Lamp,* that rules the day,
In the *Nemean Bruite* began to rage;
And the *great world* (which doth with time decay)
Limpt in his *Sixt* infirm and crooked *Age*:
Thereof (accompting in the *Church* 'is way)
Of *Sol's* incessant *Race* the Thousand stage,
      Four hundred, Ninetie Seav'nth, was running, whan
      In all their *trim* the *Shipps* to saile began.

3

Now by degrees out of our sight did glide
Parts of our *Countrey,* which abode behind.
Abode deer Tagus: and we *then* did hide
Fresh Syntra (About *this* our eyes did wind).
In the *lov'd* Kingdom likewise did abide
Our *Hearts,* whose strings could not be thence untwind;
      And, when as *all* the *Land* did now withdraw,
      The sea and *Firmament* was *all* wee saw.

4

Thus went we opening those seas, which (save
Our *own*) no *Nation* open'd ere before:
See those new *Isles,* and clymates near; which brave
PRINCE HENRY shewd unto the *world* before:
The *Mauritanian Hills* and *Strand,* which gave
ANTEUS birth, who *there* was King of yore,
    Upon the *left hand* left (for there is none
    Upon the *right,* though now suspected, known).

5

We the great *Island* of MADERA pass,
Which from it's *Wood's* abundance took the name;
The first which planted by our *Nation* was,
Of which the *worth* is more then the great *fame:*
Nor (though the last place in the *world* it has)
Doth any, Venus loves, excel the same:
    Who (rather) were it *Hers,* would lay aside
    For *This,* CYTHERA, CYPRUS, PAPHOS, GNIDE.

6

We leave adust MASSILIAS barren Coast,
Where AZENEGUES's lean *Heards* take their repast;
A People, That want *water* to their *Roast;*
Nor *Herbs* it self in any plenty tast:
A LAND in fine, to bear no *Fruit* dispos'd:
Where *Birds* in their hot stomachs Iron waste:
    Suff'ring of all things great Necessitie:
    Which ETHIOPIA parts from BARBARIE.

7

We pass the *Bound* that hedges out the *Sun*
When to the frozen *North* he bends his way:
Where *People* dwell, whom CLYMENE's rash Son
Deny'de the sweet Complexion of the *day.*
Here NATIONS strange are water'd one by one
With the fresh Currents of black SENEGA.
    Here ARSINARIUS Aloof is seen,
    That lost his name: *confirmed* by us CAPE GREEN.

8

CANARIAN ISLES (the same men call'd of old
The FORTUNATE) declined: After *These*
Among the *Daughter-Islands* we did fall
Of aged HESPER, term'd HESPERIDES:
(*Locks* in the which the *Fleets* of Portugal
To *wonder* new before had turn'd the *Keys*.)
    There did we touch with favourable wind,
    Some *fresh provisions* for our *Ships* to find.

9

It's *Name* the *Isle* on which we Anchor cast
Did from the warlike St. IAGO take,
The *Saint* That holp the SPANIARD in times past
Such cruel havock of the MOORS to make.
Thence, when the *North* renew'd his kinder blast,
We cut again the circumfused *Lake*
    Of the salt *Ocean;* And that *Store-House* leave,
    From which Refreshment sweet we did receive.

10

Winding from thence about your *Affrick shore,*
Where to the EAST (like a *half-moon*) it bends
About JALOFO's Province (which doth store
The *world* with BLACKS, whom, forc't Aboard, it sends),
The large MANDINGA that affords the *Ore*
The which doth make Friends Foes, and of Foes Frends
    (Which suck't GAMBEA's crooked water laves
    That disimbogues in the *Atlantic* Waves)

11

We pass the GORGADES, peopled by faire
Sisters, in ancient time residing *there* :
Who (rob'd of *seeing*) did amongst them share
One onely *Eye,* which they by turns did weare.
Thou onely, *Thou* (the *Net* of whose curld Haire
Caught NEPTUNE, like a Fish, in his own *Were*)
    Turn'd of them all at last the ugliest *Lout,*
    With *Vipers* sow'dst the burning sands about.

12

Ploughing in fine before a *Northern* Wind
In that vast GULPH the *Navy* went embayd;
LEONA's craggie mountains left behind,
The CAPE OF PALMS (so call'd from *Palmie* shade)
And that great RIVER, where the *Sea* (confin'd)
Against the shores, which we had planted, bray'd:
       With th'*Isle* that boasts *his* name, who would not trust
       Till in the side of GOD his Hand he thrust.

13

There lyes of CONGO the wide-spreading *Ream*,
By *Us* (before) converted to CHRIST's Law;
Through which long ZAYRE glides with crystal stream:
A *River*, this, the Ancients never saw.
In fine through this vast *ocean* from the Team
Of known BOOTES I apace withdraw:
       Having already past upon the *Maine*
       The BURNING LINE that parts the *World* in twain.

14

There we before us saw by it's own light
In this new EPICICLE a *Star* new,
Of which the other *Nations* ne're had sight,
And (long in darkness) no such matter knew.
The world's *Antartick* Henge (less gilt, less bright,
For want of *Stars,* then th'*Artick*) we did view:
       Beneath the which, a question yet depends,
       Whether more *Land* begins, and the *Sea* ends.

15

Past in this sort those *equinoxiall* clymes
By which his steeds *twice* yearely drives the *sun;*
Making two *Summers, Winters, Autumns, Primes,*
Whilst he from one to t'other *Pole* doth run:
Now *tost,* now *calm'd* (A *sufferer* in all *Times:*
By *want,* and *plenty,* equally undone)
       I saw both BEARES (the *Little* and the *Great*)
       Despight of JUNO in the *Ocean* set.

16

To tell thee all the *dangers* of the DEEP
(Which humane Judgment cannot comprehend)
Suddain and fearfull *storms*, the *Ayre* that sweep;
Lightnings, that *with* the *Ayre* the *Fire* doe blend;
Black HURRACANS; thick *Nights*; THUNDERS, that keep
The *World* alarm'd, and threaten the last *End*:
  Would be too tedious: indeed vain and mad,
  Though a *brasse* Tongue, and *Iron* lungs I had.

17

I *saw* those things, which the rude *Mariner*
(Who hath no *Mistresse*, but *Experience*)
Doth for unquestionable *Truths* aver,
Guided belike by his *externall* sence:
But ACADEMICKS (who can never err,
Who by pure *Wit*, and LEARNING's *quintessence*,
  Into all NATURE's *secrets* dive and pry)
  Count either *Lyes*, or *coznings* of the *Eye*.

18

I saw (as plain as the *sun's* midday light)
That *fire* the *Sea-man* saints (shining out faire
In time of *Tempest*, of feirce *winds* despight,
Of *over-clowded* Heavens, and black despayre):
Nor did wee *all* lesse wonder (and well might,
For twas a *sight* to *bristle* up the Hayre)
  To see a *sea-born Clowd* with a long *Cane*
  Suck *in* the sea, and spout it *out* againe.

19

I *saw* with these *two eyes* (nor can presume
That *these* deceiv'd mee) from the *Ocean* breathed
A little *Vapour*, or aeriall *Fume*,
With the curld *wind* (as by a *Turnor*) wreathed.
I *saw* it reach to *Heaven* from the salt *spume*,
In such thin *Pipe* as *those* where *springs* are sheathed;
  That by the *Eye* it hardly could be deemed:
  Of the same substance with the *Clowds* it seemed.

20

By little *this* and little did augment,
And swell'd beyond the Bulk of a thick *Mast.*
Streightning and *widening* (like a *Throat*) it went,
To gulp into it self the water fast.
It *wav'd* upon the *wavy* Element.
The top thereof (impregnated at last
  Into a *Clowd*) expanded *more,* and *more,*
  With the great load of *Water* which it bore.

21

As a black *Horse-leech* (mark it in some *Pool*!)
Got to the *Lip* of an unwary *Beast,*
Which (*drinking*) suck't it from the *water* cool,
Upon *another's* blood *itself* to feast;
It swells and swells, and feeds beyond all Rule,
And stuffs the paunch; a rude, unsober, *Guest*:
  So swell'd the *Pillar* (with a hideous Crop)
  It self, and the black Clowd which it did prop.

22

But, when that now 'tis full, the *Pedestal*
Draws to itself, which in the *Sea* was set;
And (flutt'ring through the Ayre) in show'rs doth fall:
The *couchant* Water with *new* water wet.
It pays the waves the *borrow'd* Waves, but all
The *Salt* thereout did first extract and get.
  Now tell me, SCHOLARS, by your Books; what skill,
  Dame NATURE us'd these *waters* to distil?

23

If old PHILOSOPHERS (who travayld through
So many Lands, *her* secrets out to spye)
Had *viewed* the *Miracles* which *I* did view,
Had sayled with so many *winds* as *I;*
What *writings* had they left behind! what new,
Both *Starres,* and *Signs,* bequeath'd to *Us*! What high
  And strong *Influxes*! What *hid Qualities*!
  And all pure *Truths,* without *allay* of *Lyes*!

24

But when that *Planet* (which her *Court* doth keep
In the *first sphere*) five times with speedy Race,
Had, since our *Fleet* was wand'ring on the Deep,
Shew'd sometimes *half*, and sometimes *all* her *Face*:
A quick-eyd *Lynx* cryes, from the *Scuttle* steep,
Land! Land! With *that*, upon the *decks* apace
  Leaps the transported *Crew*: their *Eyes* intent
  On the *Horizon* of the Orient.

25

At first the *dusky Mountains* (of the *Land*
Wee *made*) like congregated *Clowds* did look:
Seen *plain*, the heavie *Anchors* out of hand
Wee ready make: *Approach'd*, our *sailes* we strook:
And (that we might more cleerly understand
The parts *remote* in which we were) I took
  The Astrolabe, a modern *Instrument*:
  Which with sharpe Judgement Sages did invent.

26

We disembarke in the most open space:
From *whence*, themselves the rasher *Land-men* spread
(Greedy of Novelties!) through the wyld Place:
Which never *Stranger's* Foot before did tread.
But I (not passing the *Land's* sandie Face),
To find out where we are, with *Sea-men* bred
  Stay taking the *Sun's* heigth by th'Ocean curld;
  And with my *Compasse* trace the *painted* World.

27

We found, we had already wholly past
Of the *half-Goate,* half *Fish,* the noted *Gole*:
Between the *same* and *that* cold *Countrey* plac't
(If such there *be*) beneath the Southern Pole.
When, loe! (lockt in with my *Companions* fast)
I see a Native come, black as the *Cole*:
  Whom *they* had took perforce, as in the *Wood*
  Getting out *Honey* from the *Combe* he stood.

28

He comes with *horrour* in his *looks*: as *Hee*
Who of a *snare,* like this, could never dreame.
Hee understood not *Us,* neither *Him Wee*:
More savage then the brutish POLYPHEME.
Of COLCOS's glistring Fleece I let him see
The *mettle* which of *mettles* is supreme:
    Pure *Silver;* sparkling stones (continuing suite);
    But in all *these* was unconcern'd the *Bruite.*

29

I bid them shew him lower prized Things,
Beades of transparent crystall; a fine noyse
Of little *Bells,* thridded on *tawdry* strings,
A red Cap, Colour which Contents, and joys.
Streight saw I, by his *looks* and *beckonings,*
That he was wondrous taken with these *Toys.*
    Therewith I bid them they should set him free:
    So to the *Village* nigh away went *Hee.*

30

But the next *morn* (whilst *yet* the skyes were dim),
All *naked,* and in colour like the *shades,*
To seek such *Knacks* as had been given to *Him,*
Loe, by the *Craggs* descending his *Camerades*!
Where now their carriage to us is so trim,
So tractable, and plyant; as perswades
    VELOSE with them to venture through the *Cover,*
    The Fashions of the *Countrey* to discover.

31

VELOSO says, his Pass shall be his *Blade,*
And walks secure in his own Arrogance;
But, having now away a good while stayd,
And, I out-prolling with my countenance,
To see what *signs* for our *Advent'rer* made,
Behold him comming with a vengeance
    Down from the Mountain-top towards the *shipps*!
    And faster homeward, then he went, he skips.

32

The *long-boate* of Coellio made hast
To take him in: but, ere arrive *that* could,
An Ethiopian bold his weapon past
Full at his bosome, least escape he should.
Another, and *Another* too: Thus chac't
Velose and *those* farr off That help him would,
    I run, when (just as I an Oare lift up)
    A Troop of *Negroes* hides the mountain-top.

33

A Clowd of *Arrows,* and sharpe *stones* they rain,
And hayle upon us without any stint:
Nor were *These* uttered to the Ayre in vain,
For in this leg I *there* receiv'd a dint.
But *wee* (as prickt with *smart,* and with *disdayne*)
Made them a ready answeare, so in print,
    That (I believe in earnest) with our Rapps
    Wee made their *Heads* as *crimson* as their *capps.*

34

And now (Veloso, off, with safety brought)
Forthwith repayre we to the *Fleet* agin,
Seeing the ougly *Malice,* the base Thought,
This false and brutish people hid within:
From whom of India (so desired) nought
Of Information could we pick, or win,
    But that it is remote. So once more *I*
    Unto the *Wind* let all the *Canvas* fly.

35

Then to Veloso said a Jybing lad
"(The rest all laughing in their sleeves) Ho! Frend
"Velose, the Hill (it seems) was not so bad
"And hard to be come down, as 'twas t'ascend.
"True (quoth th'*Advent'rer* bold) Howe're, I had
"Not made such haste, but that the Doggs did bend
    "Against the *Fleet*; And I began to doubt me
    "It might go ill, that you were here without me.

36

He tells us then, he past no sooner was
The *Mountain's* top, but that the people black
Forbid him any farther on to pass
And threat to kill him if he turn not back;
And (turn'd) they lay them down upon the grass
In *Ambuscade,* whereby they *Us* might pack
  To the dark Realm, when we in haste should sally
  To rescue *Him,* before we well could rally.

37

The *Sun* five times the *Earth* had compassed
Since *We* (from thence departed) *Seas* did plough
Where never Canvas-wing before was spred,
A prosp'rous Gale making the *top-yards* bow:
When on a *night* (without suspect, or dred,
Chatting together in the cutting *Prow*)
  Over our Heads appear'd a sable *Clowd,*
  Which in thick darkness did the *Welkin* shrowd.

38

So big it lookt, such stern *Grimaces* made,
As fill'd our Hearts with horror and appall;
Black was the *Sea,* and at long distance bray'd
As if it roar'd *through* Rocks, *down* Rocks did fall.
"O *Pow'r* inhabiting the *Heav'ns,* I said,
"What divine threat is this? What *mystical*
  "Imparting of thy will in so *new form*?
  "For this is a Thing greater then a *Storm*?

39

I had not ended, when a *humane* Feature
Appear'd to us ith'*Ayre,* Robustious, ralli'd
Of *Heterogeneal* parts, of *boundless* Stature,
A *Clowd* in's *Face,* a *Beard* prolix and squallid:
Cave-Eyes, a *gesture* that betray'd ill *nature,*
And a worse mood, a clay *complexion* pallid:
  His crispt *Hayre* fill'd with *earth,* and thick *as Wyre,*
  A *mouth* cole-black, of *Teeth* two yellow Tyre.

40

Of such *portentous* Bulk was this Colosse,
That I may tell thee (and not tell amiss)
Of that of Rhodes it might supply the loss
(One of the Worlds *Seav'n Wonders*). Out of this
A *Voyce* speaks to us: so profound, and grosse,
It seems ev'n torn out of the vast Abyss.
   The *Hayre* with horror stands on end, of *mee*
   And all of us, at what we *hear,* and *see.*

41

And *this* it spake "O *you,* the boldest Folke
"That ever in the world great things assayd;
"Whom such dire *Wars,* and infinite, the *smoke*
"And *Toyle* of Glory have not weary made;
"Since these *forbidden* bounds by *you* are broke,
"And *my* large Seas *your* daring *keeles* invade,
   "Which *I* so long injoy'd, and kept *alone,*
   "Unplough'd by *forreign* Vessel, or our *owne;*

42

"Since the hid secrets you are come to spye
"Of Nature and the *humid* Element;
"Never reveal'd to any Mortal's Eye
"*Noble,* or *Heroe's,* that before you went:
"Hear from *my* mouth, for your presumption high
"What *losses* are in store, what *Plagues* are meant,
   "All the wide Ocean over, and the Land,
   "Which with hard *War* shall *bow* to your command.

43

"*This* know; As many *Ships* as shall persever
"Boldly to make the Voyage *you* make now,
"Shall finde this Poynt their enemie for ever
"With *winds* and *tempests* that no bound shall know:
"And the first Fleet Of War that shall indeaver
"Through these inextricable Waves to go,
   "So fearful an *example* will I make,
   "That men shall say I *did* more then I *spake.*

44

"*Here* I expect (unless my hopes have ly'de)
"On my *discov'rer* full Revenge to have;
"Nor shall *He* (onely) *all* the Ills abide,
"Your *pertinacious* confidences crave :
"But to your Vessels *yearly* shall betide
"(Unless, provoked, I in vain do rave)
    "*Shipwracks*, and *losses* of each kinde and Race;
    "Amongst which, *death* shall have the lowest place.

45

"And of the first that comes this way (in whom
"With heighth of *Fortune*, heighth of *Fame* shall meet)
"I'll be a new and everlasting Tomb,
"Through GOD's unfathom'd judgment. At these Feet
"He shall drop *all* his *Glories*, and inhume
"The glitt'ring *Trophies* of a *Turkish* Fleet.
    "With *me* conspire his Ruine and his Fall,
    "Destroyd QUILOA, and MOMBASSA's Wall.

46

"Another shall come after, of good *fame*,
"A *Knight*, a *Lover*, and a *lib'ral Hand;*
"And with him bring a fair and gentle *dame*,
"Knit *his* by LOVE, and HYMEN's sacred Band.
"In an ill hour, and to your loss and shame,
"Ye come within the *Purlews* of *my* land;
    "Which (kindly cruel) from the *sea* shall free you,
    "Drown'd in a *sea* of miseries to see you.

47

"Sterv'd shall they see to death their *Children* deare;
"*Begot*, and *rear'd*, in so great *love*. The black
"Rude CAFRES (out of *Avarice*) shall teare
"The *Cloathes* from *Angellick Lady's* back.
"Her dainty limbs of *Alablaster* cleare
"To *Heate*, to *Cold*, to *Storm*, to *Eyes's* worse *Rack*
    "Shall be laid *naked;* after she hath trod
    "(Long time) with her soft Feet the burning Clod.

48

"Besides all this; *Their Eyes* (whose happier lot
"Will be to scape from so much miserie)
"This *Yoake* of Lovers, out into the hot
"And unrelenting *Thickets* turn'd shall see.
"Ev'n *there* (when *Teares* they shall have squeez'd and got
"From *Rocks* and *Desarts*, where no *water* be)
    "Embracing (*kind*) their *souls* they shall exhale
    "Out of the faire, but miserable, *Jayle*.

49

The ugly *Monster* went to rake into
More of our *Fate;* when, starting on my feet,
I ask him, *Who art Thou?* (for to say true
Thy hideous Bulk amazes me to see't).
Hee (wreathing his black mouth) about him threw
His sawcer-Eyes: And (as his soul would fleet)
    Fetching a dismal groan, *replide* (as *sory,*
    Or vext, or *Both,* at the *Intergatory*)

50

"I am that great and secret Head of Land
"Which *you* the Cape of Tempests well did call;
"From Strabo, Ptolomee, Pomponius, And
"Grave Pliny hid, and from the Antients all.
"I the *but-end* that knits wide Affrick's strand;
"My *Promontory* is her *Mound* and *Wall,*
    "To the Antartick Pole: which (ne'erthelesse)
    "*You,* only, have the boldness to transgresse.

51

"Of the rough *sons* oth'Earth was *I*: and *Twin-*
"-*Brother* to *Him* that had the hundred Hands.
"I was call'd Adamastor, and was in
"The *Warr* 'gainst *Him,* That hurls hot Vulcan's Brands.
"Yet Hills on Hills *I* heapt not: but (to win
"That *Empire,* which the Second Jove commands)
    "Was Generall at *Sea;* on which did sayle
    "The *Fleet* of Neptune, which *I* was to quayle.

52

"The *love* I bare to Peleus's spouse divine
"Imbarqu'd mee in so wild an *Enterprize*.
"The fayrest Goddesse that the *Heav'ns* inshrine
"I, for the *Princesse* of the *Waves* despise.
"Upon a day when *out* the *Sun* did shine,
"With Nereus's daughters (on the Beach) these eyes
    "Beheld her *naked*: streight I felt a *dart*
    "Which *Time*, nor *scorns*, can pull out of my *Heart*.

53

"I knew't impossible to gain her *Love*
"By reason of my great deformitie;
"What *force* can doe I purpose then to prove:
"And, Doris call'd, let *Her* my purpose see.
"The *Goddess* (out of feare) did Thetys move
"On my behalfe: but with a chaste smile *shee*
    "(As *vertuous* full, as she is *fayre*) replide:
    "What Nymph can such a heavy love abide?

54

"However *Wee* (to save the *sea* a part
"In so dire *War*) will take it into thought
"How with our *honour* we may cure his smart.
"My *Messenger* to *mee* thus answer brought.
"I, That suspect no *stratagem*, no *Art*,
"(How easily are purblind *Lovers* caught!)
    "Feel my selfe wondrous light with this Return;
    "And, fann'd with *Hopes*, with fresh *desire* doe burn.

55

"Thus fool'd, thus cheated from the warr begun,
"On a time (Doris pointing where to meet)
"I spy the glitt'ring forme, ith'*evening* dun,
"Of snowy Thetys with the silver feet.
"With open Armes (farr off) like mad I run
"To clip therein my *Joy*, my *Life*, my *Sweet*:
    "And (*clipt*) begin those orient *Eyes* to kis,
    "*That* Face, *that* Hayre, *that* Neck, *that* All that is.

56

"O, how I choake in utt'ring my disgrace!
"Thinking I *Her* embrac'd whom I did seek,
"A *Mountain* hard I found I did embrace,
"O'regrown with Trees and Bushes nothing sleek.
"Thus (*grapling* with a *Mountain* face to face,
"Which I stood pressing for her *Angel's* cheek)
      "I was no *Man*: No, but a stupid *Block*,
      "And *grew* unto a *Rock* another *Rock*.

57

"O *Nymph* (the fayrest of the OCEAN's Brood)!
"Since with my *Features* thou could'st not be caught,
"What had it cost to spare me that *false* good,
"Were it a *Hill*, a *Clowd*, a *Dreame*, or *Thought*?
"Away fling I (with *Anger* almost *wood*,
"Nor lesse with *shame* of the *Affront* distraught)
      "To seek *another* World: That I might live,
      "Where *none* might *laugh*, to see me *weep*, and *grieve*.

58

"By this my *Brethren* on their Backs were cast,
"Reduc'd unto the depth of misery:
"And the *vain Gods* (all hopes to put them past)
"On *Those*, That *Mountayns* pyl'd, pyl'd *Mountains* high.
"Nor *I*, that mourn'd farr off my deep distast,
"HEAV'N, Hands in vain *resist*, in vain FEET *fly*)
      "For my *design'd* Rebellion, and Rape,
      "The vengeance of pursuing *Fate* could scape.

59

"My *solid flesh* converteth to *tough Clay*:
"My *Bones* to *Rocks* are metamorphosed:
"These *leggs*, these *thighs* (behold how large are *they*!)
"O're the long *sea* extended were and spred.
"In fine into this CAPE out of the way
"My monstrous *Trunk*, and high-erected *Head*,
      "The GODS did turn: where (for my greater payn)
      "THETYS doth *Tantalize* me with the MAYN.

60

Here ends. And (gushing out into a *Well*
Of *Tears*) forthwith he vanisht from our sight.
The black *Clowd* melting, with a hideous yell
The Ocean sounded a long way forthright.
I (in *their* presence, who by *miracle*
Had thus far brought us, ev'n the Angells bright)
    Besought the LORD to shield his *Heritage*
    From *all* that Adamastor did presage.

61

Now Phlegon and Pyröus pulling come
(With other *Two*) the *Charet* of the Day:
When that *high* Land (to which this *Gyant* grum
Was turn'd) doth to our Eyes it self display.
Doubling the point, we take another *Rumb;*
And (coasting) plough the *Oriental* Sea.
    Nor had we plough'd it long, when (underneath
    A little) in a *Second Port* we breath.

62

The *People* That this *Countrey* did possess
(Though they were likewise Ethiopians All)
Did more of *humane* in their *meens* express,
Then *Those*, into whose hands we late did fall.
Upon the sandy *Beach*, with cheerfulness
They meet us, and with *Dances* Festival.
    With *them*, their *Wives*: and their mild Flocks of *Sheep*,
    Which *fat* and *faire*, and *frisking* they did keep.

63

Their *Wives* upon straw-Pillions (black as *Jet*)
Slow-paced *Oxen* (like Europa) ride:
Beasts, upon which a higher price *they* set
Then all the *Cattle* of the *Field* beside.
Sweet *madrigalls* (in *Ryme* or Prose compleat,
In their own *Tongue*) to *rustick-Reed* apply'de,
    They sing in *Parts*, as gentle *Shepherds* use,
    That imitate of Tytirus the *Muse*.

64

These (and no less was written in their *Faces*)
Love and *Humanity* to Us afford:
Bringing us *Hens,* and *Muttons,* in the places
Of *Merchandizes* which *we* had Aboard.
But, for (in fine) our men could spye no traces
(By any *Sign* they made, or any *word*
    From their dark *Tongue*) of what we wisht to know:
    Our *Anchors* weigh'd, to *Sea* again we go.

65

Now had we giv'n the other demi-wheel
About black Affrick, And (the burning Hoope,
That girts the *World,* inquiring with my Keel)
To the Antartick Pole I turn'd my *Poope.*
By that small *Isle* (such emulous Thoughts we feel)
Discover'd by a former *Fleet,* we Soope;
    Which sought the Cape Of Tempests, and (*that* found)
    Pitcht *here* a Cross: our *then* Discov'ries's Bound.

66

Thence, many *nights,* and many sadder *days,*
Betwixt rough *Storms,* and languid *Calmes,* we grope
Through the great Ocean, and explore *new* ways:
No *Lanthorn* to pursue, but our high *Hope.*
One time above the rest (as *danger* Plays
At *Sea* the Protheus) with strange Waves we cope.
    So strong a *Current* in those parts we meet,
    As ev'n obstructs the passage of our *Fleet.*

67

More violent without comparison
(As our *reculing Vessels* plain did shew)
The *Sea* was, That did there *against* us run,
Then the fresh *Gale,* that in our *favour* blew.
Notus (disdaining much to be out-done
By *That;* and, as he thought, on purpose too
    To affront *Him*) puffs, blusters, reinforces
    His angry Blasts: and so we pass The Courses.

68

The *Sun* reduc'd the solemnized *Feast,*
On which, a King laid in a *Cratch* to find,
Three *Kings* did come *conducted* from the EAST,
In which ONE KING, *three* KINGS at once are joyn'd.
That day took *we* another *Port* (possest
By *People* like to *Those* we left behind)
     In a great *River*: Giving it the Name
     Of that *great-day* when thereinto we came.

69

Here *fresh Provisions* of the *Folks* we take:
Fresh-water from the *River.* But, in summ,
No guess concerning INDIA could we make,
By *People* unto *Us* as good as dumb.
See (*King*) how many *Countreys* we did rake
Without a *door* found *out* from that *rude scumm,*
     Without descrying the least *Track,* or *Scent,*
     Of the so much desired ORIENT!

70

Imagine, *Sir,* in what *distress* of *mind,*
How *lost* we went, how much *perplext* with *Cares,*
Broken with *Storms,* and *All* with *Hunger* pin'd,
Through *Seas* unknown, through disagreeing *Ayres,*
(So far from *hope,* the wished LAND to find,
As, *ev'n* with *hoping,* plung'd into *despaires*)
     Through *Climates* rul'd by other heav'nly SIGNES;
     And where no *Star,* of our *acquaintance,* shines.

71

The food we have, too, spoyl'd; and what we crave
As *nutriment,* ev'n turn'd into our *Bane*:
No *Entregens,* no *news,* to make us wave
Our *Griefs,* or feed us with a *hope,* though vaine.
Think'st *Thou,* if this choyce *band* of *soldiers* brave
Were *other* then of *Lusitanian* straine,
     They had obedient held to this degree
     Unto their *King,* and his *Authoritie*?

72

Think'st *Thou,* they had not risen long ago
Against their GEN'RALL (cross to their desire)
Turning *Free-booters,* forced to be so
By black *despair,* by *Hunger,* and by *Ire?*
If ever *Men* were *try'de,* These are: since *no*
Fatigue, no *suff'rings,* were of force, to tyre
    Their *great* and *Lusitanian* excellence
    Of *loyalty,* and firm *Obedience.*

73

Leaving, in fine, the sweet fresh-water Flood,
And the salt Waves returning to divide;
Off from the *Land* a prety space we stood,
Our whole *Fleet* bent into the *Ocean* wide:
Lest the cold *Southern* wind (increasing shou'd
Impound us in the *Bay* and furious *Tyde*
    Made in that *Quarter* by the crooking shore,
    Which to SOFALA sends the *golden Ore.*

74

This past (and the swift *Rudder* up resign'd
To good St. NICH'LAS, as in case deplor'd)
Towards that *Part* we steered, where the *Wind-*
Possessed *Waves* against the Beaches roar'd:
When the 'twixt *hope* and *fear* suspended mind,
And which confided in a *painted Board,*
    (Faln from *small hope* to *absolute dispaire*)
    Lookt up again by an *Adventure* rare.

75

'Twas *thus.* When to the *Coast* so nigh we drew
As to see plain the *Countrey* round about:
A *River* broacht into the *Sea* we view,
Where *Barks* with *Sails* went passing *in* and *out.*
To meet with Men That *Navigation* knew
Surpriz'd us with great *joy,* thou canst not doubt:
    For amongst *Them,* of things from *Us* so hid,
    We hop't to hear some *News:* and so we did.

76

These too are Ethiops: yet it should appeare
They had in better company been bred.
Arabick words we pickt out here and there,
By which was reacht the scope of what they sed.
A kind of *Terbant* each of them did weare,
Of *Cotton* fine, pres't close unto his head:
    Another Cotton-cloth (and *this* was blew)
    About those-parts that should be kept from *view*.

77

In the *Arabick-Tongue* (which *They* speak ill,
But Fernand Martyn understandeth though)
They say; in *Ships* as great as these *we* fill,
That *Sea* of theirs is travers't to and fro;
Even from the rising of the *Sun*, untill
The *Land* makes *Southward* a Full Point, and so
    Back from the *South* to *East*: conveying, *thus*,
    Folks, of the colour of the Day, like *Us*.

78

If with the *sight* of *These* so joy'd we were,
The *news* they give us makes us much more glad.
This (for the *signes* by *us* collected *there*)
We call The River Of Good Signs. We add
The *Land-mark* of A Cross, the which we reare,
Whereof some number in our *Ships* we had
    For such Intents: *This* bare the fair *Guide's* name
    Who with Tobiah unto Gabael came.

79

Of Slyme, scales, shell-fish, and such filthy stuff,
(The noysome Generation of the Deep)
The *Ships* (that come therewith sordid, and rough,
Through so *long* Seas) *there* do we cleanse, and sweep.
From our kind *Hosts* we had supply'de enough
Of the *Provisions* usual (as *sheep*,
    And *other* things) with smooth, and jocund *meen*,
    And as cleer *hearts*: which through their *eys* were seen.

80

But the high pregnant *Hopes,* we *there* embraced,
Bred not a *joy* unmixt with some *Allay.*
To *ballance* it, in t'other *scale* was placed
A new *disaster* by RHAMNUSIA.
"Thus gracious HEAV'NS their *Boons* have interlaced:
"*These* are the *interfearings, This* the way,
    "Of *humane* Things.   *Black sorrow* holds the *Dye*:
    "*Light joy* fades in the twinkling of an Eye.

81

And *this* it was.   The loathsom'st, the most fell
Disease, that ever these sad eyes beheld,
Reft many a *life,* and left the *Bones* to dwell
For everlasting in a *forreign* Field.
Who will believe (*unseen*) what I shall tell?
In such dire manner would the *gumms* be swell'd
    In our mens *Mouths;* that the black flesh thereby
    At once did *grow,* at once did *putrifie.*

82

With such a horrid *stench* it *putrifide,*
That it the neighb'ring *Ayre* infected round.
We had no circumspect PHYSITIAN try'de:
No *Lady*-handed SURGEON was there found.
But by a CARVER might have been supply'de
The *last.* 'Twas handling of a *dead-mans wound.*
    The rawest NOVICE with his *Instrument*
    Might *cut,* and never *hurt,* the PATIENT.

83

In fine, in this wild LAND *adieu* we bad
To our *brave* Friends (never to see them more)
Who in such *Ways,* in such *Adventures* sad,
With *Us* an equal burthen ever bore.
"How easily a burying place is had!
"The least wave of the *Sea,* any strange *shore,*
    "Serve, as to put *our Fellows's Reliques* in,
    "So of the bravest *Men* that e're have bin.

84

Thus, from this fatal *Haven* we disjoine
With *more* of joy then what we brought, and *less*:
And (coasting upward) seek some farther *signe*
Of India, to make out our present guess.
At Mozambique we arriv'd in fine;
Of whose *false* dealing, and *hard*-heartedness,
  Thou must have heard: as also of the *Vile*
  And *barb'rous* dealing of Mombassa's *Isle*.

85

Then to the *Sanctuary* of thy *Port*
(Whose soft and Royall *Treatment* may suffice
To *heale* the *sick,* to *cheer* the *Alamort,*)
We were conducted by *propitious* Skyes.
Heer sweet Repose, *Heer* soveraign support,
Heer Quiet to our Breasts, Rest to our Eyes,
  Thou doest impart. Thus (if thou hast attended)
  Thou hast thy wish; my Narrative is ended.

86

"Judge now (O *King*) if ever *Mortalls* went
"Upon so *long,* upon so *desp'rate* ways.
"*Think'st* Thou Eneas, and the eloquent
"Ulysses travayl'd so much *World,* as *These*?
"Durst *either* (of the *watry* Element,
"For all the *Verses* written in their prayse)
  "See so much through his *Prowesse,* through his *Art,*
  "As I *have* seen, and shall, or the *eighth* part?

87

"Thou, who didst drink so deep of Helicone,
"For whom *sev'n Cities* did contend in fine,
"Amongst themselves, Rhodes, Smyrna, Colophone,
"Wise Athens, *Chyos, Argos,* Salamine;
"And Thou, whom Italy is prowd to owne,
"Whose *Voyce,* first *low,* then *high* (always *divine*
  "And *sweet*) thy native Mincius (hearing) fell
  "Asleep, but Tiber did with glory swell:

88

"Sing, and advance with praises to the skye
"Your Demi-Gods, stretching your twanging lungs
"With Witches; Circes; Gyants of One Eye;
"Sirens, to rock and charm them with their *songs*:
"More, *give them* (both with *Sayls*, and *Oars*) to fly
"Ciconians; and that *Land*, where there *mates'* Tongues
    "With Loto toucht, makes them forget they're *slaves*;
    "*Give them*, to drop their *pilot* in the waves:

89

"Project them *winds* (carried in *baggs*) to take
"Out, when they list, Am'rous Calypsoes bold;
"Harpies, their *meat* to force them to forsake;
"*Hand them* to the *Elysfiian* shadows cold:
"As *fine*, and as *re-fin'd*, as ye doe make
"Your *Tales* (so sweetly *dreampt*, and so well told)
    "The *pure* and *naked Truth*, I tell, will git
    "The hand, of all the *Fabricks* of your Wit.

90

"Upon the *Captain's* honeyed lips depends
"Each gaping *Hearer* with fresh Appetite;
"When his long *Story* he concludes and ends,
"Fraught with *high deeds*, with *Horror*, and delight.
"The vast *Thoughts* of our Kings, the *King* commends:
"And their *Warrs*, known where're the *Sun* gives light.
    "The Nation's ancient *Valor* he extols:
    "The *loyalty*, and *Brav'ry*, of their *Souls*.

91

"The People tell (with *admiration* strook)
"To one another, what they noted most.
"Not one of them can *off* those People look,
"That came so *far*, That such dire *Seas* have crost.
"But *now* the *Youth* of Delos, who re-took
"The reins which Lampetusa's Brother lost,
    "Turns them to sleep with Thetys in the Deep:
    "The King leaves *that*, in his *own* House to sleep

92

"How *sweet* is Prayse, and justly purchas't GLORY
"By one's *own Actions,* when to *Heav'n* they soare!
"Each *nobler Soul* will strain, to have his story
"*Match,* if not *darken,* All That went before.
"*Envy* of other's *Fame,* not *transitory,*
"Screws up *illustrious* Actions more, and more.
      "Such, as contend in *honorable deeds,*
      "The *Spur* of high *Applause* incites their speeds.

93

"Those glorious Things ACHYLLES did in *War*
"With ALEXANDER sank not half so deep,
"As the GREAT TRUMPET That proclam'd them, far
"And neer; He envies *this, This* makes him weep.
"The *Marathonian* Trophies *Larums* are,
"Which suffer'd not THEMISTOCLES to sleep :
      "*He* said, no *Musick* pleas'd *his* ear so well
      "As a *good Voyce,* that did *his* prayses tell.

94

"VASCO DE GAMA takes great payns, to show
"Those NAVIGATIONS which the *World* up-cryes
"Deserve not in such gorgeous Robes to go,
"As *his,* which doth astonish *Earth,* and *Skyes.*
"True : But that WORTHY (who did foster so
"With *Favours, Gifts, Rewards,* and *Dignities,*
      "The MANTUAN MUSE) made *that* ENEAS sing,
      "And set the ROMAN GLORY on her wing.

95

"SCIPIOS, and CAESARS, *Portugal* doth yeild;
"Yeilds ALEXANDERS, and AUGUSTUSSES :
"But with those *lib'ral Arts* it doth not guild
"Them though, which would file off their roughnesses.
"OCTAVIUS made compt *Verses* in the Feild,
"Filling up so the *blanks* of *Business.*
      "Forsaken FULVIA will not let me lye
      "Through CLEOPATRA's charms on ANTHONY.

96

"Brave CESAR marches conquering all FRANCE;
"Nor was his *Learning* silenc't by his drumme:
"But (in *this* hand a *Pen,* in *that* a *Lance*)
"To th'*eloquence* of TULLY he did come.
"SCIPIO (whose *Wit* in other's *Socks* did dance)
"Wrote *plays,* ev'n with that *Hand* which had sav'd Rome.
        "On HOMER doted ALEXANDER so,
        "That th'ILIAD was his constant Bedfellow.

97

"*All,* That have ere been *famous* for COMMAND,
"Were learned too; or lov'd the Learned *All*:
"In Latium, Greece, and the most *barb'rous* Land,
"But only in unhappy PORTUGALL.
"I speak it to our shame; the cause no grand
"POETS adorn our *Countrey,* is the small
        "Incouragement to such: For how can *He*
        "*Esteem,* That *understands not* POETRIE?

98

"For *This,* and not for want of *Ingenie,*
"VIRGIL and HOMER are not born with *Us:*
"Nor will ENEAS, and ACHYLLES, bee,
"(This *Brave,* Hee *pious*) if the World hould *thus,*
"But (which is worst of all) for ought I see,
"FORTUNE hath shapt our *Lords,* so *boysterous,*
        "So *rude,* so carelesse to be *known,* or *know,*
        "That they like well enough it should be so.

99

"Thankt let the *Muses* be, by our DE GAME,
"To my deer *Countrey* that my zeale was such,
"As to commend her *noble Toyles* to FAME,
"And her great *deeds* with a bould hand to touch:
"For *Hee,* That's like him (only in his *name*)
"Deserves not of CALIOPE so much,
        "Or TAGUS's Nymphs, That They their golden Loom
        "Should leave, to carve his ANCESTOR a *Tomb.*

100

"*Love* to my *Brethren,* and to do things *just,*
"Giving all *Portingal-Exploits* their dues,
"To serve the *Ladies,* to procure *their gust,*
"Are th'onely *spurr,* and *int'rest* of the Muse.
"Therefore, for fear of black *Oblivion's* Rust,
"*Herroick Actions* let *no* man refuse:
    "For by *my* hand, or some *more* lofty strain,
    "Vertue will lead him into Honour's *Fane.*

End of the fifth **Canto.**

Sixth Canto

STANZA 1

The *Pagan King* could never entertain
The Navigators well enough he thought,
The friendship of the *Christian King* to gain
Of men, whose courage had such *wonders* wrought.
It troubled him, his lot should be to raign
So far from EUROPE, with all good things fraught:
    And that his *happy* Station had not bin
    Where Hercules the *Mid-Land-Sea* let in.

2

With *Games, Masks, Revels, Gambals* on the *Green;*
With *Moorish-Dances* (their sport natural):
With jovial *Fishings* (such as Egipt's *Queen*
Pleas'd the out-witted Anthony withal,
When *Carbonadoed* Fish were hang'd unseen
On her dropt *Hooks*) he *treats* the Portingall
    Each day; with *Banquets* of *unusual* Fare;
    With *Fruits,* with *Foules,* with *Flesh,* with *Fishes* rare.

3

But *now* the *Captain* (seeing time spend fast,
And that the fresh *Wind* wooes him to be gon)
From the indulgent *Land* taking in hast
Th'appointed *Pilots* and *Provision,*
Resolves to quit it: of the *Ocean* vast
Having no little Portion yet to run.
        His leave *now* takes he of the Pagan free,
        Who prays from *All* a lasting *Amitie.*

4

He prays them more, that *Port* (such as it is)
That all their *Fleets* would visit, when they pass:
For, greater good he doth not wish, then *this;*
To give such men his *Realm,* and all he has.
And, whilst he breathes, whilst what he has, is his;
Whilst the least sand is running in his Glass;
        He will be always ready to lay down
        For such a *King* and *People, Life* and *Crown.*

5

Gama was not behind in *Compliment;*
And, *weighing Anchor* without more delay,
To the rich *Kingdoms* of the Orient
(Which *he* so long had sought) pursues his way.
Now a *direct* and *certain* Course he went:
The *Fleet,* this *Pilot* means not to *betray.*
        Which (therefore) from the *hospitable* shore
        Goes now securer then it *came* before.

6

The *Oriental* Billows they divide
Now in the *Indian* Seas: and (spying than
Th'*Alcove,* whence Phebus rose as from a *Bride*)
See their desires fullfill'd within a span.
But spightful Thyoneus (grudging the *Tyde*
Of *Happiness,* which *then* to smile began
        On Portingals, who well had earn'd the same)
        Repines, fumes, curses, and with Rage doth flame.

7

He saw the *Stars* unanimous, to make
Of Lisbon, a new Rome; and that in vain
It was for *Him* to hope (alone) to shake
That, which the Supreme Power did ordain.
Desp'rate, in fine, Olympus doth forsake,
To seek *below* what *There* he could not gain;
 Enters the *humid Realm*; and to the *Court*
 Of *Him*, that bears the *Trident*, doth resort.

8

In the abstrusest *Grottoes* of the Deep,
Where th'Ocean hides his head far under ground;
There, whence to play their pranks the *Billows* creep,
When (mocking the lowd *Tempests*) they resound,
Neptune resides. *There*, wanton *Sea-Nymphs* keep;
And other *Gods* That haunt the *Seas* profound:
 Where *arched* Waves leave many *Cities* dry,
 In which abides each *watry Deity*.

9

The never fadom'd *Bottom* doth expand
A *Levell*, gravell'd o're with *Silver* fine;
Where lofty *Turrets* rise from *drayned* Land,
Of *Massive* stuff, *Transparent, crystalline:*
To which, the neerer you shall hap to stand,
The less will you be able to define
 If it be *crystal* which your *Eye* survays,
 Or *diamond*, which casts such *glorious* Rays.

10

The *Gates* are Massive *Gold*, richly imbost
With ragged *Pearlez* in their *Mother* shell;
In goodly *Sculpture* wrought, of wondrous cost,
On which vext Liber's eyes did feed and dwell;
Where first old Chaos (in it own selfe lost)
Varied with proper *shadows*, doth excell.
 Then the Fowr Elements (transcribed *faire*
 From that foule *Copy*) in their *Colours* are.

11

There active F<small>IRE</small> got highest on the wing,
Which without *matter* did *it selfe* sustayn,
Till (to give *Soule* to ev'ry *living* Thing)
By bold P<small>ROMETHEUS</small> from the *Sun* 'twas tane.
Next, subtle A<small>YRE</small> with the *invisible Ring,*
Gaping for *places* (importuning, vain)
  None *vacant* in the *world,* which *that* doth not
  Step streight into, though nere so *cold,* or *hot.*

12

Warted with *Mountains* (then) was the low E<small>ARTH</small>
In her *green gown* shadow'd with fruitful Trees:
Giving those *Creatures,* to which *she* gave *birth,*
Such *sustenance* as *best* with *each* agrees.
The carved W<small>ATER</small> serves her for a *gyrth,*
And *brancht* (like *Veyns*) ore all her *Body* is:
  Innumerable sorts of *Fishes* breeding;
  Men with her *Fish, Earth* with her *moysture* feeding.

13

Another *door* upon it carved has
The *War* between the *Gods,* and *Gyants* bold,
Beneath great E<small>TNA</small> crusht T<small>IPHOIUS</small> was,
Whence crackling *flames* in *sulphur Balls* are roll'd.
N<small>EPTUNE</small> himself stood *heer,* of *breathing Brass,*
Striking the *ground,* in that *contention* old,
  When the first *Horse,* to the rude world, gave *Hee;*
  And P<small>ALLAS</small> the first peaceful *olive-Tree.*

14

L<small>YEUS</small>'s Choler would not let him stay
To view the rest; and, passing through this *Gate,*
The G<small>OD</small>, who (told of his Approach) did stay
At th'inner Court, receiv'd him there in state:
Accompanyed with *Nymphs* in bright Array;
Of whom *each* seems to wonder, with her *Mate,*
  To see the *Water's King,* paid *one* in fine,
  Of *many Visits* made the *King* of Wine.

15

NEPTUNE (quoth *he*): O! never think it strange,
That BACCHUS comes *thy* succour to implore:
"For *highest pow'rs,* and most secure of change,
"'Tis envious FORTUNE's pride, to triumph o're.
Call all thy *Peers* that in the *Ocean* range,
Ere *more* I speak (if thou wilt hear me *more*),
  Down-weight of *misery* they shall discern.
  Let them *All* hear the wrongs which *All* concern.

16

NEPTUNE (presuming it some hideous thing
He would impart) doth TRITON streight command
To call the DEITIES inhabiting
The frigid *Waves,* on one and t'other hand.
TRITON, who vaunts himself son of the *King*
By SALACEE (ador'd in LUSUS's *Land*)
  Was a great nasty *Clown* with all that boast:
  His *Father's Trumpet,* and his *Father's Poast.*

17

His thick *bush-beard* and his *long hair* (which hung
Dangling upon his shoulders from his head)
Were spungy *Weeds;* so wet; they might be wrung:
Which never *Comb* seem'd to have harrowed.
The nitty points thereof, were tag'd, were strung
With dark blew *Mussels,* of their own filth bred.
  He had (for a *Montera*) on his Crown
  The shell of a red *Lobster* overgrown.

18

His *Body* naked, and his *genitals,*
That he might swim with greater speed, and ease:
But with *Maritine* little *Animals*
By Hundreds, cover'd, and *all hid,* were *these;*
As *Crayfish, Shrimps,* and other *Fish* that crawles,
(Receiving *theirs* from the pale *Moon's* increase)
  Oysters, and *Periwinckles* with their *slyme;*
  Snayles, with their Houses on their backs that climbe.

19

His great wreath'd *Shell*, to his black mouth apply'de,
With all the *might* he had, he now did sound;
Whose shrill and piercing noyse (heard far and wide
O're all the *Sea*) from *wave* to *wave* did bound.
Now all those *Gods* (without excuses) high'd
To the bright *Palace*, from their Quarters round,
     Of that moist God, who built the Walls of Troy,
     Which angry Greeks did afterwards destroy.

20

Old *Father* Ocean first (with all the *sons*
And *Daughters*, he begat, inviron'd) went:
Nereus (That married was to Doris) runs,
Who peopled all the *Crystal Element:*
The Prophet Protheus (his *Flocks* left for once
To range the *bitter Meade* at full content)
     He likewise came; but *He* already knew
     What, Father Bacchus to the *Ocean* drew.

21

Another way came Neptune's snowy *Wife*,
(Uran and Vesta's daughter soveraign)
Grave in her *Gate* (yet had her Graveness *life*)
And with a *Face* that calmed the woond'ring *Main.*
A *Robe* of *Lawn* (whose *Spinster* had a strife
With *Her*, That with Minerva strove in vain)
     Of her bright *limbs* was the transparent *Lid:*
     For they had too much beauty to be hid.

22

Fair Amphitrite (then the flow'rs in *May*
Fresher, and sweeter) would not wanting bee:
The *Dolphin* (who advis'd her to obay
The love of the *Seas* King) with *Her* brought *Shee.*
The *Sun* in all his glory, yields the *Day*
To *either's Eyes* (more worth then all they see).
     They marched hand in hand (an equal paire)
     For *Both*, the Spouses of *one* Husband, are.

23

That *Queen* (who, flying ATHAMAS run mad,
Came *so* to compass an *immortal* State)
Went; and with *Her* her pretty *Infant* had.
(*Him* too, the *Gods* did to their Ranks translate)
Toying before his *Mother* tript the Lad
With painted *Cockles,* which salt Seas create:
>   Whom when the looser sand molests and harms,
>   Fair PANOPEA bears him in her Arms.

24

Likewise that *God,* who had been once a *Man,*
And, through a powerfull *Hearb* he chanc'd to tast,
Was chang'd t'a *Fish*; so from that loss began
A glorious life, turn'd *Deitie* at last;
Came, adding water to the *Ocean,*
Still weeping the lewd Trick by CIRCE past
>   On his lov'd SCYLLA (*Hee* belov'd by *This*):
>   "*Hate,* where it springs from *love,* so mortall is.

25

Seated (in short) the *Powers* that rule the *seas*
In the great *Hall,* majestick, and divine;
On gorgeous *Cushions* first the *Goddesses,*
The *Gods* in carved *Chayres* of *crystall* fine,
The *King* with gracious gestures *All* did please;
His *Throne* deviding with the *King* of *Wine.*
>   The *House* is fill'd with that rich sea-bred masse,
>   Which doth *Arabian Frankinsence* surpasse.

26

When *now* the *whisprings* of the *Gods* were ceast
And *ceremonies* done between the *Kings*:
Burst THYONEUS began from hidden *Breast*
To powre the *Cause* out whence this passion springs.
Knitting his brow a little (which confest
His leaded *Heart* hung heavy on the strings)
>   *Hee,* that with *other's* weapons he may slay
>   The men of LUSUS, thus his cards did play.

27

"Prince, who (*of right*) from one to t'other *pole*
"The angry *sea* dost awe, and dost command,
"*Thou* that all *earthly* creatures dost comptroll,
"And bridlest *Nations* with a *roape* of *sand;*
"And (Father OCEAN) *Thou* whose Billows roll
"About the *world,* and circumscribe the *Land,*
    "Least those meet *Bounds* which are for *All* decreed,
    "It's proper *dwellers* should presume *t'exceed*:

28

"And you, SEA-GODS, that wont not to permit
"Your *Kingdom's* high *prerogatives* be broke;
"But, whoso dar'd to trespass upon *It,*
"Felt, what it was, *your* vengeance to provoke:
"What *tameness* this? what dull *lethargick* Fit?
"Who had such pow'r to stay your *Anger's* stroke,
    "Ready (with cause) upon *mankind* to fall,
    "Frayle as the Glasse, yet venturing at *All*?

29

"*You saw,* with what unheard of Insolence
"The highest HEAV'NS they did invade of yore:
"*You saw,* how (against *Reason,* against *sense*)
"They did invade the SEA with *Sail* and *Oare*:
"*Actions* so *Prowd,* so *daring,* so *immense,*
"*You saw*; and *We see* dayly more, and more:
    "That in few years (I *fear*) of *Heav'n* and *Sea,*
    "*Men,* will be called GODS; and but *men,* WEE.

30

"*You see* a *little* Generation *now*
"(Call'd by the *name* of one that *serv'd* me *too*)
"With haughty *Bosom,* with undanted *Brow,*
"Both *you,* and *me,* and all the *World* subdue.
"*You see,* your *Sea* with *winged* Oak they Plough,
"Farther then ROMAN EAGLES ever flew.
    "*You see,* your *Wealth* how they propose to drayn,
    "Your *Statutes* cancel, and your *walks* profane.

31

"When first the MYNIAE went about (ye know)
"To cut a *way* through the forbidden *Flood,*
"How BOREAS, and his Fellow AQUILO
"(With all the rest) the *Trespass* then withstood?
"If *They* so *stormd,* if *they* concern'd were so,
"That, as their own, *your* wrong they understood;
    "*You* (whom it touches in a *neerer* way)
    "Why sit ye *still?* for what do ye *delay?*

32

"Nor think (O *Gods*) that, for your *sole* concern,
"And for the great *Affront* which put I see
"On *you,* I have forsook the COURT SUPERN:
"But for *That* likewise which is offer'd *me.*
"For, *all* those *Honours* which my *sword* did earn,
"When (as the *World,* and *you,* can witness be)
    "INDIA I quell'd, and quell'd the ORIENT,
    "I by *this People* see trod down, and rent.

33

"For the HIGH RULER and *his Fates* (who deale
"The *under-world,* as pleases best their *mood*)
"Have *markt* these men for *Glory, Pow'r,* and *Weale,*
"Greater then ever, in the *Ocean-Flood.*
"And (*Gods*) from *you* I must not *now* conceale,
"That they teach *sorrow,* ev'n to *Gods.* 'Tis good:
    "*We* too are *slaves* to their *prepostrous* Will;
    "Which gives *Ills* to the *Good, Goods* to the *Ill.*

34

"*Now* therefore from OLYMPUS am I tost,
"To seek some *Cure,* some *Balsome* for my *wound:*
"To see, if that *esteem,* I *there* have lost,
"May happily within *your* Seas be found.
More would have said: But *Tears* the passage crost,
Which (trickling down his Cheeks in *Ropes,* that bound
    His *words*) with suddain fury did inspire
    And set the *watry Deities* on fire.

35

So rough the billows of their Anger went,
So swiftly and so high their rage did mount;
That no mature advice it did consent,
Permit no pawse, no weighing, no discount.
Orders from NEPTUNE are already sent
To mighty EOLUS, that without Count
     He slip the strugling *Winds* from their strong Caves,
     And let no Vessel *live* upon the waves.

36

PROTHEUS rose twice to speak, and went about
His judgement in the matter to propound :
Nor *Any* who were present, made a doubt
But that it was some *Prophecy* profound.
But still a rising tumult put him out,
And in their sence the *Gods* did so abound,
     That THETYS stuck not to exclaime : *Will you*
     Be teaching NEPTUNE *what he hath to do*?

37

Then doth the proud HIPPOTADES enlarge
From their *close prison* the enraged *Winds*;
And *them* with *animating* words discharge
Against the Men of never-daunted minds.
For a thick *clowd* hides *Heav'n* (as with a *Targe*)
And ARGUS's hundred Eyes, that guild it, blinds.
     The swelling *blasts* have in a trice o'rethrown
     Tow'rs, Mountains, Houses. — But of *that* Anon.

38

Whilst in the DEEP was held this *Parlament,*
The wearied *Fleet* (yet free from sad dismay)
Before a gentle Wind pursuing went
Thorough the tranquil *Ocean* their long way.
That Time it was, when from the ORIENT
Removed is the *Lamp* that rules the *Day* :
     Those of the *first* did lay them down to sleep,
     And others come the *second Watch* to keep.

39

Conquer'd they come with sleep, and (ill awake)
Repose their nodding heads against a saile.
Their Cloathes (thin, thin) but weak resistance make
To the *Night's* Ayre, which blows a nipping Gale.
Yawning, they stretch their Limbs; themselves they shake;
With their *Seal'd* Eyes to ope can scarce prevaile.
    Cures against *sleep* they *practice,* they *devise*:
    Tell thousand *Tales,* tell thousand *Histories.*

40

"What better *spur* (said one) to *post away,*
"Or *pastime* to *deceive* the hours that creep;
"Then by some *pleasant* Tale, wherewith we may
"Knock off the *leaden shackles* of dull *sleep?*
Quoth LEONARDO then (who, whilst a day
He hath to live, with faith to CUPID keep)
    "A *pleasant* Tale? then what can do so well
    "As *one* of Love? and *That,* my self will tell.

41

"Reply'de VELOSO; 'tis not *fit,* not *just,*
"To treat *soft* subjects in so *hard* extreams.
"For a *Sea-life* (replenisht with *disgust*)
"Permits not *love,* permits not *melting Theames.*
"Our *Story* be of WAR, bloody, Robust;
"For *we* (the *Wefts,* and *Pilgrims* of the streames)
    "Are onely born to *horror,* and *distress*:
    "Our *future* dangers whisper me no less.

42

To *This* they *All* agreed: and pray'd VELOSE
"What he *commended,* that *himself* would *doe.*
"I shall (*quoth He*); then listen to my *Prose*:
"I promise you an *old* Tale, and a *true*:
"And (to incite, with apt *examples,* Those
"That hear me, *great Beginnings* to pursue)
    "Of our own *Countrey-men* shall treat my *story*:
    "And let it be the *Twelve* of ENGLAND's glory.

43

When JOHN the son of PEDRO rul'd our Land
(Temp'ring his *People's* mouths with a soft *Bit*)
After he had with a *victorious* Hand
From potent neighbour's jaws deliver'd it,
In merry ENGLAND (which, from *Cliffs* that stand
Like Hills of *snow*, once Albion's name did git)
  ERYNNIS dire rank *seeds of strife* did sow,
  Whence *Lusitanian Lawrels* chanc't to grow.

44

'Twixt the *fair damsels* of the ENGLISH COURT
And *Barons bold* That did attend the same,
A hot *dispute*, beginning but in *sport*,
To end at last in *down-right-earnest* came.
The *Courtiers* (though the *Courtship* is but short
That gives reproachful terms to any *Dame*)
  "Said: They would prove, that such, and such of Them
  "Had been too lavish of their *Honor's* gem.

45

"And if with *Lance* in *Rest*, or *Blade* in *Fist*,
"To take their parts they had, or *Knights*, or *Lords*;
"That *They*, in *open Field*, or *closed List*,
"Would do them dye, with *Spears*, or else with *Swords*.
The weaker *Sex* (unable to *resist*
With *deeds*, and less to *swallow* such base *words*)
  Condemning *Nature*, That deny'de them *force*,
  Unto their *Kin*, and *servants*, had recourse.

46

But their *Accusers* (mark you?) being *great*
And *potent* in the *Kingdom;* neither *Kin*,
Nor *humble servant*, durst their *Cause* abet,
As their *Fame's Champions*, which they should have bin.
With *beauteous Tears* (which, from their blisful seat,
Might all the Gods to their assistance win)
  Distilling down each Alablaster Cheek,
  Unto the DUKE OF LANCASTER they seek.

47

This puissant *Branch* of England's *royal Tree*
Had warr'd against Casteel with Portugall;
Where his *Camrades's great Hearts* he try'de did see,
And their *good stars* which bare them out in *All;*
Like proof of their *respect* to *Dames* had *He,*
When to that *Land* his daughter he did call;
       With whose bright *Beautie's* beams our *Monarch* strook,
       The vertuous *Princess* for his *Consort* took.

48

He (loath to give them ayd with his own Hand,
Lest, so, he should foment a *civil flame*)
"Says: when I past to the Iberian Land,
"To the Castilian Crown to lay my clayme,
"Such *heavenly parts* in Portingalls I scand,
"Such *Courtship, Courage,* such high thirst of *Fame,*
       "That they alone (unless I much mistake)
       "With fire and sword your just defence can make.

49

"To *them* then (*injur'd Ladies*), if you please
"*Ambassadors* from *me* (for *you*) shall go,
"Who, with meet *Letters* and smooth *Sentences,*
"The wrong which *you* sustain to *them* may show.
"Let *Letters* likewise from *your selves,* your Seas
Of *Tears* indeare; and from your Pens let flow
       "*Nectar* of Words, to charm them to your Ayd:
       "For *there's* your *Tow'r, There* all your *hopes* are laid.

50

Th'experienc't *Duke* the *Dames* this counsell gave,
And streight to them *Twelve* valiant *Knights* did *name;*
And, that each *Dame* may know her Champion brave,
Bids them cast *Lots,* their number being the same:
And, by this way of *Lottry* when they have
Descry'de which *Knight* belongs unto which *Dame;*
       To her own *Knight,* in *varied* phrase, each writes;
       The *King,* to *All;* the *Duke,* to *King,* and *Knights.*

51

The *messenger* arives in *Portugal*:
The *Novelty* doth ravish all that *Court*:
The gallant *King* would be the first of *All*,
Might it with *Regal Majestie* comport.
Each *Courtier* longs, it to *his* chance would fall
In such a brave *Adventure* to consort;
> And each one's glory doth in *this* consist,
> To hear his name from the *Lancastrian* List.

52

In the old loyal *City* there, whence took
Was the eternal name of PORTUGALE;
He, to the *Rudder* who thereof did look,
Bad fit a *Frigat* light, with Oare, and Sayle.
Armours and *Cloathes* (delays they cannot brook)
All, of the fashion that did then prevail,
> The *Twelve* provide: *Helms, Crests, Knots, Motto's* neat,
> *Horses,* and gay *Caparisons* compleat.

53

Leave from that *King* is had, their sayles to losen
And pass out of the celebrated DWERE,
By them that had the honour to be chosen
Of famous JOHN OF GAUNT, who knew them *there*.
A *better,* or a *worse,* in all the *dozen*
(For *skill,* or *force*) there was not: *Peers* they were.
> But one (MAGRYSE) in whom new thoughts did rise,
> Bespake his valiant *Fellows* in this wise.

54

"Brothers in Arms, There hath been long in me
"A strong desire through *forraign Lands* to range;
"More *Streams,* then TEJO's and fresh DWERE's to see;
"*Strange* Nations, Cities, Laws, and Manners *Strange.*
"Since in the *World* then many *Wonders* be,
"And now I find this purpose cannot change;
> "I'l go before by Land (with your good leave)
> "To meet in ENGLAND, traversing the SLEEVE.

55

"And if (arrested by *his* Iron *Mace*
"Who is the period of each mortal thing)
"I hap to fail th'appointed time and place;
"To *you* small damage can my failing bring.
"Fight for *your selves,* and *me* too, in that case.
"But in my *aug'ring* Eare a Bird doth sing;
        "*Chance, Rivers, Mountains* (all their malice meeting)
        "In London-Town shall not prevent our greeting.

56

This said, about his valiant Friends he cast
(In fine) his Armes; and, licenc't, went his ways.
He past rough Leon: both Casteels he past:
Towns, won by *Lusitanian Arms,* survays:
Navarre: With *Pyrenean* Mountains (plac't
'Twixt Spain and *France,* as if to part their Frays):
        Survay'd (in fine) all that is *rare in* France,
        To Belgia's great *Emporium* doth advance.

57

Heer (whether sickness 'twere, or fresh *Adventer,*
Advancing *not*) He many days did stay.
But our lev'n *Worthies* the salt *Ocean* enter,
And to the *Northern Climate* plough their way.
Arriv'd in the first *Port,* to the great *Center*
Of populous England (*London*) travail'd They:
        Lodg'd by the *Duke* upon the Bank of Thames;
        Eggd on, and complemented by the *Dames.*

58

The *day* was come, and now the hour at hand,
When with the dozen English they must fight:
The *King* secur'd the *Lists* with an arm'd *Band:*
In *compleat Steel* begins to cloath each *Knight:*
Before each *Dame* (her *Honour's Shield*) did stand
A Spanish Mars in dazeling *Armour* bright:
        Themselves in *Colours,* and in *Gold* did shine,
        With thousand *Jewels,* joyful and divine.

59

But *she,* to whom Magriso (who was not
Arrived) fell, in *mourning* Rayment came;
Because to have, it was *her* hapless lot,
No *Knight,* to be the *Champion* of her *fame.*
Howe're: th'*Elev'n* (before they leave the *Spot)*
That they will so behave themselves, proclame;
    As that the *Ladies* shall victorious be,
    Though of their number wanted two or three.

60

Upon a high *Tribunal* took his place
The English King, with all his *Court* about.
The *Combattants* by *Three* and *Three* did *face,*
And *fowre* and *fowre,* their Foes; as it fell out.
The *Sun,* from Ganges till he ends his *Race,*
Sees not another *Twelve* more *strong,* more *stout,*
    More highly *daring,* then those English were,
    Who the lev'n Portingalls confronted there.

61

The golden *Bitts* the foaming *Palfreys* champ:
Upon the glitt'ring *Armes* the *Sun* curvets,
As when roll'd Cakes of *Ice* reflect his *lamp,*
Or (mingling Rays) on *Dancers* gems it beats.
Now in the *Ladyes's* hearts some little damp
(The *Troops* prepar'd to charge) the odds begets
    Of *Twelve* t'*elev'n;* when (Loe!) incontinent
    A murm'ring uproare round the *Scaffolds* went.

62

Unto that common *Center,* where the *Rout*
Began this tumult, ev'ry Face inclines.
Enters a *Knight* on Horse-back, arm'd throughout.
As one, who battail presently designes:
Salutes the *King;* the *Dames;* faceth about,
And, with th'*Elev'n,* the great Magriso joynes.
    His greedy Arms upon his *Friends* he throws
    (*Sure Card*) to lay them next upon his *Foes.*

63

Then she, that well perceiv'd this was the *Knight*
Who came *her* honour to defend and rayse,
Cloathes too with *Helle's* Fleece, which (more then bright
Vertue) the *brutish soule* loves, and obays.
The signall giv'n, the *Trumpets* blasts incite
The warlick *minds,* inflam'd with *rage* and praise.
    Spurrs are clapt to, *Reyns* slackned in a trice,
    Speares coucht in *Rest, Fire* from the struck ground flies.

64

The furious *Genets* seem, in their Career,
To make an Earth-quake with their thund'ring Hooves.
The *Shock,* in *All* that then *Spectators* were,
At once *Fear, Pleasure, Admiration,* mooves.
This, doth not *fall,* but *flye* (dismounted *cleer*);
That, *Steed,* and all (*He* better *Horseman* prooves):
    One, his *white Armour* in *Vermillion* washes:
    One, with his *Helmet's plumes* his horse-croop lashes.

65

There fell asleep for ever, *more* then one,
And a short step from *life* to *death* did make:
Here, runs a *Horse* (the Man strook down) alone:
There, stands a *Man,* whose *Horse* the Foe down strake.
The *English Honor* tumbles from it's Throne:
For two or three of *them* the *Lists* forsake.
    With *Shields, Arms, Maile,* Those who to *Arms* appeale,
    And *Hearts* of *Spanish mettle,* have to deale.

66

To lay out words in counting ev'ry *gash,*
Each cruel *thrust* in that most bloody Fight,
Is of those *Prodigals* of *Time,* and *Trash,*
That tell you *stories* which they dreamt last night.
Suffice it, I inform you at one dash,
Through *courage* high, through never-equall'd *might,*
    The *Victory* went on the *Ladies'* side:
    Ours crop the *Bays,* and *They* are *justifide.*

67

With *Balls* the *Duke*, with *Feastings*, and with *joy*,
Treats the *twelve Victors* in his *Palace faire;*
With *Cooks*, the *Bevy* of bright *Dames* imploy
Nets, *Hounds*, and *Haulks*, in *Water, Earth*, and *Aire*.
For *These*, their brave *Compurgators* would cloy,
Each *day* and *hour*, with thousand *banquets* rare,
  Whilst they in ENGLAND are content to roam,
  Without reverting to their dearest Home.

68

But great MAGRISO (if we trust reports),
Great things abroad still greedy to behold,
Clung to those parts, where at the *Gallick Courts*
Highly he serv'd the *Flandrian Countess* bold.
For *there* (as one unpractis'd in no sports
To which *Thou* MARS, inur'st thy *Schollers* old)
  He, hand to hand, a FRENCH-MAN in the *Field*
  (Like ROME's TORQUATUS, and CORVINUS) kill'd.

69

Another of the *Twelve* launcht out, into
HIGH GERMANY, where with an ALMAN *He*
Had a fierce *Combat,* who by means undue
Thought to have shorn his thred of destinie.
VELOSO come to a full point; the *Crew*
Pray him, he would not with such brevitie
  Pass the *French Duel,* but be more exact
  Therein : as likewise in the *German Fact.*

70

Just *here* (to drink his words, *they* list'ning *All*)
The *Master,* Loe! (who in the *Skye* did peepe)
His *whistle* sounds. From ev'ry Corner crawle
The *Saylors,* half-awake; and half-asleepe;
And, for the *wind* augments, he bids them fall
The *Top-sayles,* climing to the *Scuttle* steep.
  "Awake (he said) ope, and unseale your Eyes :
  "From yon black clowd, ye see, the *Wind* does rise.

71

Not fully *lor'd* the windy *Top-sayles* were
When a great *Gust* upon a suddain come.
"*Strike,* cry'd the *Master,* (so that all might hear),
"*Strike, strike* the *Main-sheet;* thrice he did exclaime.
The hasty *winds* (for *Tyrants* have no Eare)
Ere *struck* it could be, rushing thwart the same,
        Rend it to rags, with such a hideous rash,
        As if (the *World* destroy'd) the *Poles* did clash.

72

Then did the *Men* strike HEAV'N with a joynt-groane,
Themselves with *horror* struck, and pale dismay:
For (the *Sayle* split) the *Vessel,* hanging prone,
A pow'r of Water scoops up from the Sea.
"*Lighten* (the *Master* cryes with mournful tone),
"*Lighten the Ship:* if ye would *live,* obay,
        "Run others *to the Pump* (w'are at the Brink
        "Of perishing) *unto the Pumpe:* We sink!

73

Unto the Pump th'undanted *Soldiers* ran:
To which *no* sooner come, *their* parts to do,
But the *Ship* (stagg'ring like a drunken Man)
Their heels tript up, *them* to the *Larbord* threw.
Not three the sturdiest of the *Saylors* can
Manage the *Helm,* with all their strength put to.
        The *Ship* is bound with *Ropes* in every part:
        The *Land-men* lose their *strength, Sea-men* their *Art.*

74

Such the *impetuous* winds, that to have shown
More *force,* and *fury,* they could not devise;
Had they at *once* from *all* the *Quarters* blown
To throw down BABELL, which did threat the skyes.
The AMMIRALL, upon the overgrown
Mountains of *water,* shrinks into the size
        Of her own *cock-boat:* wondring *her selfe,* how
        She did to *live* in such a *sea* till now.

75

The *second ship* (in which was PAUL DE GAME)
Hod her *main mast* snapt in the midst and broke:
The *people* in her (almost drown'd) the name
Of *Him,* that came to save the *world* invoke.
With like vain *Ecchoes* to the Ayre, exclaime
In the *Third,* all COELLIOS daunted folk;
    Although that *master* so good *order* took,
    That, e're the *storm* ariv'd, *her* sayles were strook.

76

Now *All* to *Heaven* are hoysted by the fury
And rage of NEPTUNE, terrible and fell:
Now to the bottom of *his* waves *All* hurry,
As if their keels would knock the Gates of *Hell.*
The *East, West, South,* and *Northern* winds (to woory
The *world* by turns) from ev'ry corner swell.
    Her self with *Torches* the deformed *Night*
    (With which the *Pole* is all on fire) doth light.

77

The *Halcion* along the ratling shore
With *strayned* voyce cryes in a *dolefull* Key,
Rubbing with *this* the overplayst'red soare
Of her own loss, by *like* tempestuous sea.
The amorous *Dolphins* hide them, which before
Did friske and dance about the *watry* sea;
    Flying the cruell storm in *Caves* obscure,
    Nor in the very *bottom* are secure.

78

Never such red-hot *Thunder-bolts* were made,
Rebelling *Gyants* to confound and awe,
By that *foule Smith,* who (by his *faire wife* pray'd)
Forg'd a rich *Armour* for his *son in law*:
Nor ever (by the *Thunderer* displayd)
That frighted *paire* such flakes of *lightning* saw
    In the great FLOOD (*they* only left to mourn)
    Who *stones* to *people* (a *hard* race) did turn.

79

How many *mountains* did the *waves* uncrown,
Bouncing against them like a batt'ring *Ram*!
How many aged *Trees* the *wind* rusht downe,
Which by the *Cable-roots* at once up came!
Little thought *They,* the *earth* swept with their crowne,
To turn their *Heels* to Heav'n in the low *dam*
  As little thought the sands, which there were hid,
  To floate upon the *top,* as *then* they did.

80

Vasco De Gama (seeing his *Hopes* crost,
Just at the *Butt* and *end* of his desire,
Seeing the Billowes *now* to *Hell* goe post,
Now with fresh fury unto *Heav'n* aspire:
Confus'd with *horrour,* giving *All* for *lost,*
Seeing no *humane Fence* against such *Ire*)
  To that High Pow're, who is the *sov'rain Ayd,*
  And can *Impossibilities*) thus pray'd.

81

"*Protector* of the *Quires Angelicall,*
"Whom *Heav'n,* and *Earth,* and angry *seas* obay;
"*Thou,* who the *Red-sea* mad'st a double wall,
"Through which *thy* flying Isr'ell to convay;
"*Thou,* who didst keep and save thy servant Paul
"From *open Rocks,* and *Shelvs* that *hidden* lay;
  "And sav'd'st (with *His*) from *Cataracks* down hurl'd
  "The second Planter of the drowned World:

82

"If *we* have past *new* dangers numerous
"Of *other* Scylla's and Charibdesses;
"*Other* dire *Syrts,* and *Quicksands, infamous*
"Acroceraunian Rocks in *other* seas;
"Why, in the *Close,* doest thou *relinquish us*?
"Why, throw us *off,* after such scapes as *These,*
  "If with our *labours* thou art not offended,
  "If thy sole service be *thereby* intended?

83

"O *happy* men, whose lot it was to dye
"On whetted point of *Mauritanian* Lance;
"Whil'st, smear'd with *beawteous dust of* AFFRICK dry,
"The CHRISTIAN FAITH they (fighting) did advance;
"Whose *glorious deeds* remain in *History,*
"Or carv'd in everlasting *Verse* perchance,
　　"Who, losing a *short life; a long* did git:
　　"*Death* sweetned with the *Fame* attending it!

84

Whilst this he says, contending *Winds* (that roare
Like two *wild Bulls* when one with t'other copes)
Augment the *horrid Tempest* more and more,
And (*ratling*) whistle through the Spiny Ropes.
The flashing *Light'ning* never does give o're;
The *thund'ring's* such, that there are now no hopes
　　But that HEAV'N'S *Axles* will be streight unbuilt:
　　The ELEMENTS at one another tilt.

85

But, see, the *amorous* star, with twinkling Ray,
Conspicuous in the EASTERN HEMISPHERE!
Fair *Harbinger,* and *Usher* of the *Day,*
It visits *Earth,* and *Sea,* with forehead cleare.
She, from whom arm'd ORION slinks away,
And who this *Star* sits guiding in her *Spheare;*
　　Spying what *Risk* her deare *Armada* ran,
　　At once with *Anger,* and with *feare,* grew wan.

86

"*Here* hath been BACCHUS (says she) I am sure:
"Will he ne're leave this rancour? but in vain.
"He shall not *wag* the Ruine to procure
"Of *mine,* but I will have him in the Train.
She stoops like *Lightning* from OLYMPUS pure
Upon the troubled *Kingdom* of the MAYN;
　　Her *Nymphs* to crown them (as for wagers) bids
　　With *waking* ROSES that new ope their lids.

87

With *thousand-colourd* Garlands she commands
Their flowing *locks* a little be comptroll'd:
(*Who* would not judge, LOVE there, with his own hands,
Inamell'd *painted flow'rs* upon *true gold*?)
Her purpose is, to fetter in those *bands*
Th'*inamourd Winds*, where *there* they wander *bold*:
    The Faces of those loved *Nymphs* to shew them
    (More faire then *Stars*) to charm and to subdue them.

88

And so it prov'd. For she no sooner did,
But presently they faint , they dye away.
Under their wings their bashful heads they hid:
In humble posture at those feet they lay.
The slip, *Those* take them up in, is the thrid
Of that bright Hair, which scorns the mid-day's Ray.
    Then, to her servant BOREAS, thus did say
    His sweet and bosom friend, ORYTHIA:

89

"Fierce BOREAS, *This* is not the way to prove
"That e're thou *lov'dst*, as thou pretend'st to doe;
"For meek and soft as his *wings* down, is LOVE:
"And *fury* ill beseems a *Lover* true.
"Either this *madness* from thy mind remove —
"(What shall I say? couldst *thou* indure a *shrew*?)
    "I shall be frighted with it, *wee* must sever:
    "*Feare* choler may ingender, but *love* never.

90

Fayre *Galatea* likewise lays the case
To blustring NOTUS, who, full well she knows,
Hath many a *long* sigh fetcht for that sweet Face,
And is at her *devotion* doth suppose.
The *Raunter* (scarce believing such a grace)
His heart too ample for his bosome grows.
    The pleasure of his *Mistresse* to fullfill,
    He thinks it a cheap bargain, to sit still.

91

The *others* take the *other* winds aside,
And her too boystrous *lover* each reproves.
They give them to the Queen of *Beautie,* tyde,
Calme as the *Lambs,* and gentle as *her* doves.
She gives them back to *them,* and (their *faith* tryde)
Promis'd return eternal of their loves:
    Sworn on the *Nymphs's* white hands, e're thence they stir,
    In the *whole voyage* to be *true* to *Hir.*

92

Now rising SOL with *gold* those *Mountayns* lips
Which GANGES (*murmuring*) washes: when a Boy
From the tall *Am'rall's scuttle* shews the shipps
LAND, to the prow; With *that* (late *storm's* Annoy,
And halfe their *Voyage,* over) each heart skips,
Repriev'd from its vain fears. For *now* with joy,
    The *Pilot* (whom MELINDIANS to them put)
    "Cryes: if I err not, LAND of CALICUT.

93

"*This* is that *Land* (I'm sure) for which y'are *bound*:
"*This,* the *true* INDIA, which we see before:
"Then (if your vast desires *one* world can bound)
"Quiet your *Hearts,* ye *have* what ye *explore.*
Now GAMA could not hold, when as he found
(To his high joy) the *Pilot* knew the shore.
    With *Knees* sticht to the *decks, Hands* spread to Heaven,
    Eternal thanks by *him* to GOD are given.

94

Thanks he did give to GOD (and well he might)
Who was not onely pleas'd, to *Him* to show
That LAND, which he had sought through so great fright,
And for the same such *shocks* did undergo:
But snatcht him with *strong Hand* that very night
From *watry Grave,* through *winds* that raged so,
    Through *Thunder's* stroke, through blasting *Lightning's* beame,
    As one awak't out of some horrid dreame.

95

"By dreadful *dangers*, by such *Brunts* as these,
"By such *Herculean* labours, and vast *toyles*,
"*They* That in GLORIE's *Schools* take their *degrees*,
"Acquire *immortal Lawrels* and *fat spoyls*;
"Not *wholly* leaning against rotten *Trees*
"Of *ancient Houses*, not, on empty *Styles*;
 "Not, on rich *Couches*, wrapt in *Sables* soft,
 "Of the *Muscovy Merchant* dearly bought:

96

"Not, by *new-fangled dishes* exquisite;
"Not, by eternal *Visits* tedious;
"Not, by *successive pleasures* infinite,
"Effeminating Bosomes generous;
"Not, by a never quenched Appetite:
"Whereby, *old Wantons* FORTUNE makes of us
 "To that degree, We know not how to rise,
 "Or step, to any *Vertuous Enterprise*.

97

"*No*, but by tearing out of *Horror's* mouth
"*Honours*, which we may truely call our owne;
"By cloathing *Steel*, incountring *Hunger, Drowth*,
"*Watchings, high winds*, and *Billows overgrown*;
"Conqu'ring dull *cold*, in Bosome of the *South*,
"T'other *extreme* of the inflamed Zone;
 "Gulleting in, corrupt and putrid meat,
 "The Spice, and Sawce, with which the *Valiant* eat;

98

"And, by accustoming a *Face* (where doubt
"Sate once) *secure, serene*, fearless of *Harm*,
"To march through *Bullets* whizzing round about,
"And taking *here* a *leg*, and *there* an *Arm*.
"*These* (HONOUR's Brawn) make a man proof throughout,
"Make him scorn *Mony*, and *false Honour's* charm:
 "*Money*, and *Honours*, which light FORTUNE made;
 "Not VERTUE; who is *just, solid*, and stayd.

99

"SHE, shapes an understanding *round* and *cleer*,
"EXPERIENCE the *Hammer* and the *File* :
"SHE constant sits (as in a *Throne* or *Spheare*)
"Regarding busie *Mortalls* with a *smyle* :
"SHE (where *discretion* doth a *Kingdom* steer,
"Nor partiall *Favour merit* doth beguile)
　　　"Is suddainly caught up, *High Rooms* to fill :
　　　"Not by her seeking; but against her will.

End of the sixth Canto.

Seventh Canto

STANZA 1

"Wellcom, O wellcom (Friends) to that good LAND
"Which by so many hath been coveted,
"'Twixt INDUS and the silver GANGES's strand,
"In the *Terrestriall Heav'n* that hides his head.
"*Valiant* and *Happy* men, put *forth* a *Hand*
"To crop the *Lawrells* which from *others* fled :
　　　"For (*loe!*) ye see, before your faces, *loe* !
　　　"The *Territory* where *all Riches flow.*

2

"To *you* I speake, ye *sons* of LUSUS old;
"Who, of the *world* compose so *small* a stake.
"What talk I of the *world*? of that *small fold*
"Belov'd by *him,* who the *round world* did make.
"*You,* whom from conquering of *Nations,* rold
"In *Vice,* not only *dangers* doe not take;
　　　"But neither *Avarice,* or want of love
　　　"To Holy CHURCH, whose *Head* is crown'd *Above.*

3

"*You* (PORTINGALLS) as *stout*, as ye are *Few*;
"Who never care how small your numbers be:
"*You*, who are *Usurers* of *losses*: *you*,
"Who *frayle life* chaffer for *eternitie*.
"Thus PROVIDENCE was pleas'd That *him* (who drew
"The shortest *lott*) we of more use should see
    "T'extend *the Fayth*, then all the CHRISTIAN KINGS:
    "So much thou (CHRIST) exaltest little Things!

4

"The haughtie GERMANS, a *great Flock*, behold!
"In a *large pasture*, into *Factions* broke;
"Who (not to be restrayn'd within *one Fold*,
"Nor yet content to justify with stroke
"Of *Argument* what *sev'rally* they hold),
"Some *for*, and some *against* the *Roman Yoke*,
    "Their *fatall* pistols in *that Quarrell* span,
    'Which should be all discharg'd at OTTAMAN.

5

"See ENGLAND's *Monarch*, styling himself yit
"For deeds long past KING of the HOLY TOWNE,
"The filthy ISMAELITE possessing it
"(What a *reproaching* Title to a CROWNE!),
"How in his frozen Confines he doth sit,
"Feeding on empty smoake of *old* Renown;
    "Or gets him *new*, on *Christian* Foes alone,
    "Not by recov'ring what was once his own!

6

"Meane time an UNBELIEVER is for *Him*
"*Head* of JERUSALEM on *earth*, whilst love
"Of *Earth* hath made him an unuseful *lim*
"Of the JERUSALEM which is *Above*.
"Of the FRENCH then, what shall we say, or deem,
"Who (call'd MOST CHRISTIAN) doth his *style* disprove;
    "Who doth not only in her *Ayd* not come:
    "But ev'n *invites* the *scourge* of CHRISTENDOME?

7

"To Christians' Lands findst thou thy *Title* good
"(Having so fayre a *Kingdom* of thine own)
"Not to Cynifius and Nyle's sev'nfold Flood,
"*Old* Enemies to *true Religion?*
"*There* shouldst thou vent the heate of thy *French* blood,
"'Gainst the Rejectors of the *Corner-stone.*
    "Lewis, and Charles, left thee their *Name* and *seat:*
    "Not that which styl'd *one* Saint; the *other* Great.

8

"In the last place, what shall we judge of *Them,*
"Who by base *sloath,* and *Ryot* (rather *Rot*)
"Shorten their days, drown'd in their own wealth's stream,
"Their ancient *Valour* buried, and forgot?
"From *Lux, Oppression* springing; from this stem,
"*Dissensions* in a *people* giv'n to plot?
    "I speake to *Thee* (O Italie) brought loe
    "With thousand *Vices,* and thine *own* worst Foe.

9

"Ah, foolish Christians! are *you,* happilie,
"Those *Teeth* which Cadmus did to Earth commit,
"*Self*-Bane (for *Children* of one *wombe* ye bee,
"And *All* one heav'nly *Father* did begit)?
"The Holy Sepulcher do ye not see
"Possest by *dogs?* how *Those,* themselves can knit,
    "To wrest from *you* your *old Inheritance,*
    "And on your shames their name in *Arms* advance?

10

"Ye see it is a *principle of state,*
"A rooted custome, in the Hagarene,
"*Armies* on *Armies* to accumulate
"Against the *people* That on CHRIST doe leane.
"But, amongst *you,* doth sow rank *seeds* of *Hate,*
"And *Tares* of *strife,* the Enemies unclean.
    "How can ye sleep *secure,* how can ye close
    "Your *Eyes,* having both *them,* and *you,* your *Foes?*

11

"If love of *powre,* and *empire* uncomptroll'd,
"Set you a work to conquer *others Lands;*
"Both HERMUS and PACTOLUS's streams behold,
"Rouling into the Ocean *golden sands!*
"ASSYRIA spins, and LYDIA, thrids of gold;
"AFFRICK's rich *Mynes* imploy her *Negroes* hands.
  "Against THE TURKE let Bootie league you all:
  "If not to see THE HOLY CITY Thrall.

12

"That *Hellish project* of the IRON AGE,
"Those *Thunderbolts of Warr* (the *Cannon-Ball*)
"At TURKISH GALLEYS let them spit their Rage,
"And batter proud CONSTANTINOPLE's Wall.
"*Thence,* to their *Holes* in *Caspian* Cliffes, ingage
"The frighted *monsters* back again to craw'l,
  "And *Scythian* Wains, that in *your* EUROPE build,
  "With *barb'rous spawn* her *civill Countreys* fild.

13

"The THRACIAN, GEORGIAN, GREEK, ARMENIAN,
"Cry out upon you, that ye let them pay
"(*Sad Tribute!*) to the brutish ALCORAN
"Their *Christian-children,* to be bred that way:
"To scourge the arrogant MAHUMETAN
"Your *hands* unite, your *heads* together lay.
  "Unwise, ungodly, Glory cease pursuing:
  "By being *valiant* to your *own* undoing.

14

"But whilst (*mad People*) you refuse to see,
"Whilst thirst of your own blood diverts *you* All;
"*Christian-Indeavours* shall not wanting be
"In this same little *House* of PORTUGALL.
"*Strong places* upon AFFRICK's Coast has *she*;
"In ASIA a *Style Monarchicall*;
  "*Dominion* in AMERICA she has;
  "And, were there more *Worlds,* Thither she would pass.

15

And turn we to behold, in the mean while,
To our Sea-faring *Worthies* what befell;
After that gentle VENUS, with a *File*
Of BEAUTIES, the *inamour'd Storm* did quell:
After they came in sight of that vast *soyle*,
Sought with a purpose so unchangeable,
  The CHRISTIAN FAITH into the same to bring;
  To introduce *new Laws*, and a *new King*.

16

No sooner come at that *new* Land, a sort
Of little *Fisher-barks* they light among,
Directing them the way into the *Port*
Of CALICUT, whereto the same belong.
Thither they bend their *Prows*, being the *Court*
Of MALABAR, A *City* fair, and strong:
  In which a *King* his Residence did hold,
  Who, round about, a spacious LAND comptrold.

17

On this side GANGES and the YND beyand
A large and famous Province is markt forth;
On the *South* bounded by the *Ocean-Strand*,
By the *Emodian Mountain* on the *North*;
Sundry both *Laws* and *Kings* obeyth this *Land*,
Sundry pretended *Deities* ador'th;
  Some, beastly MAHOMET; some, *Idols* dead;
  Some, *Living Creatures* in that *Region* bred.

18

In that *long Mountain*, which all ASIA laces
(Running athwart so vast a *Continent*,
And borrowing sev'ral names of sev'ral places
Through which it runs), Two *Fountains* have their vent;
Whence YND, and GANGES (starting for *two Races*
At the same *Post*, and at the same length spent)
  Dye in the INDIAN SEA: Now *This*, and *They*,
  Make *all true* INDIA a *Pen-Insula*.

19

'Twixt these expiring *River's* Mouthez wide
From the broad *Countrey* a long *point* extends,
In fashion not unlike a *Piramide,*
Which (fronting CEYLAN's *Isle*) in th'Ocean ends.
And where (first thrust out of the Mountain-side)
The great *Gangetick Arm* a *Richness* lends,
  Tradition says; the *Folk,* That there *did* dwell,
  Of dainty *flow'rs* were nourisht with the smell.

20

But the *Inhabitants* That *now* are found
(In names and manners diff'ring from the old)
Are DELIIS, the PATANS, who most abound
In *People,* and in Countreys which they hold;
The DECANIES, the ORIAAS; That found
Their hopes of beeing sav'd, in what th'are told
  Of sounding GANGES. Then, BENGALA's Land;
  With which can none in Competition stand.

21

CAMBAYA's Warlike *Kingdom* (this of yore
Held great KING PORUS, as the fame doth goe):
The *Kingdom* of NARSINGA; pow'rful more
In *Gold,* and *Jewels,* then against a Foe.
Here (from the INDIAN OCEAN's Billows hoare)
Discerned is of *Mountains* a long *Rowe;*
  Serving for *Nat'ral Walls* to MALABAR,
  Inroads of those of CANARA to bar.

22

GATE the *Countrey's Natives* call this *Ridge:*
From foot whereof skirts out a narrow *Down,*
Which (*backt* by *that*) is by a natural Seige
Of angry *Seas* affronted. *Here* the *Town*
Of CALICUT (undoubted *Sov'raign Liege*
Of all her *Neighbours*) reares her lofty *Crown*:
  Seat of the EMPIRE, Fair, and Rich; and *Him*
  That's *Lord* thereof, they stile the SAMORIM.

23

The *Fleet* arriving close to that rich strand,
A Portingall is sent in a *long-Boate*
To let the *Pagan Monarch* understand
Their coming from a *Region* so remote.
He (through the *River* entering the *Land*,
Which enters there the *Sea* by a wide *Throate*)
    With his strange *Colour, Physnomy, Attire*,
    Makes all the flocking *Multitude* admire.

24

Amongst the *Rout,* which *Him* did swarm to see,
Comes *one*, trayn'd up in the Arabian's Lore,
Having been born in Land of Barbarie,
There, where Anteus was obey'd of yore.
Whether the *Lusitanian* People, *He*
Knew meerly as a *neighbour* to that shore;
    Or (bitten with their *Steel*) was sent so far
    On Fortune's errand by the chance of War :

25

The *Messenger* with jocund Face survay'd,
He, in plain *Spanish*, gave him thus the *Haile*;
"How, to *this World*, in name of Heav'n (*Cam'rade*)
"So distant from thy native *Portugale!*
"Op'ning a passage through rough *Seas* (he said)
"Which never *mortal Wight* before did sayle,
    "We come to seek of Indus the great streame,
    "Whereby to propagate the Gospel's beam.

26

Astonisht at so great a *Voyage* stood
The Moor (his name Monsayde) briefly told
Their sad *disasters* on the *azure Flood*,
And hair-breadth *Scapes,* by this same Lusian bold.
But since his main Affair (he understood)
Unto the *King* alone he would unfold;
    "He tells Him, *He* at present is not there :
    "Being retir'd into the Countrey neer.

27

"So that (until the *News* at *Court* have bin
"Of their prodigious passage through the MAYN)
"Please him, to make his homely *Nest,* his Inne;
"With Victuals of the *Land* hee'l entertain
"Him *There:* and, being well refresht therein,
"Himself will bring him to the *Fleet* again.
  "For that, the *World* hath not a thing more sweet,
  "Then in a *distant Land* when *Neighbours* meet.

28

The PORTINGALL with Bosome not ingrate
Accepts the Offer, kind MONSAYDE made.
As if their friendship were of ancient date,
With *Him* he eat, and drank, as he was pray'd.
Towards the *Ships* (that done) return they straight:
Which the *Moor* knew, when he the *Build* survay'd.
  They climb the *Am'ral:* where both Man and Boy,
  Receive MONSAYDE with a gen'ral joy.

29

The *Captain* (rapt) *Him* in his Arms did squeeze,
Hearing the *Musick* of the *Spanish Tongue;*
And (seated by him) Shreives him by degrees
Touching the *Land,* and things thereto that long.
But, as in THRACIAN RHODOPE the *Trees,*
And *Bruits,* to hear *his* golden *Lute* did throng
  Who did his lost EURIDICE deplore:
  So throng'd the *common-men* to hear the MORE.

30

He thus begins. "O *men!* whom NATURE plac't
"Neer to the *Nest* where I my birth did take;
"What *Chance,* or stronger *Destiny,* so *vast,*
"So *hard* a *Voyage,* made you undertake?
"For some *hid cause* from TAGUS are ye past,
"And unknown MINIUS, through that horrid *Lake*
  "On which no *Barke* before did ever floate,
  "To *Kingdoms so conceal'd,* and so *remote.*

31

"God, God hath brought you: *He* hath (sure) some grand
"And special buis'ness *here* for *you* to do.
"For *this* alone, he leads you by strong Hand
"Through *Foes, Seas, Stormes,* and with a *heav'nly Clew.*
"India is *this,* with sev'ral *Nations* man'd:
"Great Nature's bounty *All* beholding to
    "For glist'ring *Gold,* for sparkling *Stones* of price,
    "For oderiferous *Gums,* for burning *Spice.*

32

"The *Province* ye are anchor'd now upon,
"Is called Malabar.   In the old way
"It worships *Idols:* The *Religion*
"That bears in all *these* parts the greatest sway.
"Held 'tis, by *sev'ral Kings:* yet onely *one*
"Rul'd it of old, as their *Traditions* say.
    "The *last King* was Sarama Perimal,
    "Who in one *Monarchy* possest it *All.*

33

"But, certain *strangers* coming to this *Ream*
"From Mecha in the *Gulph* of Arabie,
"Who brought the *Law* of Mahomet with them
"(In which my *Parents* educated *me*),
"It so befell, with their great *skill,* and stream
"Of *Eloquence, These* to that hot degree
    "This Perimal unto their *Faith* did win,
    "That he propos'd to dye a *Saint* therein.

34

"*Ships* he provides and therein (curious)
"For *Off'rings* lades his richest Merchandize;
"To turn *Monastick,* and *Religious,*
"There, where our Legislative Prophet lies.
"Having no *Heir* left of the *Royal House,*
"Before he parted, he did *cantonize*
    "His *Realm.*   Those servants he lov'd best, he brings
    "From *want,* to *wealth;* from *Subjects,* to be *Kings.*

35

"To *one* Cochin; t'*another,* Cananour;
"Chale t'a *Third;* t'a *Fourth,* the Pepper-Isle;
"To *This,* Coulan; To *That,* gives Cranganour;
"The rest, to them who most deserv'd his smile.
"One young man onely (who had mighty pow'r
"On his Affections) was forgot the while.
          "For whom was left poor Calicut alone,
          "A *City since;* Rich, great, by *Traffick* growne.

36

"*This* gives he *Him* : and (to eke out the same)
"A shining Title *Paramount* the Rest.
"That done, his *Voyage* takes; his life to frame
"*So,* as to raign hereafter with the *Blest.*
"And hence remain'd of Samorim the name
"(By which *imperial pow'r,* and *height's* exprest)
          "To that *young man* and to his *Heirs:* from whom
          "This (who the Empire now injoys) is come.

37

"The Natives's manners (*poor,* as well as *rich*)
"Are made up all of *Lyes,* and *vanitie.*
"Naked they go : onely a *Cloth* they stitch
"About those *Parts* which must concealed be.
"Two *Ranks* they have, of People; *Nobles,* which
"Are Nayres stil'd : and *Those* of *base degree*
          "Call'd Poleas.   To *Both* the *Law* prescribes
          "They shall not marry out of their own *Tribes.*

38

"And *Those* That have been bred up to *one Trade,*
"Out of *another* may not take a *Wife;*
"Nor may their *Children* any thing be made,
"But what their *Parents* have been all their life.
"To touch a Nayre with *their* Bodye's *shade*
"A scandal is to his *Prerogatife.*
          "If *themselves* chance to touch him as they meet,
          "With thousand *Rytes* himself he washes sweet :

39

"Just so the JEWISH PEOPLE did of yore
"The touch of a SAMARITAN Eschew.
"But, when ye come into the *Countrey*, more,
"And things of greater strangeness ye shall view.
"The NAYRES onely go to *war*: Before
"Their *King*, they onely stand a Rampire trew
    "Against his Foes. *A Sword* they alway weild
    "With their *right-hand*, and with the *left* a *Sheild*.

40

"Their *Prelates* are call'd BRAMENS (an *old* name,
"And (amongst *them*) of great *Preheminence*):
"Of *his* fam'd *Sect*, who *Wisdom* did disclame,
"And took a *stile* of a more *modest* sence.
"They kill no *living thing*, and highly blame
"All *flesh* to eat with wondrous abstinence:
    "But *other* flesh their Law doth not forbid,
    "Yet *They* as prone thereto, as if it did.

41

"Their Wives are common: but are so to none
"Save those, who of their *Husband's* Kindred are.
"(O blessed *lot*, blest *Generation*,
"On whom fierce *jealousie* doth wage no war!)
"*These* are the *Customes*, but not *these* alone,
"Which are receiv'd by Those of MALABAR.
    "The LAND abounds in Trade of all things Isle,
    "Or *firm-Land* yields from CHINA unto NYLE.

42

Thus did the *Moor* recount. But Gossip FAME
Crying the *Newes* about the *City* went
Of a *strange people* come, with a strange name:
To be inform'd the truth when the *King* sent.
Now, through the gaping streets, invirond came
With either *Sex*, and *Ages* different,
    The *noble Men* dispatched by the *King*
    The *Gen'rall* of the *Fleet* to *Him* to bring.

43

And *Hee* (thus licenc't by the SAMORIM
To disembarque) departs without delay,
The noblest of his LUSIANS hon'ring *Him*
As his bright Trayn (*himself* more bright then *They*).
The sweet variety of colours trim
Dazles the ravisht people all the way,
    The compast *Oare* strikes, leisurely, the *water*
    Of the *Sea, first*; of the fresh *River*, after.

44

Upon the *Key* a potent *Officere,*
Whom in *their Tongue* the CATUAL they call,
Begirt with NAYRES, stood to welcome *There*
The brave DE GAME with *Pompe* unusuall:
Whom in his Arms himselfe to land did beare,
Then points him to a *Cowch Pontificall*:
    On which (*their* custome of most antient date)
    Upon *mens shoulders* he is born in state.

45

Thus *Hee* of LUSUS, *Hee* of MALABAR,
Move to the place where *them* expects *the King.*
The other PORTINGALLS, and NARYES are
Their *Infantry* advancing in a Ring.
The *multitudes* (like *Baggage* in a *War*)
Confused, pester one and t'other *Wing.*
    They would aske questions, but have not the pow'r:
    Their mouths were stopt for *that* in BABEL'S TOW'R.

46

Ride talking GAMA, and the CATUAL
Of things which the *Occasion* ministred:
MONSAYDE the *Interpreter* of *All,*
As understanding what by each is sed.
Thus marching, and ariving where the tall
And sumptuous *Fabrick* did erect it's head
    Of a rich TEMPLE in the *Citie's Center,*
    At the large two leav'd door abrest they enter.

47

There stand the Figures of their *Deities*
Carv'd in cold *stone*, in dull and stupid *wood*:
In various *shapes* presented to the Eyes,
In various *postures* as the *Feind* thought good.
Some, in yet more *abominable* wise,
(CHIMERA-like) with shapes *repugnant* stood.
  The CHRISTIANS (us'd t'adore GOD-*Man*) deride
  To see *Men, Beasts,* and *Monsters,* deifide.

48

One's humane Head a paire of *Horns* disgraces
(JUPITER HAMON stood in LYBIA so):
Another had one Body, and *two* Faces,
(Thus the old ROMANS did old *Janus* show):
A *Third,* with hundred *Hands,* fifty *embraces*
(Like BRIAREUS) pretends at *once* to throw:
  A *Fourth, Hee grinns* with a *dogs* Face (the plain
  Ador'd ANUBIS in MEMPHITICK FANE).

49

Here by the *barb'rous* people of that *Sect*
Their *Superstitious Worship* being payd;
Their course, without digression *Both* direct
To where the *King* of these vain GENTILES stayed.
The *Trayn* augments; through *Those,* who the aspect
Of the strange *Captain* to behold, assay'd.
  Women, and *Boys,* from all the *Houses* gaze:
  These *tyle* the *Roofs; Their* Eyes the *Windows glaze.*

50

Now they approach with slow and solemn pace
The beautiful and oderiferous *Bow'rs,*
Which barr'd the *prospect* of the *Royal Place;*
In *structure* sumptuous, though not high in *Tow'rs.*
For *they* their nobler *Buildings* interlace
With fanning *Groves,* and aromatick *Flow'rs.*
  Thus liv'd enjoying that rude *People's* King
  In *City, Countrey;* and in *Winter, Spring.*

51

On the fair *Frontispieces, Ours* descry
The subtlety of a *Daedalian* Hand,
Fig'ring the most remote *Antiquity*
In lasting *Sculpture* of the INDIAN-LAND.
So *lively* are presented to the Eye
Those *Ancient Times*; That *They,* who understand
    From learned *Writers* what the *Actions* were,
    May read the *Substance* in the *Shadow* There.

52

Appears a copious *Army,* which doth tread
The *Oriental* Land HYDASPES laves.
By a sleek ruddy *Warriour* was it led,
Fighting with *leavy Javelin's* curl'd in waves.
NYSA stood by her *Founder:* by *Her,* slid
The *River's* self, washing her *winy* Caves.
    So right the *God,* that THEBAN-SEMELE
    (Had she been present) would have cry'de; *'Tis* HEE.

53

Farther, a vast *Assyrian* multitude,
That drank whole *Rivers* e're they quencht their thurst.
A *Woman* Captain, with rare Form indude;
And of a *Valour,* great, as was her *Lust.*
By her side (never cold) her *Palfrey* chew'd
The foaming *Bit,* and (fiery) paw'd the dust,
    (Her NINUS's *Rival*) with whom yet 'twas done
    More innocently, then she *lov'd* her *Son.*

54

Yet *farther;* trembled in the *fancied* wind
The glorious *Ensignes* GREECE triumphant bore
(The *worlds* THIRD MONARCHY) spreading from YND
One con'qur'ing *wing* to the *Gangetick* shore.
A *young man* led them, of a *boundless* mind,
From head to foot with *Lawrells* cover'd ore:
    Who would not bee (so high his Thoughts did rove)
    The son of PHILIP, but the *son* of JOVE.

55

The Lusians feasting with these *Acts* their eyes,
The Catual unto the *Captaine* sayd,
The time draws neer, when *other Victoryes*,
Shall blot *these* out, which thou hast *now* survayd.
Heer shall be graven, *modern Histories*
Of a *strange people* that shall *us* invade.
       Such our deep *Sages* find to be our doom,
       Poring into the things which are to come.

56

By the *black Art* they doe moreover tell,
That, to prevent so great approaching *Ill*
By *humane wisdome*, 'tis impossibel:
"For vaine is *earthly wit*, against *Heav'n's will*.
But, say withall; Those *strangers* shall excell
So much in *Martiall* and in *civil* skill;
       That through the *World* it will in after story,
       Be sed: The *Conqu'rers* are the *Conquerd's* glory.

57

Discoursng thus they enter the gilt Hall,
Where leanes that Emperor magnificent
On a rich *Cowch* which (take it worke and all)
Could not be matcht beneath the *Firmament*.
His *Face* and *posture* (that *Majesticall;*
And this *secure*) his *Fortune* represent:
       His *Robes* are *cloth of gold: A diadem*
       Upon his *head*, with many a flaming *gem*.

58

An old man (at his elbow) with grave meen
Upon the knee did ever and anon
Of a hot *plant* present him a leaf green;
Which, as of custome, he would chaw upon.
Then did a *Bramen* of no mean esteem
Approach De Gama with slow motion;
       To present *Him* unto the Monarch great:
       Who *there* before him, nods him to a seate.

59

DE GAMA seated neer to the rich Bed
(*His*, keeping off) with quick and hungry Eyes,
The SAMORIM upon the *Habit* fed
Of his new *Guests*, their uncouth *hew*, and *Guyse*.
With an *emphatick Voyce* from a *deep head*
(Which much his *embassie* did authorize
    Both with the *King*, and all the *People* there)
    The *Captain* thus accosts the *Royall eare*.

60

"A potent *King* (who governs yonder, where
"*Heav'n's* ever-rolling wheeles the *day* adjourn,
"Benighting earth with earth; that *Hemisphere*
"Which the *sun* leaves mourning till his *Return*)
"Hearing from FAME (which makes an *Ecchoe* there)
"How this IMPERIAL CROWN by *Thee* is worn
    "(The sum'd up *Majestie* of INDIAN LAND)
    "Would enter with thee into *Friendship's Band*.

61

"And (through long windings) to thy COURT sent *me*,
"To let thee know; that *whatsoever* stores
"Goe on the *Land*, or goe upon the *sea*,
"From TAGUS there, to NYLE's inriched shores:
"*All* that by *Zeland Merchants* laden be:
"By *tributary Ethiopian*-MORES:
    "From *seething River*, or from *frozen Barr*:
    "Heapt up and *centred* in his *Kingdom*, are.

62

"Then if thou wilt, with *leagues* and *mutuall Tyes*
"Of *Peace* and *Friendship* (stable and divine)
"Allow commerce of superfluities,
"Which bounteous NATURE gave *his Realms* and *Thine*,
"(For *Trade* brings *Opulence* and *Rarities*,
"For which the *Poor* doe *sweat*, the *Rich* doe *Pine*)
    "Of two *great* fruits, which will from thence redound,
    "*His* shall the *glory; thine,* the *Gain* be found.

63

"And (if it so fall out, that this fast knot
"Of *Amitie* be knit between you two)
"He will assist thee in all adverse lot
"Of *Warr,* which in thy *Kingdom* may insue,
"With *Soldiers, Arms* and *Shipps;* and coldly, not,
"But as a *Brother* in that case would doe.
    "It rests, that thou resolve me in the close,
    "What he may trust to touching this *propose.*

64

This was the *Errand* of the *Captain* bold,
To whom the *Pagan Monarch* answer'd thus:
"*Ambassadours* from such farr *parts,* we hold
"No little honour to our *Crown,* and *Us,*
"Yet shall not in this case our *will* unfold
"Till with our Councell we the thing discuss:
    "What this *King* is, informing our self well,
    "The *people* and the *Land* whereof you tell.

65

"In the mean time repose you from the *Quoyle*
"Of labour past, and nauseating *Seas:*
"Whom we will back dispatch, within a while,
"With such an *answear* as shall not displease.
"Now *Night* (Task-mistresse of all *earthly* Toyle)
"Gives *humane labours* wonted stint; to ease
    "Exhausted *lims* with sweet *Vicissitude:*
    "*Eyes,* with the *leaden* Hand of *sleep* subdude.

66

In the most noble lodgings of the *Court,*
The Primere Minister of Indian Land
(With the Applause of people of each sort)
Did feast De Gama, and his valiant *Band:*
The Catuall (that he may make report
To his *dread Leige,* who gave him in command
    To find it out; which *way* the strangers came,
    What *Laws,* what *Faith,* what *Countrey,* and what *name*)

67

Soon as he spyes the fired *Axel-tree*
Of the fayre *Delian* youth the *day* renew,
Sends for Monsayde; upon Thorns, to bee
At large informed of this Nation new.
Prompt and inquisitive, he asks if *Hee*
Can give him full *Intelligence* and trew,
    What these strange people are (for he did heare,
    That to his *Country* they are neighbours neer.)

68

A punctual accompt of every thing
He knew of them, he charg'd him to afford;
As that which was a service to the *King*,
Whereby to judge of the propos'd accord.
"Monsayde answers: That which I can bring
"Of light thereto, is spoken in a Word.
    "Thus much I know; *they* are of yond same Spayn,
    "Where Phebus, and my *Nest*, bathe in the *Mayn*.

69

"*By them* a certain *Prophet* is ador'd,
"Born of a pure and incorrupted *Mayd,*
"*Conceiving* by the *Spirit* of the *Lord,*
"The *Lord* of life, by whom the *world* is swayd.
"*Of them,* that which *my Parents* did Record,
"Was that of bloody *Warr* the noble Trade
    "To it's full pitch by their strong *Arm* is wound:
    "Which to our cost *their predecessors found.*

70

"*Them* (arm'd with *vertue* above humane strayne)
"They threw out of their delectable *Seates*
"By golden Tagus, and fresh Guadiane,
"Through glorious and memorable Feats:
"Nor so content (ploughing the stormy *Mayn*
"Toth' *Affrick*) ev'n in our owne *Retreates*
    "Let us not live secure: but pull us out
    "From our Strong *walls,* and *there* our *Armies* rout.

71

"Nor have they shown lesse strength of *Hand* and *Brayn,*
"In whatsoever *other* warrs did chance
"With many warlick *Nations* of their Spayne,
"And some that fell down by the way of France.
"So that, in fine, no story doth remayne,
"That ever they were quelld by *forreign Lance;*
    "Nor for those Hannibals (I wil be bound)
    "As yet, was ever a Marcellus found.

72

"But if this *Information* (as I make
"Accompt it does) appear to *Thee* too short,
"Of *them,* let *them* inform thee.   Thou mayst take
"(So doe they hate a *lye*) their *own* report.
"Goe view their *Fleet,* their *Arms,* and how they rake
"With *founded Brass,* which tames the strongest Fort:
    "And it will please thee, of the Portingall
    "To see the *civill Arts,* and *Martiall.*

73

To see the things the Moor exalted so,
Now the Idolater is of a flame,
Calls for his *Barge* in hast, for he will goe
To view the *ships* in which De Gama came.
Together from the cover'd *shore* they rowe:
Cov'ring the *sea,* the Nayres doe the same.
    They climbe the strong and goodly *Ammirall*:
    By her long side *aboard* doth *hand* them Paul.

74

Her *waste-cloaths* Scarlet, and her *Banners* are
Of the rich *Fleece* which by a *worm* is bred:
In *them* are painted glorious deeds in War
Atchiev'd by valiant Hands of Worthies dead.
Here a *pitcht-Field,* and *there* a *single jar;*
Fierce one and t'other: *Pictures* full of dread!
    From which, since *them* the *Pagan* first did spye,
    He never could recal his greedy *Eye.*

75

To know the Things he sees, he doth beseech.
But first, De Gama prays him sit, and prove
A little of those delicacies, which
Those of the *Sect* of Epicurus love.
The foaming *Goblets* with the *Liquor* rich,
Devis'd by Noah, swell, their banks above.
      The *Pagan* sits; but cannot *Eat* (he saith)
      Truth is, it crost a *praecept* of his *Faith.*

76

The *Trumpet* (which in *Peace* doth represent
War to the Fancy) rends the Ayre. In Thunder
The fired *Diabolick-Instrument*
Speaks audibly to it's infernal *Founder.*
The *Pagan* observs *All*: but (most intent
On the *Defunct*) seems to confine his wonder
      To those brave *Deeds,* which in a little *Spheare*
      Are by *Mute Poetry* described there.

77

He starts upon his Feet; with *Him* (betwixt
Whom he was plac't) *both* the De Games: and, from
Vasco's right side, Coellio. The Moor fixt
His Eyes, upon the warlike *Transcript* dumb
Of an old man, who in his Face had mixt
Something divine, nor, till the *World's* one Tomb,
      Shall ever dye. Clad in the *Greekish mode.*
      A *Bough* in his right hand, what he was show'd.

78

His right hand held a *Bough.* — But "O blind man
"*I*! That (unwise and rude) without your clew
"(*Nymphs* of Mondego, and the *Tagan Stran*)
"A course so long, so intricate, pursue.
"I lanch into a boundless *Ocean,*
"With *Wind* so contrary; that, unless *you*
      "Extend your favours, I have cause to think
      "My brittle Barke will in a moment sink.

79

"Behold how long, whilst I strain all my *pow'rs,*
"Your Tagus singing, and your Portugale;
"Fortune (new Toyles presenting, and new Sow'rs)
"Through the *World* draggs me at her Charets-Tayle:
"Sometimes committed to *Seas's* rolling Tow'rs,
"Sometimes to bloody dangers *Martiale*!
    "Thus I (like desperate Canacee of old)
    "My *Pen* in *this*, my *Sword* in *that hand* hold.

80

"*Now* by declin'd and scorned *poverty*
"Degraded, at Another's Board to eate.
"Now (in possession of a Fortune high)
"Thrown back again, farther then ever yet.
"Now scapt, with my life onely, which hung by
"A single Thrid (ev'n *that* a load too great):
    "That 'tis no less a wonder, I am here,
    "Then Juda's *King's* new lease of fifteen yeere.

81

"Nay more (*my* Nymphs) I thus being made an *Isle*
"And *Rock* of *want* (surrounded by my *Woes*),
"The same, whom I swam singing all that while,
"Gave me, for all my *Verses*, but course *Prose*.
"Instead of hoped *Rest* for long *Exile,*
"Of *Bays* to thatch my head (which bald now grows):
    "Unworthy *scandals* they thereon did hayle,
    "Which laid me in a miserable Jayle.

82

"See, *Nymphs,* what learned Lords your Tagus breeds!
"What *Patrons* of *good Arts* we live among!
"Are *these* the *favors,* and are *these* the *meeds,*
"For *Him* That makes *them* glorious with his *Song?*
"What *Precedents* are these, what likely seeds
"To raise in future curious Wits and strong,
    "To register the Acts of all those men
    "That merit *Fame* from an *immortal Pen?*

83

"Then in this *Flood* of *Ills* let it suffice
"That *your* sole grace and favour I obtain;
"And chiefly *here,* where such Varieties
"Of honorable *deeds* I must explain.
"Give it me onely *you:* For (by your *Eyes*)
"On any that deserves it not, one grain
 "I will not spend: not flatter Dukes, nor KINGS,
 "Pain of ungrateful to your *sacred springs.*

84

"Nor think, O *Nymphs,* I'l waste *your* pretious *Fame*
"On *Him,* who to his *King* and *Countrey's weal*
"Prefers his *private interest* (The same
"Will from the *Throne,* yea from the *Altar,* steale).
"*No,* no *Ambitious man* shall hide his shame
"Under my *leaves,* who mounts, that he may deale
 "More largely to his *Lusts,* and exercise
 "His *Office,* not, but his *impieties.*

85

"No man, That stalks with *popularity,*
"Thereby to catch the *Prey* he hath design'd:
"Who, with the erring *Vulgar* to comply,
"Changeth as oft as Protheus, or the *Wind.*
"Nor (Muses) fear, that ever sing will *I*
"Whom, with grave *Face,* grave *case,* grave *pace,* I find
 "(To please the *King* in the new *Place* he's in)
 "Fleece the poor *People* to the very skin.

86

"Nor *Him,* who finds it just (and so it is)
"The *King's* Laws should be kept in ev'ry thing:
"But does *not* find it just (and that's amis)
"To pay the sweat of *those* that serve the *King.*
"Nor *Him,* who *says his Book,* and thinks with *This*
"(Though *unexperienc't*) he hath wit to bring
 "All to his *Rules:* and, with a niggard Hand,
 "Rates *services,* he doth not understand.

87

"*Those* (and those Worthies *onely*) will *I* sing,
"Who their dear lives have ventur'd and laid down,
"First for their GOD, and after for their King;
"To be repaid with *use* in due renown.
"Help me Apollo, and the *Muses's* Ring,
"With doubled *Rage* their Lawrell'd heads to crown:
    "Whilst (almost tyr'd) I *here* take breath a while,
    "So with fresh *Spirits* to renew my Toyle.

End of the seventh Canto.

Eighth Canto

STANZA 1

On the first *Figure* struck the Hagarene,
Which in the waving *Flag* did come and go:
Upon a *leavie staffe* it seem'd to leane,
With a long combed Beard, white as the snow.
Who this grave *Warriour* is, and what should meane
That same *device* he bears, he longs to know.
    Paul tells him: whose wise words which here insue,
    Monsayde rendred, who both *Idioms* knew.

2

These Figures all (which, *moving,* seem *alive*)
As *fierce* and *warlike* as they show, for here,
By the bright fame that doth of them survive,
In *truth* and *Fact,* more *fierce* and *warlike* were.
They stand *far off* in time: Through *perspective*
Of cleer Wits yet, they *loom* both *great* and *neer.*
    This thou now seest, is Lusus, from whom *Fame*
    Gives to our *Kingdom* Lusitania's name.

3

He was that THEBAN's *Son,* or else *Camrade,*
Who in so many *Lands* did *Lawrels* gaine.
Following the *Wars* (which he did make his *Trade*)
This LUSUS built at length a *Nest* in SPAINE,
With those delicious *Fields* so well apaid
(Th'*Elysian* once) 'twixt DWERE, and Guadiane;
     That *there* he set up his long Rest. *He* gave
     A *name,* to *Those;* and *Those,* to *Him,* a *Grave.*

4

The *leavy staffe* (he bears for his *Device*)
The *Thyrsus* is, That BACCHUS self did beare;
Which is to *Us,* a *letter* of *Advice*
That this was his own *Son,* or *Friend* as deare.
Seest Thou *Another,* who long *Seas* did slice
With wand'ring *Keele,* and Lands by TAGUS there,
     Where he a *Fane* to PALLAS sacred calls,
     And is the *Author* of *eternal Walls?*

5

It is *Ulysses:* who that *Temple* founded
For *Her* with Eloquence his *Tongue* that guilded.
If he in ASIA *here* fair TROY confounded,
In EUROPE there great LISBON hath he builded.
Who may this *other* be, with *dead* and *wounded*
That sows the *Field* (his sword with both hands weilded)
     Death and *Destruction* on great *Hoasts* that flings;
     Where *painted Eagles* flye with *true ones* wings?

6

Thus said the *Pagan.* Thus replyes DE GAME:
This, thou *now* seest, a keeper was of *Ewes*
(And know, that VIRIATUS was his name)
But, better then a *Hook,* a *Sword* could use.
With *this* he did affront the *Roman Fame,*
Invincible: nor *Fame* once got, did loose.
     No, Rome had ne're with *Him,* nor should (that's more)
     That luck, with PYRRHUS which she had before.

7

By *Valour* not, but creeping *trechery,*
They rob'd him of his life.   Why doest thou wonder?
In desp'rate Cases Magnanimity
It self, doth teare it's proper laws in sunder.
Behold *Another* (for Indignity
Receiv'd) with *Us* that did his *Countrey* thunder!
    To gain immortal *Honour* he chose well
    With *whom* to do it. if he must *rebell.*

8

With *Us,* behold, *He* likewise puts to flight
Those *Birds* that are the *Favourites* of Jove!
So long ago, *Nations* of greatest might
Knew how to yield, when *against ours* they strove.
See with what *wyle,* and artificial *Slight,*
Our People *he* to fight *his* Quarrel drove,
    Th'*inspiring Hind,* that helpt him with Advice!
    He, is Sertorius : *she,* is *his* Device.

9

Behold that *other* Flag!   *There* painted, see,
Of our first *Kings* the great *Progenitor!*
We make him a Hungarian; but, there bee,
That do affirm he was a Lorraignor.
After that overcome the Moors had *he,*
Gallegos, and the Leon-Warrior,
    Went holy Henry to the *Holy War* :
    To *sanctifie* the *Trunk* whence our *Kings* are.

10

Surpriz'd with wonder, *who* is *this* (demands)
Tell me, *who this* is (cryes the Catuall)
That doth so many *Troops,* so many *Bands,*
Destroy and scatter with a *Force* so small?
So many *Battailes* strikes with his own hands?
With whose fierce *Rams* so many strong *Tow'rs* fall?
    That fights in *blood* up to the Saddle-bow,
    Whilst *Flags* and Crowns fall at his feet like snow?

11

'Tis *first* ALPHONSO (doth DE GAME return),
Who from the MOOR all PORTUGALL did take.
FAME by the waters of black STYX hath sworn
Ne're more to sing of ROMAN for *his* sake.
He, *lov'd of Heav'n,* with *love* of Heav'n did burn;
Whom GOD the scourge of MOORS (his Foes) did make:
    Their *Throne* and Walls broke down to let CHRIST in,
    And nothing left there for his *Heyrs* to win.

12

Had CAESAR fought, had ALEXANDER GREAT,
With such thin *Troops,* so slender, and so short,
Against such num'rous *Armies,* as were beat
By this brave *King,* of every kind and sort:
Believe't nor *He,* nor *He,* with JOVE had eat;
Nor their proud *Fames* made such a lowd report.
    But leave *his* Acts (too glorious to unfold!),
    His *Vassails* deeds are worthy to be told.

13

This, whom thou seest upon his *pupil* (broke)
All patience lost, casting an angry Face;
Bidding him rally up his scatt'red Folke,
And turn again to justifie the place;
Turns the *young man,* turns the *old man* That spoke,
And turns with *them* the *day* in a small space:
    EGAS the name, which the brave old man hath,
    Tutor of MARS, *myrrour of Subjects faith.*

14

There, how he marcheth with his children, look,
(Barefoot, and Ropes about their Necks) t'his end;
Because the *young man,* as he undertook,
To pay CASTEEL low *Homage* could not bend!
He rays'd the *Seige* with *Craft,* and *Oaths* he took,
When vain were *Arms* the *Rampire* to defend.
    He pays the *forfeit* with his *Babes,* and *Wife*:
    And, to preserve his *Master,* gives his *life.*

15

Less did that Consull, who through folly was
Caught at the Caudine Gallows in a Trap,
When *Him* insulting *Samnites* forc't to pass
Under that *shameful yoak* they there did clap.
He (brave and constant) did *himself* disgrace,
To save his *Army* in so sad mishap:
> *This* gives to *shame, and death, himself,* his deer
> *Children,* and guiltless *Spouse* : the last goes neer.

16

Seest thou *this man,* who from an *Ambuscade*
Beats up a *King,* besieging a strong Town,
The *Leaguer* rays'd, the *King* his pris'ner made:
A *deed* great Mars could wish had been his own!
See him again (now *Head* of an *Armade*)
Massacring Moors upon the watry *Down*!
> Boarding their *Galleys,* carrying cleer away
> Portugal's mayden *Victory* at *Sea*!

17

It is Don Fuas Roupinio; on the *Land,*
And on the *Ocean,* gaining equal *Fame*:
Which from the *fired Galleys* (neer the Strand
Of Avila) shines glorious in *their* flame.
See how content he falls by the same Hand,
The Fortune alter'd, but *the Cause* the same!
> Like *Palme* (deprest in vain) through shafts of Mores
> His happy *Soule* to Heav'n triumphant soares.

18

Seest thou not, landing *there* in strange Attire,
From a great *Navy,* Troops *Auxiliar;*
Not without which, our first *King* did acquire
Lisbon (their *Prologue* to the *Holy-War*)!
Of *these,* did Henry (famous *Knight*) expire.
Behold *Palms* sprouting from his Tomb! They are
> Christ's supernatural *Badge,* for Him to weare
> Who, born a German, dyed a *Martyr* there.

19

See a *Priest* brandish (not in vain) his Blade
Against ARRONCHEZ, with revenge sharp whet,
To quit for LEYRIA, which They taken had
Who couch the *Speare* in *Rest* for MAHOMET!
'Tis PRIOR TEUTON. — But, a *Seige* is laid
To SANTAREN. Look, how *Secure*, and *Great*,
    That FIGURE plants upon her scaled wall
    The ever-winning *Cinques* of PORTUGALL!

20

Behold once more (where SANCHO overthrows
In a fierce war the ANDALUSIAN MOORE).
He kills th'*Alferez*, charging *through* the Foes,
And makes SEVILIA's *Standard* mat the floore.
MEM MONIZ 'tis (How like his *Sire* he shows,
The *Phenix* of his *Ashes*!), worthy sure
    The *Royal Flag* and *This;* who *his*, did put
    Up with his *Hand*; the *Foe's* feld at his *foot*.

21

See *Him,* that by his *Lance* descending slid
With the two *Centenells's* two *heads* by night,
To where he hath his men in *ambush hid,*
With whom he gains the *Town* by *force* and *slight!*
That takes for *Arms* the *Knight,* who take *that* did,
And the cold *Heads* in one hand of the *Knight.*
    He, That atchiev'd this unexampled *deed,*
    His *name,* is GERRARD: *Surname, Without dreed.*

22

Doest thou not see a wrong'd CASTILIAN
By their *ninth* King ALPHONSO (for old gall
To those of LARA) to the MOORS That ran,
Making himself a Foe to PORTUGALL?
ABRANTES with those *Infidels* he wan
With whom into our Countrey he did fall:
    But a bold PORTINGALL, with a small Force,
    Here takes him pris'ner; routed Foot and Horse.

23

Don Martin Lopez is the man, that crops
The *Lawrels* he was grasping. But behold
An *Apostollick Warriour,* That chops
For *Lance* of *Steel* his *Crosiers staffe* of *gold*!
See, how *erect* the *stagg'ring* minds *he* props!
How *hot* to fight the Moor, his men grown cold!
      Behold his *Vision* in auspicious skyes,
      With which the *few* he has, he fortifies!

24

Then Sevill's *King,* and *He* of Cordova,
With other *two,* Loe routed! Nor alone
Routed, but *slain*! The strength that got this *Day,*
Was not of *Man* : God claim'd it as his owne.
See now Alcacer hath no more to say,
Though, lin'd with *steel,* her *Battlements* of stone.
      To Matthew (Lisbon's *Bishop*) she submits :
      Who Sprigs of *Palme* into his *Miter* knits.

25

Behold a *Master* poud'ring from Casteel
(A Portingall by Birth) Algarves Land.
How he does conquer, his devouring Steel
Incount'ring none that can the same withstand!
Strong *Towns* (by broad day scal'd) *see,* what they *feel* :
Such his good *star,* so certain is his *Hand.*
      Big with Revenge (Loe!) Tavila he takes,
      And makes it smart for the Sev'n Hunters's sakes.

26

See, how of Sylves Master he became
By *Stratagem*! (the Moor paid dearer for't).
Correa Don Pelayo is his name,
In whom (to envy) *Wit* and *Force* consort.
But the Payr-Royal thou o'reseest of Fame,
That did such Fears in *French* and *Spanish Court.*
      By *Justs,* and *Tournaments,* and *Duels,* there,
      Immortal *Lawrels* they did win and weare.

27

Loe, by the name of Knights Adventurers,
Into the *Kingdom* of Casteel they come;
Where, in Bellonas *sports,* not one but beares
The *prize* away (they prove true *jests* to some)!
See, dead, the prowd *Castilian Cavaleers,*
That challeng'd one of them by sound of drum!
    Rivers Gonzague was *He.* Propt with his *Sword,*
    His *Gyant-Fame* did Lethe's *River* ford.

28

Mark well that *Knight,* by Fame so lov'd and sung,
That her old *Theames* are scorn'd, are out of date!
Of his dear *Countrey,* by one thrid that hung,
On his strong shoulders he sustayn'd the weight.
See, where (with *Anger* dide) a peale *he* rung
To a cow'd *People,* and degenerate,
    That they a *stranger's yoake* might from them fling,
    And take the *sweet one* of their *native King*!

29

See, through this *Counsel,* and *his prowess* too,
Guided by God, and his good *star* alone,
What was *impossible* in *humane* view,
The vast *Castilian* Army overthrown!
See, through his *Valour, force,* and *care,* a new
Cleer Victory (inferiour unto none)
    Over a *People,* fierce as num'rous, Here
    'Twixt Guadiana and Guadalquiveer!

30

Seest thou not *There* how almost routed is
The *Lusitanian Hoast,* through the retreat
Of this *Religious Leader* (whom they miss)
Th'assistance of the *Lord of Hoasts* t'intreat?
See, with pale haste he's now found out by *his,*
Who tell him, there's no dealing with so great
    A *Pow'r;* that he *himself* would look thereto,
    And with his presence cheer his fainting *Crew*!

31

But see, with what a *holy carelesness*
He answers them; *'Tis yet too soon to goe*:
As who, by *Faith,* already did possess
The *Victory* which God will streight bestow.
Pompilius thus (his *Kingdom* in distress
By suddain inroad of a potent Foe)
  To Them That bring him the *ill News,* replyes;
  And I (ye see) am off'ring sacrifice.

32

What his name is thou long'st to know (I see)
That with such boldness on his GOD did seize:
The Lusitanian Scipio it should bee,
Were not a greater Nunio Alvarez.
O *Countrey* blest in such a *Son* as He,
Indeed thy *Father*! Whilst Sol compasses
  This *Globe* of Neptune, and of Ceres yellow,
  To mourn again, thou ne're shalt own his fellow.

33

Victorious, see, in the same *war,* and *Cause,*
Another *Captain* of a *Squadron* small!
He routs *Commendum'd Knights,* and lays his paws
On the great *Prey* they marcht away withal.
See where his reeking Blade again he draws,
Rescuing his *Friend* from *Foes* That lead him Thrall:
  His *Friend,* a martyr for his loyalty!
  Pedro Rodriguez Landroal was *Hee.*

34

See yon *Faith-breaker,* paying an old score
And the base *pelfe* he up at int'rest took!
Gil-Fernand-Elvas plays his *Auditore,*
And with the *Debtor's* death crosses the Book.
Here drowns, in their *Castilian* Owners gore,
The Sherrez-*Fields* (their *sacks* they may go look).
  But see Pereyra; who, like Lightning thrown
  Upon the *Foe's Armada,* shields his *own*!

35

Behold, how poor *sev'nteen* of PORTUGALL
(Upon a *Mountain*) brave resistance make
Against *four hundred* of CASTEEL, That wall
Them in on ev'ry side, to sweep the Stake!
But (to their cost) *these* find a crew so small
More then *Defendants* in that bloody *Wake*.
       A deed deserving everlasting *Rimes*:
       Match it *elsewhere*, in *old* or *modern* Times.

36

Of *Ours* (I grant) *three hundred* did ingage
And rout a thousand ROMANS, in that Time
When VIRIATUS came upon the Stage,
And his *Fame* lightned through each wond'ring *Clime*.
Whence *Those*, who follow'd *him* in that brave *Age*,
Left to their *Race* this *Legacie* sublime,
       Never to fear a *Foe* for *multitude*:
       Which, that we do not, pretty well w'have shew'd.

37

Two *Princes* here (PEDRO and HENRY) see,
Generous *Progenie* of our *first* JOHN!
The *one* forc'd FAME into HIGH GERMANIE
To lacquay him (defrauding death of *one*):
T'other, to trumpet *Him* through the wide SEA
For *it's discov'rer*; and (his *Pen* by thrown)
       Makes enter'd CEUTA see on t'other side
       His *Lance* can prick the bladder of her Pride.

38

Behold the *Earle* DON PEDRO, holding out
Two *Seiges* 'gainst the pow'r of BARBARIE!
Behold *another Earle*, as strong, as stout,
As Mars himself, as fam'd for *Chevalrie*!
Who, not content (with Foes claspt round about)
ALCACER to defend most gallantly,
       Of his KING too the pretious *life* defends;
       And (as his *Bulwark* there) his *own* expends.

39

"Many a FIGURE, in these *Flags* that wants,
"The PAINTER (truly) did to add intend,
"But *Pencils* he doth lack, lacks *Oyle*, and *Paints*:
"*Meed, Honour, Favour*, are *Arts's Life, Nurse, Frend.*
"The fault in our degenerating *Plants*
"From those high *Trunks* of which they do descend.
      "Of *Vanitie* we see sufficient *Flow'rs*:
      "But where's the good *Fruit* of their *Ancestours*?

40

"Those *truly noble Ancestors* of theirs
"(From whom this swelling greatness had it's *Rise*)
"For VERTUE's love digested bitter *Cares*,
"And of their *Houses* to inhance the Price.
"Blind! to *intaile* (with wealth) *sloath* on their *Heirs*
"(VERTUE supplying *fewel* unto *Vice*)
      "Disfig'ring them to boot: For, in this case,
      "The *Founder's Glory* is his *Seed's disgrace*.

41

"*Others* there are, with *wealth*, and *Pow'r* that flow
"Above their Banks; nor *nobly born*, nor *faire.*
"The fault of KINGS: who on one *Minion* throw
"(Sometimes) more then a thousand *worthier* share.
"Of *These* wouldst thou behold the *Pictures*? *No*:
"It is a *vanity* their Friends can spare.
      "As *monstrous* Creatures MYRRORS fly, or break:
      "So *these men* hate the PICTURE that doth *speak*.

42

"I not deny but *some* (whom I could name)
"Deriv'd from *great* and *worthy* Ancestry;
"By high and honorable *Parts* proclame,
"And correspond with, their *nobility*:
"Who, if the *light* of their *Fore-Fathers* Fame
"Their brighter *Vertue* do not *clarify*;
      "Yet, keep it *in* they do. But, of this *Crew*,
      "The PAINTER tells me there are very few.

43

Thus Paul De Gama blazons those great deeds
Which *there* in various *Ink* are written faire;
Which by a *Master's hand* (whose skill exceeds)
In so cleer *Perspective* there painted are.
Th'intentive Catual distinctly reeds
The *History,* as legible, as rare:
     A thousand times he *askt,* a thousand *heard,*
     The *Battails delicate* which *there* appear'd.

44

But cleft was now the *Sun's* ambiguous light
Between the one and t'other *Hemisphere;*
In neither was it *day,* in neither *night,*
But *morning's twylight* here, and *Ev'nings* there:
When, from the warlike *Ship,* the Favourite
And noble Nayres, to the *City* steer
     To court dull *sleep;* which *broods* all living Things
     Of sable *Night* under the downy wings.

45

Mean time the famous *Augurs* of the Land
(Who falsly think, or so are thought at least,
To see by *magick* all things beforehand
In entrails of a sacrificed Beast)
Do their *black office,* at the *King's* command,
To scrutinize, what shall befall the East
     By the arrival through the hansell'd *Maine,*
     Of these unheard of *Guests* from unknown Spaine.

46

Of Lyes the Father shews them *here* signes true;
That a strong *yoak,* which they should ne're remove,
Their endless *Bondage,* shall, this *People* new,
Their *wealth's* consumption, and *their* people's, prove.
The frighted Augurs with pale horror flew
To tell the King, that which infernal Jove
     Made legible by their astonisht Eyes
     In the *red letters* of the *Sacrifice.*

47

Confirming *This*, T'a *Priest* (a *zealous* one,
And *pillar* of the *Law* of MAHOMET,
Whose Bosome with that Gall did over-run
Wherewith both *Sects* against CHRIST's *Law* are set),
In that *false Prophet's* shape, who from the Son
Of Bond-mayd HAGAR did descend, the yet
    Inraged BACCHUS, and who never cleers
      His filthy stomack, in a Dream appeers.

48

"And, *guard you, guard you*, People *mine* (quoth *He*)
"From *Ills* provided for you by the *Foe*,
"That cuts a passage to you through the Sea:
"*Guard you*, before the danger neerer grow.
Th'amazed MOOR starts from his Rest to see
Who gave him this *Alarum*. Thinking *Tho*,
    'Tis but a *Dream* (like common *Dreams*, in deep
      Of Night) returns into the Arms of *sleep*.

49

BACCHUS returns, and says: "Knowst thou not (MORE)
"The great *Law-Giver*, who the ALCORAN
"Shew'd thy *Fore-Fathers*, without which Thy *store*
"Would fail, and half thy *Flock* be CHRISTIAN?
"*Rude*, do I watch for *Thee*, and doest *thou* snore?
"Well, these *white Guests* (I'd have thee to know than)
    "Shall bring great dammage to that *Law*, my *Pen*
      "Deliver'd over unto *stupid* Men.

50

"*Now* whilst this People's strength is not yet knit,
"Think how ye may resist them by all ways.
"For, when the *Sun* is in his *nonage* yit,
"Upon his *morning Beauty* Men may gaze;
"But let him once up to his *Zenith* git,
"He strikes them *blind* with his *Meridian Rays*:
    "So *blind* will ye be, if ye look not too't,
      "If ye permit these *Cedars* to take root.

51

This said: both *he*, and *sleep*, vanish at once.
The Moor remains: rockt in his Bed with fright.
Th'infused *poyson* working in his sconce,
He starts, and to his servants cryes: *a light*.
When the new light (which doth precede the *Sun's*)
Disclos'd it self *Angelical*, and *white*,
  The *Chief* of that vile Sect he did convoke,
  To whom his *Dreame* in every point he spoke.

52

Then sev'ral, and cross Reasons they discourse;
As they from *others*, or *themselves*, dissent.
Secret *way-layings*, open *Feud*, and *Force*,
And sev'ral ways of each they do invent.
But, when *those* seem'd too *fine*, and *these* too *course*,
To take a middle way is their intent.
  To do *their* buis'ness with *another's* Hand,
  They mean to bribe the *Grandees* of the *Land*.

53

With *Gold*, and other *Presents* underhand,
The *ruling men* they to their *Partie* gaine;
Giving them *speciously* to understand,
These *Guests* will put a *period* to *their* Raigne:
That of lewd *Vagabonds* they are a *Band*,
Who, plying to and fro the *Western Mayne*,
  Live on *Pyratick* spoyle, without (in fine)
  Or King, or Laws, or *humane*, or *divine*.

54

"O how a Perfect King it doth behove
"To chuse his Favourites and Councell such
"As are lin'd through with Vertue, and *her* love;
"As feel of Conscience a true *inward* touch!
"For *He* (who in the *highest Orb* doth move)
"Of things *remote* can onely have so much
  "Intelligence, whereby to judge, as *They*
  "That are his outward *Organs* will convey.

55

"Nor ev'n on Vertue let him so much dote,
"T'adore't in *picture,* or without *Controule*
"T'imploy't; as some, who in a simple Coat
"Have trust an *Hypocrite* (a *preying Foule*)
"And, if a *Saint* indeed, hee'l speak by rote
"In *worldly* matters: For the *Dove* like soule
     "Seeld with an Angell's *Quill,* hath *Eyes* to find
     "The way to *Heav'n,* but to the *Earth* is blind.

56

But *here,* these avaritious Catuals,
Who did that *Pagan-Kingdom* rule and sway,
Brib'd by *infernal* People to play false,
The *Portingal-Dispatches* did delay.
Now the wise *Leader* of the Portingals,
Of all the *Indian Prince* can do, or say,
     Caring for nothing back with him to bring
     But *news* of this *discov'rie* to the King:

57

In *this alone* takes pains. For well he knew,
When he should carry back *this news alone,*
That *Navies, Arms,* and *soldiers* would insue
From Manuel, who fills the *Regal Throne;*
With which to CHRIST, and *Him,* he would subdue
The *Globe* of *Earth,* and *Sea:* That *Himselfe's* one
     Sent out but as a *Dove,* as a *Line* hurld,
     To *spy,* and *sound,* this Ocean, and this World.

58

Resolv'd he is, the *Pagan King* to find,
And pray *dispatch,* that he may take his leave;
Which *now* he sees, those spightful People mind
(If *they* can help it) he shall ne're receave.
The *King,* who with suggestions of that kind
Was shook and startled, you must needs conceave
     (Too *credulous* to *ev'ry* Augur's word,
     Much more to *All,* and when the Moors concurr'd):

59

Freez'd with this fear hath his ignoble *Brest.*
On t'other side the *sacred Thirst* of *Gaine*
(A *Vice* in *Him* that's *Paramount* the rest)
Kindles a *fire* which *thaws* that *Frost* againe.
For his *advantage* he sees manifest,
If he with *cleer intentions* entertaine,
     And with *firm Actions* cherish, and pursue,
     The *League* which PORTUGAL invites him to.

60

His COUNCELL then commanded to attend,
He found no *One* that did in this comply:
Because on *Those,* who should their judgements spend,
Money had done it's office pow'rfully.
For the magnanimous *Captain* he doth send.
To whom (arriv'd) with a *Majestick* Eye;
     "If, *here,* the pure and naked *Truth* to me
     "Thou wilt *confess,* I pardon thee (quoth *He*).

61

"I am assur'd, th' *Ambassage* thou hast done
"To *me* in thy *King's* name, is meerly coyn'd:
"For that, nor *King,* nor *Countrey* doest *Thou* own,
"But (*vagabonding*) sayl'dst with ev'ry wind.
"From farthest SPAIN's remotest *Region*
"Would any *King* or *Prince* (in his right mind)
     "A *single ship* much less a *Navy* send,
     "Through so *incertain* ways to the WORLD's *end?*

62

"And, if *thy King* support his Majesty
"With great and potent *Realms,* which he commands;
"Thy *unknown Truth* to prove and testifie,
"What pretious *presents* knit this *friendship's* bands?
"In *Presents* rich, in sumptuous *Guifts* and high,
"*Kings* speak their loves: *Their Rhet'rick's* in their *Hands.*
     "A *Hand,* that gives not, *Any* falsifies:
     "Nor will a *Sea-man's* testing it suffice.

63

"If banisht from thy *native soyle* thou *be*
"(As many a *man* hath *been* of great *Renown*)
"Welcom, by Jove, both to my *Realms* and *me*:
"For to the *Valiant* ev'ry *Land's* his *own*.
"Or if, a *Pyrat,* thou infest the *Sea,*
"Spare not through *fear,* or *shame,* to make *that* known:
  "For in all times, a vital breath to draw,
  "Necessitie hath been *exempt* from *Law.*

64

He said. De Gama (finding this *new* Face
Of *Things,* is from the greedy Catualls;
Suborn'd, by Ishmael's malicious Race,
The *Royal Ear* to poyson with things false)
With such a high *assurance,* as the Case
Required, instead of fresh *Credentials,*
  (Which Venus Acidalia did inspire)
  To his wise Breast (surcharged) thus gave fire.

65

"If the gilt *Cup* of *Lyes* (which Man betrayd
"Out of his *Paradice*) had not *pledg'd* bin
"By our *first Parents,* and by them *convayd*
"From *hand* to *hand* through foul *original sin*;
"Till in the *hand* of Mahomet it stayd,
"Who suckt the very *dreggs* that were therein:
  "Most mighty *King,* thou never had'st received
  "This *Calumny* by that damn'd *Sect* conceiv'd.

66

"But, in as much as there's no *good* that's *great*
"Done without *great Contrast;* and *Actions tall*
"(For man his bread in his Brows sweat must eat)
"That stand *on tiptoe,* are tript at by *All*;
"Therefore *they* brand me for a *Counterfait,*
"Therefore doest *Thou* my *Truth* in question call,
  "Although so *cleer,* that *see it* needs thou must,
  "Didst thou not *credit* whom thou shouldst Mistrust.

67

"For, if I liv'd by robbing on the *Sea,*
"Or (wreck of *Fortune*) banisht my dear *Home;*
"What need I go so far to seek my *Prey*?
"For unknown *Mansions* need I hither roam?
"What *gain,* what *hopes* could make me in this way
"To tempt the fury of the *waves* that foam,
          "*Antartick* colds, Heats of the *burning line,*
          "Where *Aries* hangs, the *Equinoxial sign*?

68

"If on great *Gifts* of estimation high
"The *credit* due to me thou pin and cast;
"My comming now was onely to descry
"Where NATURE hath thy ancient *Kingdome* plac't:
"But to my *Countrey,* and *Dread Leige,* if I
"Through *Fortune's* goodness get, long *Seas* re-past;
          "At my return I promise thee (O *King*)
          "That such CREDENTIALS never man did bring.

69

"If unto *Thee* an uncouth thing it show,
"That, where her farthest Arm HESPERIA flings,
"A *King* should send me to thee, *Thou* should'st know
"That nothing possible is hard to *Kings.*
"Then *Kings* of PORTUGALS (if *this* be so)
"May be allow'd, for spreading of their wings,
          "Something of greater, and of larger scope,
          "Then what is giv'n for *common Kings* to hope.

70

"Know, that for sev'ral *Generations* past
"Our Kings have firmly purpos'd in their hearts,
"With all those *Toyles* and *Dangers* to contrast
"Wherewith *Heroick* deeds whole NATURE thwarts:
"And (Enemies to *sloath*) of th'OCEAN vast
"Piercing into the undiscover'd Parts,
          "Aspir'd to know the end of it, and where
          "The farthest *Countreys,* which it washes, were.

71

"The *worthy Project* of the *learned Branch*
"Of that *victorious King,* who, to displant
"From his dear *Nest,* did through the Sea first lanch,
"Of Avila the last Inhabitant,
"*He,* joyning *one* unto *another* planch,
"(As far from *Idle* as from *Ignorant*)
    "Discover'd all those Parts which lighted are
    "By *Argo, Hydra,* th'*Altar,* and *the Hare.*

72

"Gath'ring fresh courage *then* from the event,
"In that those first endeavours prov'd not vain,
"Discov'ring farther new *Advent'rers* went
"Successively the secrets of the *Maine.*
"Th'*Inhabitants* of Affrick, That frequent
"Her Southern Cape, and never saw CHARLS WAYN,
    "Were seen by *These*: leaving behind each *Isle,*
    "And *Continent,* which Both the *Tropicks* broyle.

73

"With this so high *Resolve,* and fixt therein,
"Our *Nation* quell'd, and triumpht over *Chance*:
"Till *I,* now ending what Those did begin,
"The farthest *Piller* in thy *Realm* advance.
"Breaking the Element of molten Tyn,
"Through horrid storms *I* lead to *thee* the Dance;
    "From whom (to carry to my *King*) I ask
    "Onely a *sign* that I have done my Task.

74

"This is Truth (*King*) For, for so *doubtful gain*
"So *inconsiderable* a *Content,*
"As (were it other) I could hope; so vain
"A *lye,* and formal, I would scorn t'invent.
"No, on the *restless Bosome* of the Mayn,
"To set my *Rest* up, I would first consent
    "Forever; and by *Pyracy* to get
    "An unjust living out of others swet.

75

"So that, O KING! if my great *Veritie*
"Thou hold (as 'tis) for single and sincere;
"Dispatch me to my *Prince* with brevitie,
"Hold me no longer from my *Countrey* deare.
"But if the scruple still remain in thee,
"Ponder the *Reasons* I have render'd *Here*;
  "I lay them in thy piercing *judgements scale*
  "Secure: "For *great* is *Truth*, and will prevail.

76

The *King* markt all along the *Confidence*
With which DE GAME ev'n proved his discourse.
A full assurance of his *Innocence*,
A perfect credit did this speech inforce.
He weighs the copious *Words's* magnificence,
Th'authoritie with which they fetch their source:
  Thinks now the CATUALL *deceived* is;
  But He is *brib'd*: and so he thinks amis.

77

Added to this, his avaritious Eye
Upon the gainful Trade of PORTUGALL
Makes him obey; and rather to comply
With the brave *Captain*, then the *Moorish* gall.
In short, he bids DE GAMA presently
Get him aboard his *Fleet;* and, without all
  Suspect of harm, whatever *Merchandice*
  To send ashore, to sell, or truck for Spice.

78

In fine, he bids him send of every thing
That in *Gangetick Kingdoms* is not met;
If ought that fits them from that *Land* he bring
Where the *Land* ends, begins the *ocean* great.
Now from the awful presence of the *King*,
Illustrious GAMA parteth; to intreat
  The CATUALL, That of the *Ports* had charge,
  (His *Own* from shore) to order him a *Barge*.

79

A *Barge* he prays from this illustrious Lord :
But this is more, then he is well content
(As ruminating mischiefe) to afford :
Pretending this and that impediment.
Yet (as in order to his going abord)
Far from the *Royal Court* with *Him* he went,
    Where *he* (unnoted by the *King*) may write,
    To *Avarice* what *malice* did indite.

80

He tells him, yonder afar off, that He
Hath imbarcation fitter for his turn;
Or that to morrow it may better be,
If he till then his going will adjourn.
Now did abused GAMA plainly see,
By this *put off* unto another morn,
    The *great one* too is in the *Moorish* plot :
    Which till that instant he suspected not.

81

This CATUAL was *one* (and *first*) of Those
That were corrupted by that crooked *Sect* :
And whom the SAMORIM (that lov'd him) chose
Th'Affairs of all his *Empire* to direct.
In *Him alone* those *devils* now repose
To bring their plotted Treason to effect.
    He (who consents to break his *Master's* faith)
    Steps not an inch beside *their* chalked path.

82

To be dispatcht DE GAMA begs, and prays,
But begs in vain, in vain he pray'rs lets fall :
Protests th'*Embargue;* nor will this please (he says)
The noble *Successor* of PERIMAL.
Why these *Impediments,* why these *delays,*
When he should fetch the *Goods* of PORTUGAL?
    Since, what commands the *Sov'raign* of a *Land,*
    None hath authority to countermand.

83

The bribed Catuall small reck'ning made
Of this *Protest:* rather in spightful mood
Some never-heard of *Treason* (to be waigh'd
Out of the Stygian dam) within did brood.
Or, how he may imbrew his cursed Blade
In those detested veins, consid'ring stood:
    Or, how the *Ships* he may blow up, or burn;
    That they may never into Spaine return.

84

That's it (ev'n that they never see Spaine more)
For which the Moors infernal *Junta* bribe:
That so they may not wealthy India's shore
Unto the *King* of Portugal describe.
In fine De Game goes not: the Regidore
Forbids, in favour of that barb'rous *Tribe.*
    Nor without his permission can it be:
    For a stop laid on all the Boats had He.

85

To all the *Captain's* importunities,
The *Pagan* bids him in a word, command
(For the more ready truck of Merchandize)
To have his *Ships* brought close up to the Land.
It is the way of *Thieves* and *Enemies*
(He says) at distance with their *Fleets* to stand.
    "No sign so sure of one that *Ill* intends
    "As to suspect *ill dealings* from his *Frends.*

86

Wise Gama understood by half a word,
The Cause the Catual did neer desire
To have the *Ships,* was, that with *fire* and *Sword*
He *openly* might wreake on them his Ire.
'Twas time (he thought) he *now* himself bestir'd,
That he assemble *now* his Wits intire.
    His *Fancy* musters, to defeat all plots:
    All things he fears, and all things counterplots.

87

As of a *Mirrour,* the reflected light,
Of burnisht *Steel,* or *Cristal* without stain,
Which struck by Sol (as if in fell despight)
Strikes the next *man* it meets, or *Thing,* again :
And (mov'd by nimble Hand of some young *spright*
About the *House,* who is in gamesome *vain*)
    Skips on the *Floor,* the *Roof,* the *Wall,* the *Chaire;*
    And has you *here,* and *There,* and *ev'ry where* :

88

So shot the wav'ring *Fancy* to and fro
Of circumspect De Game; imagining
That possibly the Boats Coellio
Might to the shore (as he had order'd) bring.
Back to the *Navy* (if that were) to row,
He sends to Him forthwith advertising;
    On *Him,* or *That,* lest ought attempted be
    By the Moors cruel *Infidelitie.*

89

"Such should be *All,* who in *war's* Trade profound
"Would imitate and match illustrious men;
"Fly like the *Needle* all the *Compass* round,
"*First* divine *Dangers,* and prevent them *then,*
"With martial skill try ev'ry depth, and ground,
"And, for the *Foe's one* fence-play shew Him *ten;*
    "Believe all *is,* that *may be;* For (in briefe)
    "To say, *I thought,* is ugly in a Chiefe.

90

The Malabar protests, that he shall rot
In prison, if he send not for the *Ships.*
He (constant, and with noble *Anger* hot)
His haughty *menace* weighs not at two chips.
All that base *malice* dares or *do,* or *plot,*
When her black trailing bowels forth she rips,
    Alone hee'l bear, e're he will dis-ensure
    His *King's Armada* which he hath secure.

91

All that long *night,* and *part* he *there* was held
Of the next day, when to the Samorim
He means again to go: but was withheld
By a strong *Guard* plac't in the entry dim.
The *Pagan* (seeing how he still rebell'd,
And fearing less the *King* should punish Him
　　　In case he knew, as know he must e're long,
　　　If this restraint proceed, the barb'rous wrong)

92

Bids him then send for, and expose to sale,
Not *some,* but *all* the *Merchandise* he brought;
That men may buy and truck in open scale:
"For where *free Trade* is barr'd there *war* is sought.
De Gama (though he pierce through this thin vaile
And plainly views the *Evil* of his *Thought*)
　　　Consents thereto: because he well doth see
　　　That with his *Goods* he buys his *libertie.*

93

The'agreement is, that *Boats* the *Pagan* find
Such as are fit to Land the *Merchandise,*
For to send *his* the *Captain* doth not mind
To be *embargu'd,* or *sunk* by Enemies.
To fetch such *Spanish wares,* as *vend* in Ynd,
Are soon dispatcht the *Indian Almadies.*
　　　The *Captain* to his Brother writes, to lade
　　　The *Goods* with which his *Ransom* must be payd.

94

Landed they are: which wondrously doth please
The Catual's infamous *Avarice.*
There with doth Diego stay, and Alvarez:
With pow'r to truck, or sell them at a price.
That (*more,* then King, *Pray'rs, Honor,* or *All* these,
Upon a soul infected with that *Vice*)
　　　A *Bribe* can do, the *Pagan* heer doth show:
　　　Who for the *Goods* did let De Gama go.

95

For *Those,* he lets *Him* go : before he quit
The *Pawn,* on which he *now* hath layd his hand,
Meaning a better penny thence to git
Then if he kept the *Captain* still on Land.
He (scapt out of the Trap) thinks it no wit
On t'other side, to come within command
     Again : but (safely got aboard his *Fleet*)
     In his own *Nest* takes sleep secure, and sweet.

96

At leisure *then* he walks upon his *Decks*
To see what *Time* and *Patience* will bring forth.
No *Ruler* hath he *there* to make him vex :
Imperious, brib'd, without or *shame,* or *worth.*
"*Now* let the judging *Reader* mark what *wrecks*
"The *Idol Gold* (which all the World ador'th)
     "Plays both in *Poor* and *Rich:* by *Money's* Thurst
     "All *Laws* and *Tyes* (Divine, and Humane) burst.

97

"Slain by the *Thracian* King, to seize a vast
"Intrusted Treasure, Polidoro was.
"When stern Acrysius thought his *Daughter* fast,
"A *Show'r* of *gold* did pierce a *Tow'r* of *Brass.*
"The yellow *Bracelets* of the *Foes,* did cast
"Such tempting beams on the Tarpeian Lass,
     "That she, for Those, the *Tow'r* of Rome unbarr'd :
     "Who brain'd her with the *Bribe* for a reward.

98

"*This* strongest *Forts* subverts, and overthrows :
"Makes Kindred, *Kindred*; and Friends, *Friends* betray.
"*This* noble-men *ignobly* doth dispose :
"Delivers *Captains* to their Foes a Prey.
"*This* blasts of pure *Virginitie* the Rose :
"Trampling on *Fame* and *honour* by the way.
     "*This* bribes ev'n Lib'rall Arts (it's pow'r is such)
     "Makes Judgement have no *sight,* Conscience no *touch.*

99

"*This,* in unheard of Sences *Texts* doth take:
"*This* makes an unmakes *Laws* in the same case:
"*This* perjures *Subjects,* and *This* KINGS doth make
"Stoop to the *Lure,* like *Eagles* from their place.
"Ev'n *golden minds* (of *those* That *All* forsake
"For GOD) this *Antichimist* doth debase
    "To vilest mettle: with this *Diff'rence* though,
    "That still *These* glister with a *holy show.*

End of the eighth Canto.

Ninth Canto

STANZA 1

Long in the *City* the Two *Factors* lay,
Without dispatching *off* the *Merchandize.*
So many *rubbs* are scatter'd in their way
By the false INFIDELS, that no man buyes.
All *These* design thereby, is to delay
INDIA'S *Discov'rers* There (whom *they* call *spyes*)
    Arriv'd, till they the Fleet of MECHA see,
    With which this *other* overwhelm'd may be.

2

At the far end o'th ERITHREAN Sea
Where (calling it by his dear *Sister's* name)
The goodly *City* of ARSINOE
(Which afterwards to be call'd SUEZ came)
Was founded by EGYPTIAN PTOLOME,
The Port of MECHA lyes: which hath it's fame
    From MAHOM's superstitious *Lavatory,*
    Promising *Heav'n* through watry *Purgatory.*

3

GIDDA the *Port* is call'd, in which did meet
The *Trade* of that RED SEA and flourisht most:
The *Gain* whereof was not a little sweet
To EGYPT's *Soldan* who then rul'd that *Coast*.
From *hence* to MALABAR a warlike *Fleet*
Of INFIDELLS the *Indian* Ocean crost
  Each yeer; in that EMPORIUM to find
   Health-giving *Drugs,* and *Spices* of each kind.

4

The *Ships* expected by the MOORS are *These,*
With which (not onely *great,* but built for *Fight*)
Them, who supplant their *Traffick* in those Seas,
To wrap and burn in crackling flames and bright.
In this Sure *Card* themselves they so much please,
That, all they wish to gorge their Appetite,
  Is that the *Strangers* will but stay so long
   Till from fam'd MECHA come this *Navy* strong.

5

But the GREAT GOVERNOR of *Heav'n* and *Earth*
(Who, for what *He* before all Time did doom,
Likewise decreed fit means, which to the birth
Should bring the same when the full Time should come)
Kindled unlikely love on the cold Hearth
Of a MOOR's breast (MONSAYDE's) sending whom
  Before, He to DE GAMA gave advice
   Of *All,* and for his payns had PARADICE.

6

This man (of whom the MOORS had no suspition,
Being *one* himself, but on the contrary
To all their secret *junta's* gave admission)
Did to the *Captain* this *foule play* descry.
He visits oft the *Fleet,* and repetition
Makes of his visits oft, though far it lye:
  To heart he lays the danger it is in,
   Through the black *Project* of the SARACIN.

7

He tells the cautious GAMA of the *Fleet*
Which from ARABIAN MECHA comes each yeere,
And how those Countrey men do thirst to see't,
As a sure *Engin* to destroy him there.
That it comes stuft with *Soldiers,* and in *It*
Doth horrid *Thunderbolts* of VULCAN beare:
    So that, consid'ring, how his own is brusht,
    It may thereby be overpowr'd and crusht.

8

DE GAMA, besides *this,* considering
That now the time it self calls him away;
And that for better answer from the *King*
(Who loves the MOORS) he may till doomsday stay:
Sends one ashore, the *Factors* summoning
To come aboard forthwith; and, lest that *They*
    Be stopt, if their intent perceiv'd should be;
    Commands them do it with all secresie.

9

But long it was not e're a rumour went
(And it fell out to be a rumour true)
That the two *Factors* were to prison sent,
'Cause from the *City* they by stealth withdrew.
The *Captain,* seeing which way the world went,
Seiz'd (by *Reprisal*) without more ado
    Some, That were then aboard his *ship,* lin'd well
    With *Precious Stones* which they desir'd to sell.

10

Grave *Citizens,* and wealthy were *These* all;
Well known, and well allide in CALICUT:
Therefore, to see them bound for PORTUGALL,
Into an *uproare* did the *City* put.
For streight to work the sturdy *Sea-men* fall:
The *Capstone* roles, their *sev'ral* strengths set to't
    In *sev'ral* manners: *some* the *Cable* halling,
    With the *Bar* others their hard *bosoms* galling.

11

This, hangs by the *main-yard;* and now untyes
The flowing *Saile,* with a great *cry* displayd:
When to the SAMORIM with greater cryes
Is told how hastily the CAPTAIN waigh'd,
Their Wives and *Children* (trust up in this wise
That are) a noyse, as they were murther'd, made
    In the KING's hearing; screaming they should lose,
    These their dear *Fathers:* their deare *Husbands,* Those.

12

The *Lusitanian Merchants,* with the *Ware,*
(There's no delaying) freely he remands,
Although thereat the MOORS do stamp and stare.
Or else his *own* must visit uncouth Lands.
With all *excuses,* to make things look faire,
Sends to *his* King.   DE GAME (who understands
    The *Restitution* better then the *Cringe*)
    Returns some BLACKS, and gives the *ships* their swinge.

13

He *coasts it homewards,* fully satisfy'de
That he in vain solicits with *that* King
A *peace and friendship,* to be ratify'de
By mutual Trade, as he propos'd the thing.
But, having now that noble Land descry'de
Which lay much hid under the *Morning's* wing,
    For his deare *Countrey* with this *news* is bound:
    Carrying sure *signes* of that which he hath found.

14

He carries MALABARS, retained by Him
Perforce, of Those, who the stopt Factors brought
Aboard from the inforced SAMORIM.
He carries burning *Pepper,* which he bought;
Nutmegs, (the which their own dry'de flow'rs up trim)
From BANDA; the black *Clove* (for which is sought
    MOLUCO's ISLE) and *Cinnamon,* through which
    CEYLAN is noble, beautiful, and rich.

15

All *these* provided by the diligence
Of good MONSAYDE, whom he carries too:
Who fir'd with *Evangelick* influence
To have his name writ in CHRIST'S book doth sue.
O happy AFFRICAN! whom PROVIDENCE
DIVINE, out of *infernal darkness* drew;
    And, so far from thy *Countrey,* found a way
    To thy *true Countrey* to reduce thee, stray!

16

Thus vanish from the spicy Territory
The happy *ships,* whose *Prows* directly stand
OF GOOD HOPE pointing at THE PROMONTORY
(*South-Bound* of NATURE fixt by her own Hand);
Bearing the evidence and welcom story
To LISBON of the *oriental* Land:
    Once more committed to the rude annoy
    Of *Seas* uncertain betwixt *fear* and *joy.*

17

That they are going to their *Countrey* deare,
To their dear *Parents,* and *Aboads* at last,
To tell their wond'rous *Navigation,* there,
The various *Nations* seen, and *Dangers* past;
That now the *Harvest* of their *Toyles* is neare,
The *Fruits* of their *Adventure* ripe to tast;
    Is such a *joy* as cannot be *exprest*
    By their faint *Tongue, pent* in their narrow *Brest.*

18

But CYPRUS'S *Queen,* who by the *King* of HEAV'N
Was made the LUSITANIANS'S *Patroness,*
And for a *Guardian Angel* to *them* giv'n,
To whom she many yeers hath prov'd no less;
Glory for which they have so *bravely* striv'n,
Amends for their so *well indur'd* distress,
    Means them by way of *earnest* beforehand;
    And in sad *Seas* the *Pleasures* of the *Land.*

19

Having a while revolved in her thought
The world of *Sea* which they have back to pass,
The world of Woes, *that* God on them had brought
In Amphionian Thebes twice-born that was:
It is her purpose, *joys,* so dearly bought
With *Griefs,* to fill them in an ample glass;
    To cook them some *delights,* find them some nest,
    Where in the rolling *Empire* they may rest;

20

In fine an *Inn* of *pleasure* by the way
To *bait* and *strengthen* tyr'd *Humanity:*
To give her gallant *Sea-men* (not their *Pay,*
But) the use *here* of fair Eternity.
She means to tell't her *Son,* and well she may;
For, with *his shafts* it is, she makes the *high*
    Gods stoop to the *base ground:* and, with *his fire,*
    Unworthy mortals to *bright Heav'n* aspire.

21

This well digested, she resolves, in fine
There, in the middle of the *briny frost,*
To have in readiness an *Isle* Divine,
With flow'rs on green inameld and imbost:
For she hath many in those *Seas,* which joyne
To that *blest Land* which our *first mother* lost;
    Besides those sweet ones in the *Midland Seas,*
    Impounded by the Gates of Hercules.

22

There will she have th'*Aquatick maids* prepare
To these rare men their graces to impart;
All that are honor'd with the name of *Faire*
(The *glory* of the *Eye, Bane* of the *Heart*)
With *Balls,* and *Banquets, blithe* and *debonayre:*
For she inspires into their brests the dart
    Of secret love, that *they* with all their might
    Of their *Gallants* may study the delight.

23

Such once her *Project* for the man she bare
To TROY's ANCHISES neer to SIMOIS's flood;
To get him *welcome* in that *City* fair
Which in the compass of an *Oxe-hide* stood.
Her *boy* she seeks (for, without *Him*, her rare
Beauty is nothing), CUPID giv'n to blood:
     That, as to Him *of yore* she recommends
     Her *sayling son*, so *now*, her *sayling* Frends.

24

She yoaks those *Birds* unto her Coach of gold
Which sing their own sad *Dirge* with long white necks:
And *those*, into the which was turn'd of old
PERISTERA, That gather'd flow'rs by pecks.
The flying Goddess *These* in Rings enfold,
Exchanging kisses with lascivious Beaks.
     She, where she passes, makes the *Wind* to lye
     With gentle motion, and serenes the *skye*.

25

Over *Idalian* Mountains *now* she hung,
The *winged Boy* residing in that Land,
To get an *Army* up of *Bow-men* young,
For a great *War* which he hath then in hand
Against the rebel WORLD; where late have sprung
Much *Weeds*, as he is giv'n to understand:
     Loving those things, wherewith 'tis richly stor'd,
     To be made use of, not to be ador'd.

26

He sees ACTEON hunting, so inclin'd
To that mad *sport*, and brutal *exercise*,
That a deform'd *wild-beast* to follow (blind)
The Beauty of a *humane* Face he flyes:
And (to torment him with a *Fair Unkind*)
Shews stript DIANA to his gazing eyes.
     Now, let him take good heed he do not prove
     A *Prey*, ev'n to those *Hounds* he doth so love.

27

He sees the *great ones* of each Land, that none
Have *Publike Good* so much as in their *Eye:*
Sees they love nothing but themselves alone;
Which is part *Intrest,* and part *Philautye.*
Courtiers he sees (men That besiege a *Throne*)
How for *true Doctrine* they vent *Flattery.*
    'Tis husbandry *these* like not in a *King*
    To weed the *Flow'rs* out of his *Corn* in *Spring.*

28

He sees, how *Those* that owe a *vowed* love
To *Povertie,* and *Charitie* to *Men,*
Love *Riches* onely, and to floate Above,
Pretending *justice,* and a *Conscience* clean.
They tell the *People,* what doth *Them* behove;
OBEDIENCE, in the *deed,* the *Tongue,* the *Pen.*
    Laws they set up in favour of the CROWN,
    Laws in the *People's* favour they pull down.

29

He sees, in fine, none love that which they should
But onely what complies with some vain lust:
Therefore his hands can *he* no longer hold
From *punishments* that may be *sharp,* yet *just.*
His *Captains* prickt, his *Soldiers* are inrol'd
Fit for a *War* which undertake *he* must,
    With the misgovern'd *World:* whereby to quell
    All that persist against him to rebel.

30

Swarms of these little *Hov'rers* (newly flown)
At sev'ral *works,* busie as *Bees,* are all:
Some whetting *Arrow-Heads* on *bloody Hone,*
Others the shafts of *Arrows* shaving small.
Working they *sing,* and *sing* of *love* alone,
And then that *Love* it is *Seraphical:*
    In *Parts;* and in the *burthen* all do joyne;
    The *Ditty* excellent, the *Tune* Divine.

31

On the immortal *Anviles* (where their Arts
They use, the *steeled points* to forge, and fit)
Instead of *Embers* there are burning *Hearts*,
Which bring their *Bellows* with them (panting yit):
The *streams,* with which they *temper* their *steel'd darts,*
Tears, which from miserable Lovers flit:
    The sparckling *flame*, the never quenched *fire*,
    (Which *burns,* and not *consumes* them) is *desire.*

32

Some of these *Archers* exercise their *Hand*
On the hard Bosomes of the *Vulgar* rude;
The *bor'd Ayre hiss't* (by this we understand
The *sighings* of the wounded *multitude*);
For *Surgeons, Nymphs* to *Cure* them ready stand,
With *Sov'raign Vertue* to this end indu'd:
    Who, to the *Hurt* not onely life can give,
    But make, ev'n *them* that ne're were *born,* to *live.*

33

Some of these *Nymphs* are faire, and some are not,
According to the Nature of the *Wound:*
Into the *blood* if once the Taint be got,
Oft ugly *Treacle* gives the *Patient* sound.
There are, whom *Spells* and *Philters* do besot;
Nayl'd to their *Seates*, they wiss not how, and *bound:*
    Where *this* is, Love hath us'd against fraile *Hearts*
    Unlawful weapons, shooting *poyson'd darts.*

34

From these *raw Soldiers*, out of *ranke* and *file,*
A thousand rash and senceless *Darts* are sped:
A thousand senceless *loves* are born the while
In the low People, to be pittied.
Ev'n amongst *Those* in *highest Forms,* of *vile*
And *horrid Love* are thousand *patterns* read:
    Biblis, and Myrra, for one *sex;* for *t'other,*
    The'Assyrian Son, and the Judean Brother.

35

And *you* (Great *Lords*) by *shepherdesses* meane
Under the *yoke* of LOVE have oft been brought,
And *you* (great *Ladies*) with rude *Clowns* uncleane
In VULCAN'S subtle *Nets* have oft been caught:
Some, watching the dim fall of the *Serene;*
Some, pitchie *Night*, o're *Tiles*, or *Walls* to vaut.
     Though for these *sordid fires* (if *right* we *did*)
     More then the *Son* the *Mother* should be chid.

36

But the swift *Coach* now softly on the *Green*
The white *Swans* (ballanc't in their Harness) put;
On which DIONE (in whose *Cheek* is seen
The Snow-mixt *Rose*) sets light her milky foot.
The *Archer* meets her with a jocund meen
Who shoots at HEAV'N, and doth not miss the *But*.
     With *Him* in *Squadron* his SUB-CUPIDS move,
     To do their *Homage* to the QUEEN OF LOVE.

37

She (not to spend the pretious time in vain)
Snatching her Child up, confidently said;
"Dear Son, in *whom,* and whose strong *Arm,* I raign;
"And the Foundations of my *Pow'r* are laid;
"Son, in *whom* all my *strengths* always remain;
"*Who* feard'st not *Them,* That made great JOVE afraid;
     "I have a special buis'ness to be done,
     "In which I greatly need *thy* pow'r, *my* Son.

38

"The LUSITANIANS, harast out, behold!
"Who are *my Care* of long Antiquity;
"Because my Friends (the *Fates*) to me had told,
"Wheree're *They* go, my worshipt name should fly.
"And, for they imitate my ROMANS old
"In all *Heroick* Actions, therefore *I*
     "Resolve, for them to do a *Guardian's* duty,
     "And raise the *Posse* of the *Realm* of Beauty.

39

"And, since the malice of the God of Wine
"Spun them new troubles upon *Indian*-ground,
"When from the furies of the swelling *Brine*
"They crope out weather-beaten, and half-drown'd;
"Therefore in middle of the *Seas* (in fine)
"Which they their bitter enemie have found.
 "And neer that India, I would have them breathe,
 "And of their *Labours* the *first-fruits* receave.

40

"As wanton *Fishes* then therein are strook,
"So do *Thou* strike the fair Nereides;
"That on these Lusitanians they may look
"With *amorous* eyes, who carry home the Keys
"Of their discover'd World. Sick with the Hook
"Let them on shore an *Isle*; an *Isle* (in *Seas*
 "*Immense*) which *I* have deckt with all the Flow'rs
 "Or Zephyrus breathes out; or Flora pow'rs.

41

"*There* with a thousand *dishes* delicate,
"With oderiferous *Wines*, and *Roses* sweet,
"In crystal *Palaces* immaculate,
"In *lillie sheets* (they whiter then the sheet),
"In fine with thousand joys past Vulgar rate,
"Let the obliging *Nymphs* their *Heroes* meet
 "(Wounded with *love*) and yield up *Nature's* treasure,
 "To be all ransackt at the *Victor's* pleasure.

42

"In Neptune's *Realm* (to which I owe my birth)
"A fair and manly *Off-spring* would I have;
"To serve for *pattern* to the Bastard-Earth,
"Which with rebellious Heart thy *pow'r* doth brave:
"That men may know, From *Thee*, the Foe of mirth
"*Hypocrisie*, nor *walls of brass* can save.
 "Ill can it be resisted on the *Land*,
 "If in the *Sea* burn thy immortal *Brand*.

43

She had not ended when the *Wag* her Son
Prepares himself to do as he was told:
Calls for his *Iv'ry Bow*, ingrav'd upon,
Whose *Arrow-points* are tagg'd with heads of *Gold*.
Ravisht with joy the Cyprian Parragon
Sets the *Boy* by her in her Coach, which troll'd,
    The reins enlarged to those *Birds*, whose *Song*
    The death of Phaethon laments so long.

44

"But we do want a certain necessary
"Woman, to broke between them, Cupid said;
"Whom, though to *Him* she had been oft contrary,
"Yet, of his side, he had as often made:
"*Rash Boaster*, who both *Lyes* and *Truths* doth carry,
"*Sister* to *Them* that did the *Gods* invade,
    "Who with a *thousand Tongues* spreads where she flyes,
    "That which she saw but with a *hundred eyes*.

45

Her find they out, and make her go before:
Who with a ratling *Trumpet* doth proclame
The *Praises* of the *Navigators* more
Then of all else she e're vouchsaf't to name.
Now in the hollows of the *Rocks* did roare,
And the hoarse *Waves*, the piercing voice of Fame.
    Truth she relates, and *Truth* esteem'd to be,
    For with the *Goddess* went Credulitie.

46

Brib'd with this *Praise*, this excellent *Report*,
The *Gods* (whom Bacchus so inflam'd had erst
Against these gallant men, in Neptune's *Court*)
With passion for them are a little pierc't.
The *female Breasts* (that quit with less *effort*
The prejudices *they* receiv'd at first)
    Now call it an *ill zeale*, a *cruel mind*,
    Which to such *Vertue* made *them* prove *unkind*.

47

The bloody *Boy* strikes while the Iron's hot.
Shafts follow shafts, the *Sea* roares with his shoots.
Some, through the fickle *Waves,* point blanck are shot:
Some, hit on *Rocks;* nor, to be rocks, it boots.
Down drop the *Nymphs, each* hath her deaths wound got,
All dart out burning *sighs* from their heart-Roots;
    No *Face* yet seen: "For Shafts, which Love lets flye,
    "Kill in the *Eare* as sure as in the *Eye.*

48

With *doubled* force the *Lad,* that tam'd was never,
Makes the two *horns* meet of his Iv'ry *Moon.*
More then of *All,* he ayms at Thetys's Liver,
For more then *All* hath she against him done.
Now not *one shaft* is left in *all* his *Quiver,*
In all the *Sea* Nymph left alive not one:
    Or if (being hurt) they *live,* it is for *This,*
    That they may feel how sweet such *dying* is.

49

Make room, ye azure Billows of the Deep:
Loe! Venus comes, and brings the *Med'cine* with her!
The pregnant *Sayles* on Neptune's surface creep,
Like her own *Swans,* in *Gate, out-chest,* and *Fether.*
That their *desires* like *equal* pace may keep,
And *neither* to great Love complain of *either,*
    The *Mens* bold *fires* shall press chaste Hymens bands;
    The *Female-Blush* do Beautie's Queen's commands.

50

All the faire *Quire* of the Nereides
Is now prepar'd, and in a lofty Dance
(After their *loving* custome) through the *Seas*
To th'*Isle* by Venus shew'd, *at once* advance.
The skilful *Goddess* there erudiates *These*
In all *she* did, when Love her Breast did lance.
    They, whom the *Son* had conquer'd, are not nice
    To listen to the *Mother's* sweet advice.

51

The lofty *ships* went cutting the vast sea
In their long *Voyage* to their *Countrey* deare,
Least *that,* they had, should fail them by the way,
Prolling about for water *freshe,* and *cleare.*
When (to their suddain joy) at break of day
Th'*inamour'd Isle* doth to them *All* appeare.
     Streight MEMNON's mother, delicate and faire,
     Spread all her sweetness through the purged Ayre.

52

They see *Aloofe* the *Island* fresh, and green,
Which VENUS carries floating on the *Main.*
Just as the *Wind* does their white *Sayles*; and seen
The *ships* are from the *Isle* too, but not plain.
For, left by *Them* o'reshot it should have been,
Making her *Wish,* and *Preparations,* vain,
     (What cannot VENUS ACIDALIA do?)
     She mov'd it *plum* in the *Armada's* view.

53

But fixt it; when she saw, *They* saw, and sought
The *Island* with their Keels: so, on the *Floods*
Was DELOS fixt, when forth LATONA brought
APPOLLO, and the GODDESSE OF THE WOODS.
Thither through sliced *Seas* their way they wrought
Where a calm *Bay* the crooking *shore* includes,
     Whose gliss'ning *Sands* with interfused *vains*
     Of purple *Cockles* CYTHEREA stains.

54

Three goodly *Mountains* with a graceful pride
Thrust their majestick *Heads* into the Ayre
(With green imbroydred *Hangings* beautify'de)
In this gay *Isle* delicious, fresh, and faire.
From their three *Tops* three crystal *Springs* did glide,
Lacing the *Liv'ry* their rich *Margents* ware;
     Jumping on *Peebles* while their *Crystals* brake:
     Such *Musick* never *Water-works* did make.

55

In a pure *Valley* which those *Hills* divides,
As by appointment the three *Currents* meet,
Shaping a *Table* with proportion'd sides,
Broad, and beyond imagination, sweet.
A *Frenge* of *Trees* hangs over it, and prides
It self, in so cleer *Glass* it self to greet:
    Now prancks its *locks* therein, and *now* retires;
    Now looks again, and its own form admires.

56

A thousand gallant *Trees* to *Heav'n* up-shoot
With *Apples,* odoriferous, and faire:
The *Orange-tree* hath in her sightly *fruit*
The colour DAPHNE boasted in her *Haire*:
The *Citron-tree* bends almost to her Root
Under the yellow burthen which she bare:
    The goodly *Lemmons* with their *button-Caps,*
    Hang imitating *Virgins* fragrant *Paps.*

57

The *savage-trees* (That doe the *Forest* there
With *leavie-Haire* innoble and adorn)
Are, *Poplars* of ALCIDES; *Laurels,* deare
In vain unto the GOLDEN GOD UNSHORN;
Myrtles of VENUS; the proud *Pine* severe,
That CYBELE for meaner love did scorn.
    The speared *Cypress,* from this *vale* of *Vice,*
    Stands pointing at CELESTIAL PARADICE.

58

The fruit POMONA gives, NATURE bestowes
Heer lib'rally, and in the kinds all good;
Better then *elsewhere* it in *Gardens* growes,
'Tis *heer* undrest, unplanted, in the *Wood*;
The *Cherry,* that begs *outside* from the *Rose;*
The *Mulberry,* stain'd with *true-Lovers* blood;
    The *Peach,* translated from its *Mother-soile*
    In PERSIA, and made better by *Exile.*

59

Th'ingenuous *Pomgranat* shews his Heart,
With which Thou, *Rubie,* losest thy esteem:
From her lov'd *Elme* the *Vine* doth not depart,
Her Clusters loading *Him,* some red, some green:
And, *Pear* pyramidall, if loth thou art
To dye before thy time, hide thee between
    The Leaves; for to anticipate thy Fate
    Ten thousand *feather'd-Minstrels* lye in waite.

60

The fine and noble *Carpets* then (which *there*
Lye to be trod on by the meanest Plant)
Make those of Persia, *course;* and *pleasanter*
These of the gloomy Valley *All* will grant.
Narcissus, there, over the water cleere
Hangs his sick head, who what he had, did want.
    There flaunts the *Grand-child-Son* of Cynaras,
    For whom Thou, Paphian Queen, cry'st Yet, *alas!*

61

It was not easie to be understood
(The self-same *colours* seen in *Skyes* and *Bow'rs*)
Whether Aurora lent the *Flowers* blood,
Or borrowed *complexion* of the *Flow'rs.*
There Zephyrus and Flora painting stood
The *Vi'let* with the *Pale* of *Paramours;*
    The *Flow'r-de-lis,* with *blew;* the lovely *Rose,*
    Just *such,* as in a *Virgin's cheek* it blows.

62

The *Lilly,* white; in whose pure snow the print
Sits of the *Morning's* Tears: and *Marjorame:*
The doleful *ay,* read in the *Hyacint;*
A Flow'r Latona's son loves for the name.
Flora bets high, Pomona knows no stint,
She Vyes with *Flow'rs,* with *fruits* This sees the *Game:*
    Nor *Flow'rs,* and *Fruits,* are *All* that place affords;
    The Earth hath *Beasts* besides, and the Ayre *Birds.*

63

Along the *Lake* the snowy *Swan* did sing,
Him Philomela answers from a *Bough;*
Acteon drinks out of the crystal *Spring,*
Nor fears the *shadow* of his *horned* Brow.
Here the close *Hare* (to whom her fear gives wing)
Starts from her *Form;* or, from a *Brake* the *Row*:
    The wanton *Sparrow,* there, to his dear *Nest*
    Bears in his *Bill* the little *Chirpers* feast.

64

The *second* Argonauts now disembarke
From the tall *ships* into an Eden green.
There, in this *Isle,* this *Forest,* or this *Parke,*
The fair *Nymphs* hide, with purpose to be seen.
Some touch the grave *Theorba* in shades darke,
Some the sweet *Lute,* and gentle *Violeen*:
    Others with golden *Cross-bows* make a show
    To *hunt* the *Bruits,* but do not *hunt* them though.

65

Thus counsell'd them *their Mistress,* and her *Arts*:
That so, the more their own desires they Master,
And seem *a flying prey* to their *sweethearts,*
It might make *them* to follow on the faster.
Some (who are *Conscious* that their *skins* have *darts,*
And put their trust in *naked Alablaster*)
    Bathe in *Diaphane* streams, their *Roabs* by-thrown,
    And ask no *Ornament,* but what's their own.

66

But the bold *Striplings,* setting on the sand
Their nimble feet, which long'd to touch the ground,
(For not a man of them but came a land
To see what *Savage Game* might there be found)
Dreamt not to finde Game ready to their hand,
In that sweet *Forest* (without snare, or Hound)
    So *Debonayre,* so *tender,* so *benigne,*
    As was *there* hurt by means of Ericine.

67

Some (who with *Guns* and *Cross-bows* make account
The *Royal Stag,* and *Lordly Buck,* to slay)
Through the sharp *Bushes* resolutely mount,
And lofty *Forest;* where no *Foot-path* lay.
Others in *Shades* (which PHEBUS'S Arrows blount)
Walking, or resting, *while* the *Heats* away
  By those sweet *Brooks,* which (stumbling as they past
  Over white *Pebbles*) to the *Sea* made hast.

68

When suddainly, thorow the Green-wood leaves,
Variety of *Colours* they descry;
Colours, which soon the judging eye perceives
Are not of *Roses,* or fresh *Flow'rs* the *dye*:
But of fine *wool;* or *That,* the rich *worm* weaves,
Of which LOVE makes his *Lure,* and *Sawces high*;
  Of which their Garments *Humane Roses* make,
  To make the *Bird* sell for the *Feathers* sake.

69

Amaz'd VELOSO with a lowd voice cry'd;
"Strange *Game* (my masters) in this *Forest* rise:
"The ancient *Poets Tales* are verify'd,
"And this *Isle's* sacred to the DEITIES.
"Nay, what to *humane-fancy* is deny'd
"To hope, or comprehend, see with your *Eyes*!
  "And see, what *wonders,* what great *blessings* then,
  "The *world* and *Nature* hide from *vulgar* men!

70

"Chase we these *Goddesses*; it shall be seen
"If they be *Real* or *Fantastical.*
This said (more swift then *Bucks* o're *Pastures* green)
Through the rough *Brakes* and Woods darted they *All.*
The *Nymphs* went flying the thick boughs between,
Yet not so *Swift* as *Artificial.*
  Shreeking, and laughing softly in the close,
  They let the *Greyhounds* gain upon the *Does.*

71

One's golden *Tresses* up the wind did blow,
The light *coats* of *Another* as she fled:
The *desire*, kindled by the *naked Snow*,
Upon the dainty *Prospect* (greedy) fed.
This falls on purpose, and whilst she doth go
To rise (with *kindness*, more then *Anger*, red)
    He that *pursues*, falls over her; like *one*
    That rubs the *Mistress* when his *Bowle* is gone.

72

Others (who *Game* in other Parts did seek)
Chop on the *Goddesses* that bathing were.
These suddainly begin a fearful shreek
As if they wonder'd to see *Mortals* there.
Some (sliding through the *Laund* their Bodies sleek,
As who should say; *shame* less, then *force* We fear)
    Scud to the *Cops,* exposing to the *Eye*
    What to the greedy *Hand* they did deny.

73

There *is,* That (hiding with a *Veile* of *Glass*
(Diana-like) if not her *Lims,* her blushes)
Sinks where she stands: There *is,* That (on the grass
Snatching her *Cloaths* that lye) shoots through the Rushes.
Amongst the Rest, an eager *Lad* there *was,*
Rayments and all, into the *Bath* that brushes
    (For, whilst he stript, he feard to lose the *Game*)
    To quench in *water* his tormenting *flame.*

74

As a rough *Water-dog,* to fetch and seek
That's us'd, and wait upon his *Master's gun,*
Seeing *him* lay the *Steel-Cane* to his Cheek,
Aym'd at a *Duck,* or *Teal,* to *him* well known;
Before the *blow,* into the *stream* or *creek*
(Sure of the *Quarry*) doth impatient run,
    And, barking, swims: The *Lad* so, from the shore
    Swam to the *Nymph* whom *Love* had shot before.

75

Another (LEONARD) whom *Books* adorn,
Stout, noble, handsom, amorous, and young;
On whom GOD CUPID had not cast *one* scorn,
But *all* his *gall* into *his potion* wrung;
So that he well might think, he was not born
To any luck in loving; yet, among
  His *faults,* 'twas *one,* that *on* he *still* would play
  (As *Gamesters* use) in hope 'twould turn one day,

76

'Twas *here* his fortune, in pursuit to fall
Of fair EPHYRE (LOVE'S own *sister-Twin*)
But *one,* who would give dearer then they *All,*
What *Nature* gave to *Her* to give *agin.*
On Her, *He* (spent with running) lowd doth call.
"O *Cruelty,* lodg'd in too fair an *Inn,*
  "If to thy *Shrine* (quoth *he*) I'm vowed whole,
  "Stay for my *Body,* since thou hast my *soul!*

77

"All (out of breath, and weary) *Nimph* divine,
"Are yielded to the pressing *Enemy.*
"Through Bryers and Thorns *Thou* onely still fly'st *Thine*:
"Who told thee, I am *I,* that follow thee?
"If thou were't told it by that *star* of mine,
"Which, wheresoe're I fly, *shoots* after me;
  "Ah! do not credit *That*: For when as *I*
  "Did so, thou canst not think how it would lye.

78

"I tire with tyring *Thee,* my *spirits* wast;
"And if thou *fly,* thereby to flye my touch,
"I can assure thee (fair one) *stay* thou may'st,
"And yet I ne're the neer, my *star* is such.
"Stay, if thou please; and see but (if thou *stay'st*)
"The *slight of hand,* the which my *Fate* (so much
  "In vain deplor'd) will finde at last, to reare
  "A *Wall,* between the *Sickle* and the *Eare.*

79

"O flye me not! So may *Time* never flye
"Thy *Beauty* out of sight. For, do but turn;
"Dasht with the beams of thy *Majestick Eye*,
"No *sawcy* fire in me will dare to burn.
"What KING could break the force of *destiny*?
"What ARMY conquer it? and *mine* hath sworn
 "To thwart *me* still. Yet stay: I'm happy than:
 "And thou shalt do what KINGS, nor ARMIES can.

80

"With my *malignant star* doest *Thou* take part?
"To help the stronger is not *nobly* done.
"Carriest *Thou* with thee my *Grief-loaden* heart?
"Send it me back, and thou wilt faster run.
"That *Soul* of mine, grown heavy with long smart,
"Hang'd in those *Tresses* which out-shine the *Sun*,
 "Does it not *clog* them? Or, since it came *there*,
 "Hath it chang'd *mood*, and weighs but for one *Here*?

81

"With this *hope* onely thy white feet I trace,
"That either *Thou* her weight will not indure,
"Or *she*, by being in that *heav'nly* place,
"Will change her *luck*, and *better stars* procure.
"And, if *that* change, flye never such a pace,
"LOVE can hit *flying* I am very sure;
 "And, if he hit, Thou't stay; and, on *this* score,
 "If thou do stay, of *Heav'n* I ask no more.

82

The fair *Nymph* now fled not so much to sell
The *Jewel* dear, for which the *Lad* pursu'd her;
As the sweet *Tunes* to *hear*, that from him fell,
And amorous *laments* with which he woo'd her.
Her *Eyes* (now bath'd in *smiles* and *tractabell*)
Turn'd upon *Him*, who with his *charms* subdu'd her;
 All melted in pure *love*, languidly *sweet*,
 She lets her self fall at the *Victor's* feet.

83

O what *devouring Kisses* (multiply'd)
What *pretty whimp'rings,* did the *Grove* repeat!
What *flatt'ring Force*!   What *Anger* which did *chide*
It self, and *laught* when it began to *threat*!
What more then this the blushing Morning spy'd,
And Venus (adding *Her's* to the Noon's heat)
     Is better *try'd,* then *guess'd,* I must confess:
     But *Those* who cannot try it, let them *guess.*

84

For first with all the *Rites* of *wedlock* joyn'd
Were the *lov'd Sea-men* to th'Aquatick Pow'rs:
What gentle *Tongue,* and what white *Hand* could bind,
The *Nymphs* had added in those *sacred Bow'rs.*
And now their *Lovers* heads they crowned (kind)
With *gold,* and *Lawrel,* and abounding *Flow'rs*:
     Promise, to keep them company for ever;
     Whom *life,* or *death* with *honor,* shall not sever.

85

The *Chief* of them (whom all the *rest* went after,
And did obey in all things her behest,
Of Uranus and Holy Vesta Daughter,
As by her Face was easie to be guest,
Filling with wonderment both *Earth,* and *Water*)
Th'illustrious *Captain,* worthy of the Best,
     With *grave* and *Royal Ceremonies* took:
     Shewing her *Greatness* in her *Pompe* and *Look.*

86

Him (whom she first acquainted with her *name,*
Then, in a kind *exordium* mixt with state,
Gave him to understand she *Thither* came
By the immutable decree of *Fate*;
To *Him* of the promiscuous *Globe* and *Frame*
Of the *vast* Earth, and Ocean, to relate
     Parts undiscover'd by *Prophetick* Spirit:
     Which *He* alone, and his brave Spaniards merit)

87

Taking up with her by the hand, she led
Unto a *Mountain's* top, high and divine;
Where a rich *Pyle* erected the prowd head,
Of crystal all, with massive gold and fine.
Here all the live-long day they rioted
In full delight, and sports to sports that joyn.
    Within the *Palace* she injoys *her* love:
    The others *theirs* within the flow'ry *Grove*.

88

Thus the fair *Bevy, thus* the Valiant *Crew,*
Divide the *How'rs* by innocent, by chast
Delights, and such as *Mortals* never knew,
In recompence of so long labours past.
And *thus* the *meed,* to such high Actions due
Of noble *Prowess*; ev'n the *World* at last
    Pays (in despight of *Envy*) with the sound
    Of a great *Name*; which *Time* nor *Place* shall bound.

89

"For these fair *Daughters* of the OCEAN,
"THETYS and the *Angellick* pensil'd ISLE,
"Are nothing but sweet *Honour,* which *These* wan;
"With whatsoever makes a *life* not vile.
"The *priviledges* of the MARTIAL MAN,
"The *Palm,* the Lawrell'd *Triumph,* the rich *spoile*;
    "The *Admiration* purchac't by his sword;
    "*These* are the *joys,* this *Island* doth afford.

90

"So those *false Godships* which ANTIQUITIE,
"To all *illustrious Men* a zealous Frend,
"In *Starry Heav'ns* created, to which *shee*
"Made them on towring wings of *Fame* t'ascend,
"For honorable *Acts* they did, for free
"And noble *Suff'rings* (VERTUE'S *path,* the *end*
    "Whereof is *smooth* and *pleasant* like *our Isle,*
    "Though it self *craggie, steep,* and full of *toile*)

91

"What meant they but an *Immortality*
"Giv'n by the *World* for Actions Soveraign,
"To *such* as Arts, or Arms, advanc'd t'a high
"And *heav'nly* pitch, being born of *humane* strain?
"For Jove, Apollo, Mars, and Mercury,
"AEneas, Romulus, the Thebans Twain,
 "Juno, Diana, Ceres, Pallas; *All*
 "Dwell (as *you* doe) in brittle *Earthen* Wall.

92

"But Fame (the *Trumpet* of deeds great and good)
"Gave them *new* Names and *Titles* on the Earth;
"Gods of the *whole*, and Gods of the *half-blood,*
"Gods by *Adoption*, and Gods by *Birth.*
"If ye love *Fame* then, if make *These* ye wou'd,
"(As *Men*) your *patterns*, though (as *Gods*) your *Mirth,*
 "Fly Sloath; by *which* the Soule, which *Heaven* gave
 "To be the Body's *Queen*, becomes its *Slave.*

93

"Curbe, with a *Bit* of *Iron*, Avarice;
"Ambition curb, to which y'are too too prone;
"And curb the black and detestable *Vice*
"Of Tyranny, and base Oppression.
"For these *vain Honours*, this *false Gold*, give price
"(Unless he have it in *himself*) to *none,*
 "Better *deserve* them, and to goe *without;*
 "Then *have* them *undeserved*, without doubt.

94

"Either in *peace* promote *impartiall Laws,*
"That so *great Fish* devour not the *small Fry;*
"Or (armed) tear out of the *Great* Turks jaws
"The *Christian prey*, on which he stretcht doth lye.
"The *Kingdom's greatness,* by this means ye'll cause;
"Nor *lesson*, but *augment*, your *own*, thereby.
 "In *Riches merited* ye will abound;
 "And with *true Honor* have your Temples crown'd.

95

"And to your KING ye so pretend to prize,
"Ye shall bring honour; *now*, with *Councels* grave:
"*Now*, with your *Swords*, which will immortalize
"*You*, as they have done your *Fore-Fathers* brave.
"I ask you not *Impossibilities*:
"*He* That *will*, always *can*. Then, *each* shall have
      "A HERO's place: or (if *that* more may move)
      "Be *Denizen'd* into this ISLE OF LOVE.

End of the ninth Canto.

Tenth Canto

STANZA 1

But now the *Larissean* Lasses Frend
(Who for a wealthier *Lover* did foregoe
The *God* of *Verse*) his setting Steeds did bend
O're the great *Lake* of silver MEXICO;
SOL's burning Rays FAVONIUS did suspend
With that cool breath which makes, where it doth blow,
      Becalmed *Jesamines* erect their heads,
      And sickly *Lillies* sit up in their *Beds*:

2

When the fair *Nymphs* and *Lovers*, two abreast,
Now Frends and well contented, hand in hand
Towards the *Palace* bright their steps addrest,
Which upon *Pillars* of pure *gold* did stand;
To a most splendid and *Opiperous Feast*
All summon'd thither, by the *Queen's* command
      Who had prepar'd it for them, to repaire
      Consumptive *Nature* with delicious Fare.

3

There, in rich *Chaires* of substance *crystalline*
They sit by *Two's* and *Two's, Gallant* and *dame.*
At th'upper end, in *other* of *gold* fine,
Sits the fair GODDESSE by renown'd DE GAME.
With *Viands* delicate in *sawce* divine
(Such as to CLEOPATRA's *Board* ne're came)
    Are heapt the *dishes* of red burnisht *gold*:
    Part of the *Treasure* which *their Seas* infold.

4

The *fragrant Wines* not onely are above
Falernian Liquor of *Italian* growth,
But that *choice-Nectar* sent about by JOVE
When Rebel *Gyants* felt IMMORTALS wroth.
In *Di'mond-Cups* (tempting to *mirth,* and *love*)
The *Ruby* sparckles: bubbles the curl'd froth
    With the powr'd spring. Thus, of their *Lovers* true
    The greatest *Foe,* the *watry Nymphs* subdue.

5

A thousand pleasant *Arguments* they touch,
Still-laughters pass, quick witty *Repartees,*
'Twixt *dish* and *dish*; whereby, without too much
Of *Those,* to whet the appetite to *These.*
Musical Instruments not wanting (such,
As to the *damned spirits* once gave ease
    In the dark Vaults of the *Infernal Hall*)
    Joyn'd with a SIREN's *Voice Angelical*:

6

The fair Muse sang, and with her shrill *Accents*
(Which from the lofty Battlement rebound)
In equal harmony the *Instruments,*
Keeping just time, their softer *Notes* confound.
A suddain *Silence* curbs the *Winds,* indents
With the hoarse *waves* to whisper under ground;
    And the *bruit Creatures* in their Houses (made
    By *Nature's* hand) asleep are *sung* and *playd.*

7

With a sweet *Voyce* she raises to the skies
Rare men to come into the world; whose cleare
Ideas were beheld by Protheus wise
In a *Diaphane* and *Phantastick Sphere,*
Which in a *Dream* Jove shew'd to his shut *Eyes;*
And after, *He,* by *Prophecy* appeare
  Made it in *humid Realms* : where this *Nymph* (took
  Therewith) got the brave story without book.

8

Matter for *Buskin* 'tis, and not for *Sock,*
In the Vast Lake that which the *Mermaid* heard;
Beyond what Yopas knew, or Demodoke :
This King Alcinoo's, *That* Queen Dido's *Bard.*
Now, my Caliope, I *Thee* invoke
To my *last Labour* : begging, for reward
  Of all I write (which I in vain pretend)
  I may come off with a good *tang* ith'end :

9

I sink into the *Vale* of *years;* and, past
My *Summer's* pride, to *Autumn* speed amain.
And my *Wit* (more then *years*) Misfortunes blast;
Which *Wit* I own not *now,* nor boast my *Vein.*
Sighs blow me to that *Port,* where all must cast
The *Anchor* never to be *weigh'd* again.
  Yet, great *Queen* of the Muses, grant that *I*
  May close my Nation's *Poem* e're I dye.

10

The Siren sang, how from the *Tagan* shore,
Through *Seas* first open'd by *De Gama* now,
Should *Navies* come; which all within the Rore
Of *Indian Seas* shall to that *Empire* bow :
And how each *Pagan King,* who the sweet *Lore*
And *yoak* those *Guests* will bring, shall from them throw;
  With *fire* and *sword* by their brave Arm so bit
  Shall be, that they shall yield to *Death,* or *It.*

11

She sang of *One*, who (being dignify'd,
With the *High-Priesthood* of all MALABAR)
Because, the knots of Friendship he had ty'd,
He would not break with men so singular;
Shall let his *Fields* and *Cities* be destroy'd
With *fire* and *sword*, and all the rage of *war*,
    Before him, By the potent SAMORIM:
    So hateful shall those *strangers* be to *Him*.

12

And sings, in BETHLEM there, how shipt shall be
The Sov'raign *remedie* of this *Disease*,
The great PACHECO knowing not, that He
Carries with *Him* the *Pelian Lance* through *Seas*.
But the *Sea* shall; when, to such great *Guests* she
Unus'd, shall feel his *weight*: The *groaning* Trees
    Of his *prowd ship* shall know't, which two foot more
    Shall draw of water, then it did before.

13

But, treading now the *Oriental* Strand,
And left, the *Pagan King* of spoyld COCHIM
To ayd, of PORTINGALS with a small Band,
Upon the salt and crooked *River's* Brim;
Rout shall he, at the pass of CAMBALAND,
Th'infernal NAYRES, That *there* set on Him:
    Turning with fear the burning ORIENT cold,
    So much done with *so little* to behold.

14

The SAMORIM shall raise an Army new;
The *Kings* shall come of BIPUR and TANORE
From Highlands of NARSINGA; what they'll do
For their *chief Lord,* making large Brags before.
All the arm'd NORTH he shall assemble too,
Which lyes 'twixt CALICUT and CANANORE,
    Of both *Religions,* 'gainst the *True* that band,
    The MOORS by *Sea,* the PAGAN POW'RS by *Land.*

15

And once more *All* defeats on *Land* and *Mayn*
The bold Pacheco, Thunderbolt of War;
The multitude unnumberd of the slain
Amazing all the *Realms* of Malabar.
The undespairing *Emperor* again
Shall hast to try his Fortune militar;
　　　Rating his *Men,* pouring vain *pray'rs* and *tears*
　　　To his vain *Gods* That have nor *eyes* nor *ears.*

16

Your Troops shall *passes* now no more defend,
But burn the Pagan's *Houses, Towns,* and *Fanes.*
The *Dog* (inrag'd to see they make no end
Of laying flat his goodly *Towns*) ordains
His Men, whom he doth prodigally spend,
Pacheco's then divided in two Lanes,
　　　To charge between them. *He* together brings
　　　His *Jaws,* and makes two *Pincers* of his *Wings.*

17

In person then the Samorim shall come
To see what's done, and reinforce his men.
Dasht (by a shot which through the Aire doth humme)
In his high *Chair* with blood he shall be then.
That *Force,* nor *Policy* can overcome
This *Warriour;* now he shall to see begin.
　　　Treasons, and *Poisons* base he shall invent;
　　　Which *Heav'n* (Pacheco's keeper) will prevent.

18

That a *sev'nth* time he shall return, she sings,
To fight the brave unconquer'd Portingall;
Whom no Toyls tyre, who dreads no dreadfull Things,
Yet this a little *discompose* him shall.
To horrid battail the fell *Tyrant* brings
Engines of *Wood,* dire and unusuall,
　　　To board the *Caravels* upon the *Mayn,*
　　　Which he till then shall have assay'd in vain.

19

Mountains of *Fire* shall on the water float
The little *Navy* to consume with flame.
The great Pacheco (like himself) this hot
And fierce *Bravade* shall in a trice make vain.
No *Master* in the *Art* of War (That got
Never so high upon the wings of *Fame*)
    With all his *Palms* can neer this Worthy come:
    Pardon me noble Greece, and nobler Rome.

20

For with a hundred men, or little more,
Unto the end so many Battails fought;
With such high *Stratagems* unseen before,
On *Warlike-Hoasts* so many wonders wrought;
Seem either *Fables* dreamt by men that snore,
Or that *celestial Quires* (with *Pray'rs* down brought)
    Their *Champion* in those Exigencies Ayd
    With *Wit, Sleight, Force,* and courage undismayd.

21

He, who in *Marathonian* Fields of old
O're vast Darius's pow'rs victorious was;
Nor *He,* who, with three hundred Spartans bold,
Of fam'd Thermopilee maintain'd the *Pass;*
Nor Rome's young Cocles, who at bay did hold
All the prowd *Tuscan* pow'r, till cut he has
    The *Bridge* behind him: nor old Fabius is
    Or *wise,* or *valiant,* when compar'd with *This.*

22

But at this point, her high and ratling tone
The *Nymph* abasing, made it hoarse and sad;
And with low *Voyce* (drown'd in her *Tears*) did moan
Of so strange *Valour* a Requital bad.
"O Belisarius (said she), That art *One*
"Who by the Muse will still in price be had;
    "If Mars himself *affronted* were in *Thee,*
    "Here is a man that may thy *Comfort* be.

23

"*Here* thou a *Rival* hast, as in thy *Deeds*,
"So in their cruel and unjust *return*;
"In *Thee*, and *Him*, misused Vertue bleeds:
"In *Thee*, and *Him*, doth begging Valour mourn:
"*Both* Bulwarks of your King, *Both* of your *Creeds*:
"Both dye in Hospitals ragged and torn.
    "*This* those *Kings* do, whose *justice* is their *will*;
    "Their *Evidence* what Malice shall instill.

24

"*This* those *Kings* do, who (with smooth Tales misled
"Of *Flatterers,* by whom asleep th'are sung)
"Give the *Rewards* by Ajax merited
"Unto the fraudulent Ulysses's *tongue*.
"But 'tis reveng'd at full, when, hand o'rehead,
"They deal their *Boons* those Sycophants among:
    "By *whom*, of their ill choice they will be made
    "Ashamed first, and afterwards betraid.

25

"But *Thou*, That such a man couldst leave, to Scorn
"And Want, O King unjust in *this alone*!
"If *Thou*, to build *his Fortunes*, wert not born;
"*He* was, to give to *Thee* a potent *Throne*.
"And (credit me) whilst Phebus's locks unshorn
"To light the *Earth* and *Heaven* shall be known,
    "Like that *Sun* glorious shall Pacheco be,
    "And *Thou* in *this* Eclipse thy *Majestie*.

26

Another, loe! (proceeding in her *Song*)
Comes, with a *Regal Title*, and his *Son*;
Who, on the *Sea* shall do such things, e're long,
As by no antient Roman were out-done.
They *Both*, shall *win* by armed Hand and strong
Wealthy Quiloa, and shall sack it, *won*:
    Placing therein a mild and loyal *King*
    For a false *Tyrant*, whom they out shall fling.

27

Also, the City of Mombassa (Crown'd
With sumptuous *Houses,* and aerial *Spires*)
Shall by them *Both* be levell'd with the ground,
For an *old fault* which a *new rod* requires.
But, afterwards, upon the Indian Sound
(Cover'd with *Ships* and *Artificial Fires*
　　T'o'rewhelm the Portingalls) with Oare, and Sayle,
　　Alone the *young* Lorenzo shall prevaile.

28

The Caracks of the potent Emperore
(Peopling the scorched Ayre with *Iron Ball*
Which from the burning Brass, like Thunder, roare)
Tear shall he, *Canvas, Rudder, Mast* and all.
His *grappling-hooks* thrown resolutely o're
Her lofty Decks, *Himself* their *Admiral*
　　Shall enter first; and cleer, with *Lance* and *Sword*
　　Four hundred Moors she will have then aboard.

29

But God (whose secret *doom* is over *All* :
Best judge, of what's his service, and *Man's* good)
Shall bring him *then,* where *Wit* nor *Prowess* shall
Have pow'r to stop his Foes prevailing Flood.
Neer Choul (where cheaply yet he shall not fall :
The purpled Sea *there* boyling o're with blood)
　　He will be forc't to leave his life behind,
　　By *Fleets* of Egypt and Cambaya joyn'd.

30

There shall *innumerable* Enemies
(Who, with *great* force alone, great *Vertue* tire)
The *Wind* that fails, *Danger* that multiplyes,
Upon the *Sea*; against him *All* conspire.
Now from their *Graves* let all the *Antients* rise,
A *pattern* to *behold* of *noble Ire* :
　　They shall *behold* another Sceva, skill'd
　　How to *dye* piece-meal, but not how to *yield.*

31

Rob'd of a *Thigh* (which an unlucky *shot*
In splinters with it through the ayre shall beare)
Still does he use his *Arms;* These fail him not,
Nor his great *Heart,* uncapable of Feare :
Until another *Bullet* breaks the knot
Wherewith his *Soul* and *Body* marryed were.
　　　The *prison* open, *she* escapes : and straight
　　　Doth find her self in a triumphant state.

32

Soule, go in *Peace;* from furious *War* retire,
In midst of which *Thou* inward *Peace* shalt find.
The Body, *Him* who got it will inspire
With *high revenge,* when he shall see't disjoyn'd.
I *hear* a rumbling *storm,* I *see* the *fire*
Of *Sacres, Drakes,* and *Basilisks,* combin'd
　　　With fell and home-destruction to rebuke
　　　The fierce Cambayan and black Mamaluke !

33

Behold ! the *Father* comes a mad man like,
In whom for mast'ry *Grief* with *Fury* vyes;
Whilst at one time paternal love doth *strike*
Fire on his *Heart, pumps water* from his *Eyes.*
A noble *Anger* whispers him, his *Pyke*
Shall blood his *Foes, so* that the *Tyde* shall rise
　　　In their down'd *Decks* knee-deep : Nylus shall bear,
　　　Indus shall *see* his *Blows,* and Ganges hear.

34

As a *Corrival'd Bull* That (practising
For a fierce *duel*) fences with the *Oakes;*
Or, at the Trunck of a broad *Beech,* doth fling
In Thrusts, and with his *Horns* the Ayre provokes :
So Don Francisco (e're his *Fleet* he bring
In swoln Cambaya's *Gulph* to desp'rate strokes)
　　　On Dabul's wealthy City whets his Blade,
　　　The *Mountain* of her *Pride* a *Level* made.

35

Then enters (horrid with *her* blood) the Bay
Of Dio: fam'd for *Sieges*, and *pitcht-Fields*.
The *great* but *Coward-Fleet* his *look* doth fray
Of Calicut: which *Oars* for *Lances* weilds.
That of Melique Yaz (which makes away
More slow) with *Bolts* of Vulcan he unbuilds;
    To the low *bottom* of the Ocean sent:
    Cold *mattrice* of the *humid Element.*

36

But *that* of Mir Hozem (which with close *bords*
The rowzed wrath of the *Avenger* stands)
Shall swimming see, ith'*Ocean* of their *Lords,*
Hands without *Bodies, Bodies* without *Hands.*
The rage-blind *Victors,* waving their bright *Swords,*
Shall seem to toss so many *flaming Brands.*
    What *there* shall be perceiv'd by *Ears,* and *Eyes,*
    Will be *Smoke* onely, *Iron, Fire,* and *Cryes.*

37

But ah! Of a defeat great Mars might boast
(Bound for his Native-Tagus back again)
The Fame and glory shall he lose almost
By a sad traverse I foresee too plain.
The Cape Of Storms (which in it's Desert Coast
His *Bones* and *Memory* shall ay retain)
    Shames not to ravish from the world a *Soule*
    Whole India could not, and Egypt whole.

38

By savage Cafres, there, shall *that* be done
Which dext'rous *Enemies* could not perform:
And by rude *Clubbs* (hardned with fire) alone,
What *Arrows Shower* could not, *Bullet's* storm.
"God's secret *judgements* are not to be known.
"Vain Gentiles (being a *Book* above their *form*)
    "Call it ill *Fate,* cross *Fortune, star* maline;
    "Being solely, purely, Providence Divine.

39

O! What *new light* beginneth *there* to bud
(The SIREN said, and rais'd her Voyce thereat)
From the *Melindian* Sea, dy'd with the blood
Of LAMO, OCHA, BRAVA, all laid flat
By great DE CUNIA; who through all the *Flood*
Which laves the *Southern-Isles* and *Shores* (but *That*
    Of MADAGASCAR chiefly) the wide mouth
    Of FAME shall fill, and threat the unknown *South*.

40

This *light* is of those *flames* and glitt'ring *Arms*
Wherewith the stubborn PERSIANS of ORMUZE,
Spurning the *yoake,* and valiant to their harms,
Fierce ALBURQUERQUE afterwards subdues.
There shall the hissing *Shafts* (like living swarms)
Turn'd in the Ayre, their *shooters* Helmets bruize;
    That they may see, with Eyes though ne're so dim,
    How GOD will fight for *Them*, that fight for *Him*.

41

The MOUNTAINS then of SALT will not be able
To keep those *Bodies* from corruption
Which on the *Coasts* shall lye out (miserable)
Of CALAYAT, MASCATE, and GERUN;
Until the easie *yoake* and honorable
They learn (with all their fierceness) to put on:
    Forc't by the *Conquerours*, to pay to *Them*
    Rich Tribute of their *Pearles* of BAHEREM.

42

What glorious *Palms* do I see weaving *There,*
With which his forehead VICTORY will crown
When without shadow or least touch of fear
He shall win GOA's Isle of bright renown!
But then (the *Storm* obeying) will not bear
So great a *Sayle,* and takes that *Bonet* down:
    To reattempt the thing in fitter season.
    "FORTUNE and MARS fear *Valour* joyn'd with Reason.

43

And (see) he does it; charges undismay'd
Through *walls,* through *Pykes,* through *Bullets,* and
        through *fire:*
Opens the quilted *Squadrons* with his *Blade*
Of MOORS and PAGANS knit in *Leagues* intire!
His gallant *Soldiers* in more blood shall wade
Then *Lyons* pin'd, *Bulls* prickt with love and Ire;
    Upon the *Feast* (as pat as by designe)
    Of EGYPT's *Virgin Martyr,* KATHERINE.

44

Nor *Him* shalt *Thou* (though potent) scape, and flye,
(Though sheltred in the Bosome of the *Morn*)
MALACCA (and the Apple of her Eye)
Prowd of thy wealthy Dow'r as her *first-born.*
Thy *poyson'd Arrows,* those *Auxiliary*
CRYSES I see (thy *Pay* That do not scorn)
    MALACCANS amorous, valiant JAVANS,
    Shall all obey the LUSITANIANS.

45

More *Stanzas* had the SIREN in the praise
Of the illustrious ALBUQUERQUE sung;
But she remembers one harsh Act, which weighs
Him down, though through the *world* his *Fame* be rung.
"A *great Commander* (whom to crop bright *Bays*
"On precipitious *Cliffs* his *Fate* hath hung)
    "Should to his *Men* a *Camrade* rather be,
    "Then a *Judge* made up of *Severitie.*

46

"But in a time of *Famine,* and hard *Toyle,*
"Of *Sickness, Arrows,* and of thund'ring *Ball,*
"Of *Season sad,* of *discommodious soyle,*
"And the poor *Soldier* patient under *All;*
"It seems to me of *Savage Breasts* the style,
"Of an *inhumane* and *insulting* Gall,
    "To make a *Man* for such a fault to dye
    "As *Love* and *humane frailty* qualifie.

47

"*Incest's* detested Brand it shall not be,
"Nor boyst'rous *Rape* upon a Virgin pure,
"Nor blot injurious of *Adulterie,*
"But with a *Slave* lascivious and obscure.
"Then whether fir'd with *zeale,* or *jealousie,*
"Or else to keep his bloody hands in Ure,
        "Against his *own* he give his rage the reins,
        "With a *black Action* his *white Fame* he stains.

48

"With his Campaspe Alexander spy'd
"Apelles took, and upon *Him* bestows
"Her cheerfully: being not his *Soldier try'd*
"Nor serving at a *Siege* of desp'rate Foes.
"That sowr Araspas in the Rays is fride
"Of his fair Charge Panthea, Cyrus knows;
        "Having profest to be her *Guardian* true,
        "And that no ill desire should *Him* subdue.

49

"But the illustrious Persian, seeing love
"Is in the fault ('gainst whom there's no defence)
"Acquits him streight, and onely doth remove,
"Where he may serve him well in recompence.
"The *Iron* Baldwin (much his Rank above)
"By stealth Espouses Judith; yet th'offence
        "Her great *Sire* pardons (needing such a man)
        "And gives them Flanders, whence those *Earls* began.

50

But her long *Song* the *Nymph* continuing,
Of Suarez (who his *Standard* doth display
On the *red coast* of Arabie) did sing:
Abasia's hindmost shore, and Barbora
(Neighb'ring Zeyla's *Emporium*) fear the Thing
She feels; nor less then *Mecha,* and Gidda,
        Filthy Medina quakes, where Mahomet
        In his *Steel-Hamac* lies in a cold swet.

51

Also the noble *Isle* of Taprobane:
For by *that name* it was as fam'd *of yore*
As by *another now* 'tis *Soveraign*
Of the hot *fragrant Barke*, of which 't has store,
Of which, she to the Standart Lusiane
    Shall pay sweet Tribute: when (percht prowdly o're
        Columbo's highest steeple) *that* shall be
        More fear'd by *Her*, then by her *Neighbours, she*.

52

Through the *Red-Sea* Sequeyra a new way
To *Thee*, vast Land of Prester John, shall show;
Candace's Nest, and *Her's*, who, to survay
The *Wisdome* of great Solomon, did go.
From *Cisterns water'd, He*, shall see Macua:
Shall see her neighb'ring *Port* of Archico:
        And cause *new Isles* to be discover'd, which
        With *Modern wonders* shall the *World* inrich.

53

Meneses comes the next, whose *sword* shall serve
In Affrick for the *wreaths* he here shall weare.
He prowd Ormooz (That from her faith will swerve)
A double Tribute shall constrain to beare.
Thou Gama too (who wilt it well deserve
With two *exiles*), the third time thou com'st there
        (An *Earl, Vice-Roy*, and *Admiral*), the *Land*,
        Which thou hast now *discover'd*, shalt *command*.

54

But then that rude *Necessitie* (which none
Can scape, who from a humane womb doth spring)
Arrests thee in thy *Robes*, and painted Throne,
Where thou shalt act the person of thy *King*.
Streight will another Mennes (old alone
In *wisdome*) have the *Sov'raign* managing
        Of the *Affairs*: And *Happy* Henry shall
        Behind him leave a name perpetual.

55

For he shall quell not onely MALABARS,
Razing PANANE and COULETE's walls,
Incountring *Cannon,* clapping on *Petars,*
And hurling *wild-fire* in sulphureous Balls;
But (arm'd with *Vertues* past the *Sphere* of Mars)
Quell the SOULE's *Enemie's* sev'n Generals:
        Quell *Avarice,* quell foul *Incontinence,*
        In a *young man* the sum of excellence.

56

His *Stars* now calling *Him* to tread on *Them,*
Thou, valiant MASKARENIAS shouldst succeed:
But (if usurpt on) know, a *Diadem*
It self, thy *brighter honor* will not need.
Thy courage, *Admiration* and *Esteem*
(Although not *love*) ev'n in thy *Foes* shall breed,
        If unjust FORTUNE shall deny the *might,*
        VERTUE will give the *merit,* LAW the Right.

57

Great *Actions* in the *Kingdom* of BINTAN
Thou shalt perform, MALACCA's Foe: her *score*
Of *Ills* in one day *paying,* which *That* ran
Into, for many a hundred year before.
With patient courage, more then of a man,
Dangers, and *Toyles,* sharp *Spikes, Hills* always hoare,
        Spears, Arrows, Trenches, Bulwarks, Fire and Sword,
        That thou shalt break, and quell, I pass my word.

58

Meane while *Ambition, Avarice* to boot,
In INDIA setting up with open face
Against GOD and his *justice,* are a Root
Of *discontent* to thee, but not *disgrace.*
"To trample on *weak Right* with a prowd Foot,
"Presuming on the pow'r, and upper place,
        "No *Conquest* is: *He* conquers with Renown
        "Who dares be just ev'n though it lose a CROWN.

59

Yet I deny not, but SAMPAYO shall
Be of rare Valour for all this; on *Seas*
Shewing himself a thund'ring GENERALL,
Which he shall people with Foes Carcasses.
In BACANORE begins he to appall
The MALABAR, that he may after tease
    (Prepar'd with that rough *Prologue* to submit)
      Bold CUTIALE, and his num'rous *Fleet*.

60

Ev'n *that* of DIO (so *resolv'd* and *great*
That *his* at CHOUL will give it self for lost)
By HECTOR OF SILVEYRA shall he beate,
And to *peccavi* turn their furious boast.
The LUSITANIAN HECTOR: who shall get,
Upon the always-arm'd *Cambayck* Coast,
    A name, that *He* doth GUZARATS annoy,
      No less then GREEKS the HECTOR did of TROY.

61

CUNIA is fierce SAMPOYO's successour.
The *Ship* of *State* he long doth wisely steer.
Of CHALE he erects the lofty Tow'r,
Whilst famous DIO quakes to be so neer.
The strong BAZAIN shall render to his pow'r,
But with much blood; MELIQUE groaning here
    To see a way o're his prowd *Rampire* made
      By the sole dint of *Lusitanian* Blade.

62

After *Him* comes NORONIA, whose good *Star*
From DIO the fierce RUMES packing sends:
DIO, which the through-practis'd Breast in War
Of ANTHONY SILVEYRA well defends.
Death's Writs upon NORONIA served are:
When a brave Branch of Thine (O GAMA!) bends
    His shoulders to the *Government*; the fright
      Of whose great name shall turn the *red Sea* white.

63

Out of thy STEPHEN's hand shall take the rain
One in BRASILE before high fame that wan;
The great *French Pyrat* overcome and slain,
Who shall be terrour of that *Ocean.*
Made after *Gen'ral* of the INDIAN MAIN
The no less prowd, then fortifide DAMAN,
     He enters first: where, having made a *breach,*
     'Tis clos'd with *Flames,* and *Shafts,* his way t'impeach.

64

To *Him* CAMBAYA's King, prowd above measure,
Of wealthy DIO gives the famous *Fort;*
Against the GREAT MAGUL, mighty in treasure,
To ayd him his *Dominions* to support.
Then doth he, in his yet unquencht displeasure,
The Pagan King of CALICUT take short
     That would have past him: with no little loss
     Sending him home again by weeping cross.

65

Destroy shall *He* the City REPELIM,
Making her *King* with many quit the place,
And after by the *Cape* of COMORIM
Perform a deed that shall the *Nine* disgrace.
The *Navy Royal* of the Samorim,
That thinks it may to all the world give chace,
     With fire and sword he overcomes, and breaks.
     In BEADALA shall his *Blade* play *Rex.*

66

INDIA, thus weeded with his *Sword* of Foes,
He comes to rule with *Scepter* afterward;
Finds dangers *none,* finds none so bold t'oppose.
All hush, *All* tremble like a Lark that's dar'd.
Onely BATICALA a longing shows
To fare as well as BEADALA far'd.
     She's fill'd with blood and Trunks in dead heaps cast:
     With *fire* and *Ball* disfigur'd and defac't.

67

This shall be MARTIN, or a little MARS,
From whom his *Deeds* he'l take, as well as *name*:
As *stout* for execution in all *wars*,
As *wise* to play the fairest of his Game.
CASTRO succeeds; advancing to the stars
Of PORTUGAL the *Standart* and the *Fame*,
    Fit successour to MARTIN: DIO's *Fort*
    The *one* shall *raise,* the *other* shall support.

68

Fierce PERSIANS, *Abassins,* RUMES (who boast
Their name from ROME) complexions various,
And various *Modes* (for to this *Leaguer* post
A thousand *Nations* keen and furious)
Heav'n to the *world* accuse with labour lost,
That so few men should nestle in their House.
    In blood of PORTINGALLS, by their *no faith*
    They swear, their turn'd up whiskers they wil bathe.

69

Drakes, horrid *Basilisks, Engines* of *Wood*
As bad as *either,* secret *Mines* and *Plots,*
Hath MASCARENIAS with his Men withstood,
Meeting their certain Deaths with willing Throats:
When, in the utmost stress of Flesh and Blood,
CASTRO (their *Freer*) his two Sons devotes,
    That everlasting Honour they may gain,
    And *Sacrifices* to their God be slain.

70

FERNAND (this lofty *Cedar's* highest *Bough,*
Where with a hideous crack a close *Mine* sprung
Th' unrooted Wall into the Ayre will blow)
Shall in a sheet of Fire to *Heav'n* be flung.
ALVAR, when *Winter* swathes the Earth in Snow,
And hath on humid Gates cold Padlocks hung;
    These burst, through dangers to seek dangers goes,
    And fights the *Elements* to fight the *Foes.*

71

Loe, *now* the *Father* follows with full sail,
And the Remainder of the *Lusian* force!
He, with strong *Hand* and *Head* of more avail,
Gives a brave lucky Battail to the Mores.
Where no way is, he makes one with his Flail;
And where there is, the *Rampires* are his *dores.*
　　　Such that day's *Feates,* so terrible the *Blowes,*
　　　They will not *stand* in *Verse,* nor *lye* in *Prose.*

72

Then (loe!) he to the great Cambayan King
Presents himself a *Victor* in the Field:
Pale *Fear* into the *Face* of him doth fling,
And of his furious *Horse,* which ground shall yield.
Nor Hydalcan shall from the Conquering
Army, with all his might, his Countrey sheild.
　　　Dabul sack'd on the *Coast; In-land* Ponda
　　　Scapes not it self, by being out of the way.

73

These, and the like, into all *Quarters* hurl'd,
(All worthy *wonder,* and *Fame's* strongest blast)
Making themselves brave Marses in the *World,*
The joyes of Venus's Isle shall fitly tast;
Trayling triumphant *Standarts* through the curl'd
Amphitheater of the *Ocean* vast:
　　　And they shall find these *Nymphs,* these *furnisht Bords,*
　　　Which are the Harvest of Victorious Swords.

74

Heer the Nymph ended: And the others *All*
Give their applause with an Harmonious noyse;
Congratulating this grand Nuptiall:
Where, look how many *Hearts,* so many *joys*!
Though Fortune Stands Upon A Tott'ring Ball
(They all reiterate as with one Voyce)
　　　Renowned People You Shall Never Lack,
　　　Wealth, Valour, Fame, till the Worlds Henges Crack.

75

When now Corporeall Necessity
Suffic'd with noble Nutriment they had;
And seen the Acts the *Nymph* did prophecy
In *Musicall Poetick Raptures* clad:
THETYS, adorn'd with grace and gravity,
(That she of *glory* may new *quilats* add
     To the high bliss of that triumphant day)
     Unto the *Happy* GAMA thus did say.

76

The SUPREME WISDOME hath vouchsaf'd thee, *Knight,*
The grace to see with thy corporeall Eyes
What the *vain Science,* what the *erring Light,*
Of miserable *Man* cannot comprize.
Thou, with the rest, up this dark *Cops* forth-right
Follow me, strong and constant, stout and wise.
     This having said, shee hands him through a *Wood,*
     Steep, thick with Thorns, and hard to flesh and blood.

77

They marcht not long, when of the arduous *Hill*
They gain the top; where an inameld *Flat*
(In a *Field Em'rauld*) *powdred Rubies* fill,
Making them think old PARADICE was *That.*
Heer, in the Ayre a GLOBE (by wondrous skill
So fram'd with *Thorough Lights*) they contemplat,
     That th'unresisted Eye the *Center* sees,
     As plainly as the *superficies.*

78

The matter of it did their Eye-sight pose:
That it consisted yet discern'd they well
Of *Orbs,* which the *Divine Hand* did compose,
And in the middle did the *Center* dwell.
Rouling, it *sometimes fell,* and *sometimes rose,*
And yet it *never rose,* it *never fell*:
     Throughout *one Face,* throughout its *period*
     Begins throughout. In fine, the Work of God.

79

Infinite, perfect, uniform, self-poiz'd;
Brief, like the ARCHITECT that made the same.
Seeing this admirable *Globe,* surpriz'd
With wonder and desire was our DE GAME.
To whom the GODDESS thus: Epitomiz'd
I shew thee heer the UNIVERSALL FRAME,
     That thou maist read, in *Print* and *Volume* small,
     Whither Thou *goest,* and *shalt* goe, and Thine *shall.*

80

The WORLD's great *Fabrick* thou doest *heer* descry
Heav'nly and *Elementall*: for just so
'Twas made, by that *All-wisdome,* that *All-eye,*
Which no *beginning* knew, no *end* shall know:
Which *interweaved* in each *part* doth lye,
And round the fair *Work* like a *Border* goe:
     'Tis GOD. But what God is, poses *Man's* wit,
     Nor can *short Line* fathome the INFINIT.

81

This, which is *first,* and doth (as in a *Nest*
Of Boxes) all the other *Orbs* comprize,
Darting such radiant Beames, as Mortall *Brest*
Cannot *conceive,* much less *behold* Mans *Eyes;*
Is call'd the EMPYREAN, where the *blest*
Enjoy that *good,* the *World* wants *similies*
     To cast a shadow of, and which *good* None
     Can understand, except *it self* alone.

82

"There is no *true,* no glorious GOD, but *There*:
"For SATURN, JANUS, JUNO, JOVE, and *I,*
"Vain *Creatures* only, and blind *Figments* were
"Betwixt *Mans pride,* and *Mans Idolatry,*
"To stick as *Stars* in the *Poetick Sphere*:
'From whence again w'are borrow'd, by and by,
     "For to distinguish the *true Stars* in *Heav'n,*
     "To which ASTRONOMERS our Names have giv'n.

83

"As likewise because HOLY PROVIDENCE
"(Which shadow'd is by JUPITER in Verse)
"Doth by a thousand *Ministers* dispence
"His *Gifts* to the supported *Universe,*
"And sacred *Prophets* oft impart their sence
"In mystick *Parables* which they reherse;
  "And tell us Men are favoured by the *good,*
  "By the *ill spirits* hurt, unless withstood:

84

"*Now comes* THE POET, who would *teaching please,*
"And *pleasing teach,* and mix *variety;*
"And *He* the self-same Names bestows on *These*
"The HEATHENS did upon their *Genii*
"And *feigned* Gods; for I can shew with Ease,
"That ANGELLS ev'n in *holy* Poetry
  "Are called *Gods;* nor *Sacred Writ* denyes
  "That ev'n the *Ill* this *glorious Name* belyes.

85

"In fine, ALMIGHTY GOD (who rules the round
"*World*) by his *Second Causes* He commands.
"But (to return to open the profound
"And heav'nly *operations* of his *Hands*)
"Within this *Spheare,* where the *pure Soules* abound
"In endless Bliss (which sphere *unmoved* stands)
  "Another runs so *swiftly,* and so *still,*
  " 'Tis not perceiv'd: 'Tis the FIRST MOVABIL.

86

The *motion rapt* of this FIRST MOBIL draws
All the rest after, which with it are linkt.
The hurried *Sun* from his own bent and laws
Makes *Night* and *day* by this RAPT ORB's instinct.
The NINTH moves next, so curb'd, with so great pawse,
That whilst SOL's lamp (which never is extinct)
  Ends it's *true* course about the ZODIAKE
  Two hundred times, *This* but one step doth make.

87

Behold the EGHTH goes under *That,* imbost
With *Sleek* and *radiant Bodies*! These likewise
(Besides the *motion rapt* with which they post)
Move on their *proper Axe* with twinckling Eyes.
See with how rich a *Belt* this *Orb* is crost!
How broad, how glitt'ring with *Embroyderies*!
  Where the twelve *Starry Animals* do make
  The *Sun's twelve Houses* in the ZODIAKE.

88

Behold in other Parts what knots of Gold
This FIRMAMENT displays! the DRAGON there
Behold! CHARLES-WAYN, and CYNOSURA cold!
ANDROMEDA, and her old *Sire* severe!
CASSIOPEA's sparckling eyes behold!
And turbulent ORION, Sea-mens feare!
  Behold the SWAN, which dying is not mute,
  The HARE, the DOGS, the SHIP, and the sweet LUTE!

89

Under this great and spangled Canopy,
Loe, in the SEV'NTH dull SATURN takes his place!
Propitious JOVE inthron'd in the SIXT sky:
Next (Foe to *Man*) MARS rides with fiery Face:
Plac't in the MIDDLE is the WORLD'S GREAT EYE:
The QUEEN OF BEAUTY the THIRD ORB doth grace:
  Eloquent HERMES rules the SECOND SPHEAR:
  Three-shapt DIANA marches in the *Rear.*

90

In all these PLANETS motions different
Thou maist perceive, some *speedy,* and some *slow*:
Now climbing nearer to the FIRMAMENT,
Now stooping closer to the *Earth* below,
As seemed best to the OMNIPOTENT,
Who made the *Fire* and *Ayre,* the Wind and Snow:
  Which *Fire* and *Ayre,* thou seest more neere the pole:
  And *Earth* and *water Center* of the whole.

91

Upon this *Center* is the seat of MAN:
Who, not content in his presumptuous pride
T'expose to all *Earth's* Mischiefs his life's span,
Trusts it to the unconstant *Ocean* wide.
Behold the various *Parts* that *Ocean*
With interfused dangers doth divide!
       Where various *Nations* dwell, various *Kings* raign,
       Who various *Worships,* various *Laws* maintain.

92

See CHRISTIAN EUROPE, higher by the head
In *Arms* and *civill Arts* then all the rest!
See untill'd AFFRICK, covetous, ill-bred,
Wanting ev'n things whereof shee is possest,
With her great CAPE (by *you* discovered)
Which NATURE towards the *South-Pole* addrest!
       See all this *Neck* with People infinite
       Almost, who neither *doe* nor *know* what's right!

93

See the great *Empire* of MONOMOTAPE,
With naked savage People black and grim;
In which the good GONSALVO shall not scape
A cruel death for CHRIST, who dy'd for *Him*!
In this blinde HEMISPHERE (short of the CAPE)
The *Mettle* grows for which pale *Mortals* swim
       Through Seas of *Sweat,* and *Blood.* See that great *Lake*
       From whence, with QUAMA, NYLE this way doth make!

94

Behold the NEGROES Houses, without doores,
Whom both the Poverty of their *Straw-nests,*
The *Laws,* and *justice* of their King secures,
And the black *Candor* of their Neighbours Brests!
Loe, a vast Army of these bruitish MOORES,
Like a dark Band of *Stares* (devouring Guests)
       Against SOFALA's batter'd *Fort* will bend
       Their strength, which NAYA bravely shall defend!

95

See *there* the very *Spring* and *Head* of NYLE,
Which fled (though dearly sought) the ANTIENTS eys!
See how it laves (spawning the CROCODYLE)
The ABBASIN, who upon CHRIST relyes!
See where (a better Fence then *Walls*) a File
Of *Hills* they *man* against their Enemies!
    See MEROE, an *Isle* of antient Fame:
    Which now NOVA the *Natives* of it name!

96

In this *In-land* a *Son* of *Thine* great fame
Shall win against the proud CIRCASSIAN;
And DON CRISTOVAL shall be *that Son's* name:
But against *Fate* can stand no mortal man.
See, see, that way thy shatter'd *Navy* came
MELINDE's dear and hospitable stran!
    Mark well the RAPTO (Natives call't OBE)
    Which at QUILMANCE rouls into the *Sea*!

97

See the *Cape* call'd of old AROMATA,
But GUARDAFU which now the *Dwellers* call;
Where the RED-SEA (so famous) doth Embay,
Dy'd with her Bottome's shade! This is the *Wall*
Or running *Boundarie*, which ASIA
Divides from AFFRICK: And the principal
    Cities, that on the *Affrick-side* are seen,
    Are ARCHICHO, MACUA, and (chief) SUANQUEN.

98

See farthest SUEZ, HEROPOLYS of old,
City of Heroes (so do some conceave)
Others, that this was the ARSINOE hold:
But EGYPT's *Navies* it doth now receave!
The very place great MOSES past, behold,
When with his *Rod* he did the *Waters* cleave!
    ASIA begins. Her self she doth present
    In *limits* vast, in *Kingdoms* opulent.

99

Mount SINAI see, and tremble ev'ry lim,
From whence when MOSES came his face did shine!
See TORO, and GIDDA, in *wealth* that swim,
Yet want *Spring-water* pure and crystalline!
See the *Streight's* other jaw, having for Brim
The Realm of dry ADEN, which doth confine
>   With *Mountains* of ARZIRA, which (they tell)
>   Are all one Rock, whereon *Raine* never fell!

100

Behold the THREE ARABIAS, so wide-spred,
All *Tawny-Moors,* All *Thieves* therein that dwell:
Whence come the *Horses* for the *Warriour* bred,
Of noble Race, Fleet, lasting, terrible!
Behold the *Coast* by which thine Eyes are led
T'another *Gulph* (the *Persian*) there to swell
>   Into a CAPE; which by FARTAQUE's name
>   (Ow'd to the *there* known *City*) shuts the same!

101

See famous DOFAR, which did ever boast
The sweetest *smoke* to make the *Altar* steam!
Mark *here* (where ROSOLGAT your eye hath lost
And barren shores) begins ARMUZA's *Ream*!
It lyes extended all on the *Sea-Coast,*
And shall fit FAME with an immortal Theam,
>   When TURKS's fierce *Fleet,* and blushing *Moons* dismayd,
>   Shall see unsheathed CASTELBRANCO's Blade.

102

Behold the CAPE OF ASABOR, they call
At present MOSANDAN who sail that way;
At bottom of the *Gulph,* which hath for wall
Rich PERSIA here, There BLEST ARABIA!
Mark well BAREM, an *Island* bord'red all
With *Pearls,* whose colour mocks the springing day!
>   In the salt waves commanded by her eye
>   The famous TIGRIS and EUFRATES dye.

103

The noble *Empire* of great Persia see,
Always on horse-back, always in the War:
Who think it base to have *Artillerie,*
Or Hands not hardned with the *Cymetar!*
But mark the Isle Gerun, what a proof *she*
Is of the pow'r of Time to *make,* and *mar!*
    Of Ormuze City (which was once elsewhere)
    She *now* the *glory* and the *name* doth beare.

104

Heer Don Phelipe Of Meneses shall
Approve himself a glorious *Man at Arms,*
When with a very few of Portugall
He shall at Lara quell whole *Persian* swarms.
Likewise shall Sousa on their Quarters fall,
Give them bold *charges,* give them sharp *Allarms,*
    And the *Reversion* of that *Sword,* whose dint
    Struck fire before, on raz'd Ampaza's flint.

105

But let us leave the *Streight,* and *Cape* well known
Of Jasques (call'd Carpella anciently)
With all that *Land* (which *Nature* doth not own
By any Act of Liberality)
Whilom Carmania, Habitation
Of the old Itiophagues. Now wipe thine Ey,
    And see fam'd Indus, born in yonder Mountain,
    Near which flows Ganges from a higher Fountain!

106

See *heer,* where *Nature* prodigall hath bin,
The *Kingdom* of Ulcinde; and the long
Bay of Jaquete, where the Waves flow in
With speed incredible, as fast out-throng!
Cambaya see, where this *Gulph* doth begin,
In *wealth* and *people* infinite and strong!
    A thousand *Cities* here un-nam'd I leave,
    Which shall the *yoake* of Portugall receave.

107

See where the celebrated *Indian* shore
Runs *Southward* to the CAPE of COMOREE
(Call'd in old time COREE), which lyes right ore
Against CEYLAN (TAPROBANE anciently).
Along this Sea the LUSIAN (who, with more
Forces shall be dispatched after Thee)
    Lands, Victories, and Cities shall obtain,
    In which they many *Ages* shall remain.

108

Behold in various *Countreys* (plac'd betwixt
These Rivers) Nations almost infinite:
Some *Pagans*, some *Mahumetans* (well mixt)
To whom the *Devil* did their Laws indite!
Behold NARSINGA's Realm, to which is fixt
A *holy Relique* of a blessed Wight,
    St. THOMAS's body, who was not deny'de
    To thrust his Fingers into JESUS's side.

109

Heer stood the *City* call'd MELIOPORE,
Beautifull, wealthy, and magnificent;
The *Idols* ancient she did adore
As still doe those of her prophane descent:
Farr was she seated then from the Sea-shore,
Whenas the *Gospel*, through the whole *world* sent,
    THOMAS came preaching *there;* and did the same
    In all the *Provinces* through which he came:

110

Arrived *preaching*, and administring
Life to the *dead*, and *health* unto the *sick*;
The *Sea* chanc'd hither on a day to bring
A floating *Tree*, unmeasurably thick.
For a vast *Pyle* in hand desires the *King*
To frame a *Beame* of this *prodigious stick*;
    And makes accompt on shore to drag it then,
    By force of *Engines, Elephants,* and *Men.*

111

So *heavy* 'tis, *All these* have not the might
To stir the *Log* that on the Water lyes.
But the true CHRIST's true *Nuntio* hath a slight
To doe it without trouble, without noyse.
He draws it to him like some Matter light
With a small *Cord*, which to the *Trunk* he tyes:
 Wherewith a *sumptuous House* for GOD to raise,
 To stand a *pattern* for succeeding days.

112

Full well he knew, with lively *faith if* Hee
Should say unto a Mountain deaf, *Remove*;
Ev'n that *deaf Mountain* would *removed* bee:
As CHRIST once said, and THOMAS now doth prove.
This doe the *people* stand aghast to see,
The BRAMENS know it must be from *Above*:
 Seeing his *Miracle*, seeing his *life*,
 These fear the fall of their *prerogatife*.

113

They are the HEATHENS PRIESTS, in whom alone
Envie the bowels of her *Gall* hath shed.
A thousand plots and Trains they think upon,
How THOMAS may be *silenc'd*, or be *dead*.
A horrid Act performs, as ere was known,
The *Chief* of *These* That wear the *Triple-thred*:
 Which proves, "No *Foe* so *bloody*, so *severe*,
 "As *Hypocritick Vertue* to *sincere*.

114

He murthers his own Son, and charges it
Forthwith on THOMAS who was innocent:
False witness brings (*There* nothing hard to git)
Through which the *Man's* condemn'd incontinent.
The *Saint* (having no way to be acquit,
But by *Appeal* to the OMNIPOTENT)
 Resolves, in presence of the *King* and *Court*,
 To work a *Miracle* of the great sort.

115

He bids the *Corps* be laid in view of *All,*
That it may rise and be examin'd There
Touching the question'd *Fact,* and whom *that* shall
Accuse, let *him* be held the *murtherer.*
In name of JESUS crucifi'd, i' th' *Hall*
They see the *Youth* stand up, record to bear:
    Who (thanking THOMAS for his life) describe
    His *Father* to have been the *Homicide.*

116

This struck such fear, that streight his *Christendome*
The *King* receives, and *many* with the *King.*
Some kiss the *Hem* of THOMAS' garment, Some
The praises of the *God* of THOMAS sing.
The BRAMENS swell with such an *odium*
Through *Envy's* now imposthumating sting,
    That (therunto perswading the blind *Rout*)
    They vow to put so bright a *Taper* out.

117

One day, as preaching to the same he was,
They feign'd a quarrell 'mongst the multitude
(For CHRIST himself hath sign'd him now his *Pass*
To climbe to *Heav'n* by way of *Martyr-hood*).
A showre of Stones, which GOD's commission has,
Flyes in his Face: who all their Tempest stood.
    One (whose *Bloud-thirstiness* could not abide
    Delay) with cruell *Spear* did broach his side.

118

GANGES and INDUS did Thee, THOMAS, weep;
Wept thee the Countreys all which thou hadst trod:
But, *holy Shepherd,* wept thee most thy *sheep,*
Whom thou didst deck with *Faith* (the *Cloth* of GOD).
Only the ANGELS holy-day did keep
For *Thee,* whom God did comfort with his Rod:
    Laughing, and Singing, These thy *Soule* transport
    With *golden sailes* to her *celestiall Port.*

119

You then, who claim the honor (like this *Saint*)
To be the great *Ambassadours* of GOD;
(Pray give me leave) why are ye lame, and faint,
When with your *Errand* ye should go abroad?
If *y'are the Salt oth'Earth*, and at home taint
(No *Prophet* being esteem'd in his *Aboad*)
Who now shall salt (I bayte you *Paganism*)
So much of *Heresie,* so much of *Scism?*

120

But tread we light a bog so dangerous,
Returning to the *Coast* from whence we stray'd.
With this great *City* and illustrious,
Begins the GULPH GANGETICK to be made;
NARSINGA, next, lies rich and populous;
Next ORYXA her cloth of gold doth lade;
Fam'd GANGES at the bottom of the *Bay*
To the *Salt Realm* doth *Silver Tribute* pay:

121

GANGES, in which his Borderers dye lav'd;
Holding it as a certain principle
That (be they ne're such *Sinners*) they are sav'd,
Bath'd in those streams that flow from *Sacred Well.*
The City CATHIGAN would not be wav'd,
The fairest of BENGALA: Who can tell
The plenty of this *Province?* but *its post*
(Thou seest) is *Eastern,* turning the *South-Coast.*

122

The *Realm* of ARRACAN, *That* of PEGU
Behold, with *Monsters* first inhabited!
Monsters, which from a strange commixtion grew:
Such ill effects oft *Solitude* hath bred.
Here (though a barb'rous misbegotten Crew)
Into her way was erring *Nature* led
By an invention rare, which a *Queen* fram'd,
To cure the *Sin,* that is not to be nam'd.

123

Behold the City of TAVAY, with which
The spacious *Empire* of SIAN begins!
TENASSERI! QUEDA: with pepper rich
For which the praise she from all other wins!
MALACCA see before, where *ye* shall pitch
Your great *Emporium,* and your *Magazins*:
     The *Rendezvouz* of all that Ocean round
     For *Merchandizes* rich that *there* abound.

124

From *this* ('tis said) the Waves impetuous course,
Breaking a passage through from *Main* to *main,*
SAMATRA's noble *Isle* of old did force,
Which *then* a Neck of Land therewith did chain:
That *this* was CHERSONESE till that divorce,
And from the wealthy *mines,* that *there* remain,
     The *Epithite* of GOLDEN had annext:
     Some think, it was the OPHYR in the *Text.*

125

But at that *Point* doth CINGAPUR appeare:
Where the pincht *Streight* leaves *Ships* no room to play.
Heer the *Coast,* winding to the *Northern Beare,*
Faces the fair AURORA all the way.
See PAN, PATANE (ancient *Realms* that were)
And long SYAN, which *These,* and *more,* obay!
     The copious *River* of MENAM behold,
     And the great Lake CHIAMAY from whence 'tis roll'd!

126

In this vast *Tract* see an Infinitie
Of *Names* and *Nations* to your WORLD unknown!
LAOS, in *Land* and *men* That potent bee!
AVAS, BRAMAS, in those long Hills o'regrown.
In yon far MOUNTAINS other *Nations* see
(GUEOS they're call'd) and savage ev'ry one!
     They eat *Mans flesh,* and paint their *own* in knots
     With *fire,* as ye doe *Rooms* with *watring-pots.*

127

The River Mecon (which they *Captain* style
Of Waters) see, Camboya on his brink!
He overflows the *Land* for many a mile:
So many other *Rivers* doth he drink.
Set times he hath of *flowing* (like cool Nyle):
The near Inhabitants *brutishly* think,
     That *pain* and *glory*, after this Life's end,
     Ev'n the *brute Creatures* of each kind attend.

128

Upon his soft and charitable Brim
The wet and ship-wrackt Song receive shall *Hee*
Which in a lamentable plight shall swim
From sholes and Quicksands of tempestuous *Sea*,
(The dire effect of *Exile*) when on *Him*
Is executed the unjust Decree:
     Whose repercussive Lyre shall have the Fate
     To be *renowned* more then *Fortunate*.

129

Heer, (mark it!) runs the Coast that's call'd Champa,
Whose *Groves* smell hot of *Calambuco* wood:
Heer Cauchinchina, and heer Aynam's Bay;
Both *One* and t'*Other* little understood.
Heer the great *Empire* (famous for *large sway*,
And its vast *Wealth's* unfathomable Flood)
     Of China runs: calling *all this* her *Owne*
     From *burning Cancer* to the *Frozen Zone*.

130

See the stupendious *Monster* of a Wall
'Twixt *this* and the Tartarian Empire set:
A witness to the World perpetuall
Of *Regall Pow'r* immeasurably great!
The King these have, was *born* no *Prince;* nor shall
Reign after him the *Children* he shall get:
     But one chose by the People of Renown
     For *qualities* proportion'd to a Crown.

131

Much of the WORLD being now conceal'd from *You*
A time will come when it shall *all* be show'd.
But by all means the *Islands* thou must view,
Where *Nature* seems most cost to have bestow'd.
This, shadow'd *half,* which CHINA answers to,
(By which, at distance flanking it, 'tis Woo'd)
    JAPAN is, yeelding the best *Silver-mine* :
    Which th'*Evangellick Furnace* shall *refine.*

132

Through all these *Oriental* Seas, behold
Sown infinite of *Isles* that have no name !
TIDORE *see* ! TERNATE, whence are roll'd
(Holding black *Night* a Torch) thick *Plumes* of *Fame* !
See *Trees* of burning *Cloves,* that shall be sold
For LUSIANS blood, and water'd with the same !
    Heer are those *golden Birds,* which to the ground
    Never descend, and only *dead* are found.

133

See BANDA's *Isles,* inameld curiously
With various *Colours* which the *red fruit* paints;
With various *Birds,* from Tree to Tree that fly,
To take their *tribute* of the NUTMEG-PLANTS !
Behold BORNEO likewise, in which dry
Coagulated Liquor never wants
    From a fat Tree which CAMFORA they name,
    For which this *Isle* is in the B*ook* of FAME !

134

There (look you !) is TIMOR, that sends the Wood
Call'd *Saunders, Physicall* and *Odorous.*
See SUNDA, painted at half face, so broad
That the *South-side* lies now quite hid from *Us* !
The *Natives* here (and *Those* who from abroad
Travail the *Land*) of a miraculous
    River report; which, where it slides alone,
    The *wood* that falls therein, converts to *Stone.*

135

In *that* (which Time, I told you, made an *Isle;*
Which lifewise trembling flames with smoke expels)
Two wonders see, a *Fountain* that runs *Oyle;*
And *Balsamum* that from *Another* wels,
Sweeter then *that* Adonis' Mother vile
Weeps in the Blest Arabia where she dwels!
　　And see how, having *these* (which none else have)
　　She with soft *silk too,* and fine *Gold* is brave!

136

See in Ceylan a *mountain* whose proud Head
Above the Cloudy Region doth appear!
The *Natives* count it *holy* for the tread
Of a *Man's* foot which on a Stone is *there.*
In the Maldiva Isles a *Plant* is bred
(Of vertue under-water) which doth bear
　　The Coco-Apple, against working *Bane,*
　　An *Antidote* approved Soveraign.

137

Against the Red-Sea's mouth Socotora
Fam'd for the bitter *Aloes* behold!
See other *Isles* of sandie Affrica,
Whose Coast too *ye* shall conquer!   Hither roll'd
That *Lump* is, which Divine Panchaya
Out-smels: of unknown birth, more rare then Gold.
　　Behold St. Lawrence his renowned *Isle,*
　　Which otherwise they Madagascar stile!

138

Thus hast thou all the *Regions* of the East,
Which by *Thee* giv'n unto the World is now:
Opening a way with an undaunted Brest
Through that vast Sea which none before did plough.
But it is likewise reason, in the West
That of a Lusian too *one* Action Thou
　　Shouldst understand; who (angry wih his *King*)
　　Atchieves a great and memorable Thing.

139

See *there* another WORLD, which from the *North*
Extends it self to the opposed *Pole*,
And shall be one day proud to have brought forth
The *Ore,* that imitates the beams of SOL!
Your Friend CASTEEL (as guerdon of her worth)
Shall throw the *Collar* on this ragged *Foale:*
> Where various *Nations* dwell, various *Kings* raign,
> Who various *worships,* various *Laws* maintain.

140

But PORTUGALL shall have her share there too,
Mark't with *red wood,* and SANTACRUZ call'd than;
Descry'd by the first Fleet, *she* after *you*
Shall send, by Tempest thrown upon that stran.
Alongst this *Coast* (to find out, and to view
The end thereof) shall wander MAGELLAN;
> Who in reality of *Fact* shall be
> A PORTINGALL, but not in *loyaltie.*

141

When he shall thus have past above half way
Towards the POLE ANTARTICK from the LINE;
Men of *Gigantick* bulk he shal survay,
Inhabiting the *parts* which *there* adjoin;
And (farther on) that STREIGHT, which shall for ay
Be honor'd with his name. *This* leads in fine
> To a new Sea, and by a new Land brings,
> Which the *South-wind* doth hide with his cold wings.

142

Thus farr, O PORTINGALS, ye are allow'd
Your *Nation's* future Actions to survay,
Which through the *Sea* by *you* left ope, her prowd
And never wearied *Ensigns* shall display.
Now then, since ye have found not to be bow'd
Under *Herculean labours,* is the way
> To please your *Angell-Spouses* bright and fair,
> That knit immortal Garlands for your Hair;

143

Ye may embarque (for Wind and Weather fit,
And the Sea courts you) for your *Countrey* dear.
Thus said *shee* to them; and and *they* forthwith quit
The *Isle* of *Love,* the *Harbour* of good chear.
Noble *Provisions* they take out of It;
Take their desir'd desirous *Nymphs* to bear
  Them company: Whom nothing shall divorce,
  Whilst in the *Heav'ns* the *Sun* shall run his course.

144

Thus went *They* ploughing the appeased Main
With always *prosp'rous Gale,* and always *fair*;
Till sight long wisht, much long'd for, they obtain
Of that dear *Earth* where first they suck't the *Ayr.*
Sweet Tagus's Mouth they enter once again:
Where to their *King,* and *Master* (whom they *fear*
  And *love*) for having sent them, the *Renown*
  They give; and add *new titles* to his Crown .

145

"No more, my Muse, no more; my *Harp's* ill strung,
"Heavy, and out of tune, and my *Voyce* hoarse:
"And, not with *singing,* but to see I've sung
"To a deaf people and without remorse.
"*Favor* (that wont t'inspire the Poet's *tongue*)
"Our Countrey yeilds it not, she minds the *Purse*
  "Too much, exaling from her *gilded Mud*
  "Nothing but *gross* and *melancholy* blood.

146

"Nor know I by what *fate,* or duller *Chance,*
"*Men* have not *now* that *life,* and gen'rall *gust,*
"Which made them with a cheerful countenance
"Themselves into perpetual *Action* thrust.
"*You* then, O King! whom *Heav'n* reserv'd t'advance
"At this time to the *Throne* to scoure our Rust;
  "Behold (mark else what other *Nations* doe)
  "The Best of *Subjects* doe belong to *You!*

147

"Behold how cheerfully, a thousand ways,
"Like *fearlesse Lions* and *wilde Bulls* they run;
"Expos'd to *watch* whole *Nights,* to *fast* whole *days,*
"To *fire* and *sword,* the *Arrow* and the *Gun* :
"To *torrid Regions,* and to *frozen Bays,*
"To Moors, and People that adore the *Sun;*
 "To unknown perils a *new* World to find;
 "To *Whales,* to *shipwracks,* to *tempestuous Wind* !

148

"To *doe* and *suffer* All for *You* prepar'd;
"And to obey in the remotest *Land*
"(Though ne'r so *bitter,* and though ne'r so *hard,*
"Without *Reply,* or *stop*) what *You* command.
"With *You* they'll charge the *Devill* and his *Guard*
"Ev'n to the Gates of *Hell,* did You but stand
 "A meer *Spectator* by : and never feare
 "But they will make you too Victorious *there.*

149

"Then warm and glad them with your *present* Rayes,
"*Sweetly majestick,* and severely kind :
"Their shoulders of their heavie *Taxes* ease :
"Thus, thus, the path to *Honour* you shall find.
"Men of *Experience* to your Councell raise,
"If with *Experience* they have goodness joyn'd :
 "For such have a more certain *Rule* to tell
 "The *How,* the *When,* the *Where* to do things well.

150

"In their respective Places count'nance *All;*
"But choose Men rightly qualifi'd thereto.
"Let Rev'rend Churchmen to their *Prayers* fall,
"That God would bless the *Government* in *you;*
"And (for the Nation's sins in generall)
"To *Disciplines* and *Fastings* : for the true
 "Churchman (exempted from *Ambition's* heat)
 "Seeks neither to be *Rich,* nor to be *Great.*

151

"Your Nobles and your Gentry highly prize,
"For *they* their boyling blood undaunted spend,
"Thereby not only Christianitie's,
"But ev'n your *Empire's* limits to extend :
"And *He* who to a *Clyme* so distant flyes
"Your *Royall Service* duely to attend,
        "O'recomes *two* Enemies; the Living *first,*
        "Excessive Toile the *second* and the worst.

152

"*Great Sir,* let never the astonisht Gall,
"The English, German, and Italian,
"Have cause to say, the fainting Portugall
"Could not *advance* the Great Work he *began.*
"Let your A*dvisers* be *experienc'd* All,
"Such as have seen the *World,* and studied *man.*
        "For, though in Science much contained bee,
        "In speciall Cases Practice more doth see.

153

"Phormian (an elegant *Philosophar*)
"You may have read how Hanniball did foole;
"When, in *his presence,* of the Art Of War
"He made a long Discourse by Square and Rule.
"No, no, the brave Profession Militar
"Is not learnt, Sir, by *Fancy* in the *Schoole,*
        "*Dreaming, contemplating,* to *spelling* held;
        "But *seeing, sweating, fighting* in the Feild.

154

"But *I,* who speak in rude and humble *Ryme,*
"Not known nor dreamt of by my Liege at all;
"Know yet from *mouths of little ones* sometime
"The *praise* of Great Ones doth compleatly fal.
"I want not *honest studies* from my *Prime;*
"Nor *long Experience* since to mix withal;
        "I want not *Wit* (such as in *this* you see)
        "Three things, which rarely in *Conjunction* be.

155

"An *Arm* (to serve you) trayn'd in *War* have *I*,
"A *Soul* (to sing you) to the *Muses* bent:
"Onely I want acceptance in your *Eye*,
"Who *owe* to Vertue fair encouragement.
"If Heav'n afford *me*, This; and *you,* some high
"And brave Exployt; worthy a *Monument*
  "*Of Verse,* as my *prophetick* Thoughts presage
  "By what I see now in your tender Age:

156

"Making Mount-Atlas tremble at your sight,
"More then at *that* of dire Medusa's Head;
"Or putting in Ampleusian Fields to flight
"The Moors in Fez and black Morocco bred;
"I'll gage, my Muse (then in *esteem* and *plight*)
"*You* in such manner through the World shall spred,
  "That Alexander shall in *you* respire,
  "Without envying the Meonian Lyre.

FINIS

Textual Notes

Except in a few insignificant details, wherever our text departs from the 1655 edition, the 1655 reading is given below. This is followed by (Ed.) if the present text gives a correction by the editor. Otherwise all emendations indicated were made by Fanshawe in the Leventhorpe copy now owned by Professor C. R. Boxer.

1655 READINGS

LUIS DE CAMOENS. 7 Lost 8 tost.

Dedicatory Epistle: 20 have all Homer 30 Who, what is right, . . . what brave,

SATYRICON (Latin prose) 4 *Helliconem* 11 utilitate,
(Latin verse) 29 vilibus   60 furoque   79-90 etc. F. added the inverted commas.   90 professa   120 confisaque   224 debillatique   257 mortis (Ed.)
Out of the Satyr: 4 common   13 fields, 14 Lo other   18 deare, . . . *Graine.*
67 sets on   69 *can make*   73 Asia . . . Affrick   86 *fatal hue.* 89-121 etc. F. added inverted commas.   104 *There . . . stone.*   161 *rocks*   164 *Head to* 182 *beams* 187 *one shame* 242 *hand* 263 *shame)* 271 *and* 274 *broke)* 283 *and . . . hurl'd* 291 GRANDSON *and* 292 *acts) The* 295 *a blotted* 306 world *with . . . intentions*: 313 *spirits*

TORQUATO TASSO. 1 te 8 *Subjetto.*   13 ferina

THE LUSIAD.

Canto 1.   2.5 Glebe;   9.4 climbe (Ed.)   11.8 grant their   12.7 GANIA   13.8 ALPHONSO, 24-29 F. added the inverted commas. 24.4 LUTUS 34.3 That at 35.5 Air   38-40 F. added inverted commas.   39.8 GOD's   40.6 *Brooke.*   46.3 they'd   50-55 F. added inverted commas.   52.2 INDIES   58.6 dark-pent 64-66 F. added inverted commas.   64.5 nor breed   68.7 indure (Ed.)   74-76, 78-81 F. added inverted commas.   84.3 with his   86.3 on one 102.6 *task*

Canto II. 2-6 F. added inverted commas. 4.4 good or 27.8 alone. 30-32 F. added inverted commas. 36.5 *Cesto's* 39-41 F. added inverted commas. 39.6 is bated in the heat; 44-55 F. added inverted commas. 47.6 find : 47.8 makes . . . . afraide. 51.1 MOOR, 53.2, 5; 54.7 F's brackets. 55.7 HEROS (deifide) 59.5 "For 64.1 and 69.4 sides 69.6 falls. 69.7 His (Ed.) 71.6 Charactere. 83.2 Coming to see 83.7 this command 90.2 Ed. adds full stop. 98.8 *a toe* (Ed.) 79-88; 104-5; 109-13 F. added inverted commas. 110.6 *Coasts*

Canto III. 7.3 plough 7.4 Meotick 8.1 Where she is most beneath 22.6 Anan, (Ed.) 35.7 matter 38-39 F. added inverted commas. 41.5 cry, 41.6 *1655* omitted the line. F. wrote it vertically up the left margin and indicated the omission by small crosses between the lines, 49.4 next which *Field, Furzes* 59.1 did hide 61.9 F. left this as in *1655.* 68.8 keep, 70.5 Here 71-73 F. added inverted commas. 74.3 been; 79.8 guarded in 84.6 kept; (Ed.) 87.2 FREDRICK; 87.5 GUIDA 87.6 SOLDAN 93.2 who *Kings* in SYRACUSA were : 93.4 the *Tyrants* 96.3 the way 103-5 F. added inverted commas. 105.6 seal, 121.8 IDEA's (Ed.) 123.7 *Sheaths,* 124.8 feare :) 125.7 made 128.1 MORE, 132.3 thought set, 137.8 THESUS, 138.7 its (Ed.) 140-43 F. added inverted commas. 143.8 *his* case

Canto IV. 3.8 Cry'd 11.1 drives 13.1 no such, 15-19 F. added inverted commas. 18.3 *World,* (Ed.) 20.1 *Youth* 21.6 Lances, and Darts. 27.8 put 30.7 makes, (Ed.) 34.8 pause. 35, 37, 38 F's inverted commas. 36.4 Ed. adds full stop. 38.5 The irrefragable 43.2 did leave 44 F's inverted commas. 47.7 the unequall'd 48.3 toyle) 54.3 night 55.2 bit, (Ed.) 55.7 ALAOER's F. miscorrected ALACER's 58.3 therefore. 58.6 plaine. (Ed.) 59.3 the 60.1 Inserted by F. 65.8 come 66.3 *Thee* 67.1 person, (Ed.) 71.7 Taun'd 72.1 heads, (Ed.) 73.4 *world,* now (Ed.) 73-4 F's inverted commas. 75-79 wrongly numbered 35-39 in *1655.* F. did not correct. 75.1 *River,* sed (Ed.) 76.7 find to 78.1 phraise 79-80 F added inverted commas. 80.4 brave. 81.1 *Boons;* and *words,* . . . exceed; (Ed.) 83.2 him more : 84.6 benmms 88.3-4 dismay, . . . solitarinesse, Ed. lightens punctuation. 89.2,4 lost, . . . Ghost, (Ed.) 89.6 most.) (Ed.) 89.8 That she 90-91 F. added inverted commas. 92.1 speches 94.6 shrow'ds) 94.7 *science,* (Ed.) 95-104 F. added inverted commas. 96.1 *soules* ! 99.1 Since with 99.8 (Since so 100.6 *Power's* availe, 103.7 *Statute* 104.6 *Calm* and

Canto V. 2.7 running whan, 3.4 Ed. adds full stop. 4.4 before. (Ed.) 8.5-6 F. added brackets. 9.2 take. (Ed.) 10.1 Winding withal 10.2 bends; (Ed.) 10.4 sends.) (Ed.) 10.7 GABMEA's 14.2 new : (Ed.) 18.4 Heav'ns.

18.4 despayre:) (Ed.) 19.8 which the 25.4 strook, 26.5 But O 27.4 F. inserted second bracket. 29.2 transformed crystall; 31.1 his pledge 31.3 stayd 31.4 countenance. 32.8 *Negroe's* (Ed.) 35,38 F. added inverted commas. 38.6 is? Ed. *adds* this 39.7 hard as 40.4 *Wonders*) out (Ed.) 41.8 owne. 41-59 F. added inverted commas. 50.7 (neverthelesse) 51.1 *Twin,* 51.2 *Brother* . . . an hundred 53.2 F. added; 54.6 F. added ! 56.7 No but 60.2 vanish 61.1 Pʏʀous 61.7 F. inserted bracket. 68.1 *Sun,* 68.6 *People,* (Ed.) 74.1 This part . . . streight up 74.8 up by 78.7 bar 78.7 Guides's (Ed.) 78.8 Who, (Ed.) 79.5 we, supply'de, 82.7 Novɪcᴇ, 82.8 *hurt* 86-91, 93-100 F. added inverted commas. 87.4 Salamɪnᴇ, 89.7 git. 94.6 *Gifts* 95 Alᴇxanᴇdʀs 95.6 *Business,* 96.7 Our 97.3 or the 98.4 (This *feirce,* 99.8 Ancᴇstoʀs 100.3 *gusts,*

Canto VI. 5.1 went 5.6 not, (Ed.) 9.8 cast 10.4 dwell. (Ed.) 11.7 Now 13.4 *Batts* 16.4 one, and tother 21.4 wand'ring 23.4 Ed. adds full stop. 23.7 harms; (Ed.) 24.2 though 24.6 Tricks 26.4 out of his *sufferings.* 27-34 F. added inverted commas. 28.2 *perogatives* 30.5 Plough. (Ed.) 34.6 Cheek 35.7 slipt 40-42, 44-45, 48-49, 54-55 F. added inverted commas. 55.5 *me to,* 61.2 *Armes,* 61.8 went, 63.5 blasts, 64.6 prooves: 68.5 sports, 70-72 F. added inverted commas. 72.8 sink: (Ed.) 79.6 *dam,* 80.5 *horrour* 81-83, 86, 89 F. added inverted commas. 81.3 *Read-sea* 83.3 F. *added* dry, 83.4 advance 83.8 F. added ! 88.5 in; (Ed.) 89.4 true, 89.5 remove. 89.6 F. added second bracket 91.4 *Lambs* 91.7 Worn 93, 95-97, 99 F. added inverted commas. 93.6 shore, 94.7 beame 95.5 leaning, (Ed.) 97.8 eat. 98 F. put no inverted commas before this stanza.

Canto VII. 1-14 F. added inverted commas. 1.7 see; (Ed.) 2.5-6 *Nations* . . . .*Vice* . . . *dangers* did 6.6 disprove. 8.4 *Valour,* (Ed.) 8.6 plot: 8.8 *Vices.* 11.1 uncomptroll'd. 11.8 Thrall, 13.7 Glory; (Ed.) 17.4 *North,* 17.8 bred, 18.8 *the true* 21.3 Naʀsɪɴɢa; 22.1 Gatᴇ 25, 27, 30-41 F. added inverted commas. 26.5 since, (Ed.) 27.7 sweet; (Ed.) 32.4 sway, (Ed.) 34.5 *Heir,* . . .*House;* (Ed.) 38.7 touch them 41.7 things; (Ed.) 43.7-8 leisurely . . . *Sea* first . . . *River* after. 47.8 . . . Men Beasts, and Monsters deifide. 48.7 *Fourth Hee* 49.8 Eyes, (Ed.) 54 Misnumbered 53 in *1655.* Numbering righted at St. 59. 54.2 *Ensignes,* (Ed.) 55.4 survayd, (Ed.) 56.1 tell; (Ed.) 57.3 On the 57.3 worke, (Ed.) 60-65, 69-72, 78-87 F. added inverted commas. 60.2 wheles 60.6 worn. 61.2 the 64.5 unfold) 74.3 deeds, 74.5 *pitcht-Field* and 76.6 wonder. 77.2 plac't 77.3 ride side (Ed.) 79.4 -Tayle): (Ed.) 79.6 *Marteale*! 81.7 therein 82.7 men.

Canto VIII. 5.5 which *dead* (Ed.) 6.1 Gamᴇ. 6.7 nor shall 20.8 Up,

(Ed.)   St. 25-29 misnumbered 29-33 and not corrected by F. (Ed.) 25.4 F. added !   28.8 F. added !   29.8 GUADOANA   37.1 see (Ed.)   38.4 and fam'd   39-42, 48-50, 54-55, 61-63 F. added inverted commas.   49.6 those 51.4 cryes a (Ed.) 51.6 white: (Ed.)   60.8 confess; (Ed.)   62.7 not   66.2 *Contract;*   67.4 roam.   65-75, 89, 96-99 F. added inverted commas.   68.4 place: 76.2 F. *inserted* With   76.8 amis,   77.8 ashore   78.4 ends   81.5 repose.   82.3 now   86.2 ne'er   87.4 *Thing*   88.2 GAMA;   88.3 Boats,   89.6 And   93.4 *embarqu'd,* F. embargu'd, (i.e. embargoed) 94.5-6 F. inserted brackets.   97.1 *Tracian*   99.1 *Text*

Canto IX.   5.6 MONSAYDES   11.6 murther'd   12.1 *Merchants;* (Ed.)   14.4 brought;   17.8 *Tongue*   22.5 *Banquets*   25.3 young. (Ed.)   32.5 *Sugeons,* 32.8 *born*   34.1 *life,*   37-42, 44 F. added inverted commas.   37.6 *Them;* (Ed.)   37.8 pow'r *my* (Ed.)   39.6 enemies   40.8 Or ZEPHYRUS breathes, out; or FLORA, pow'rs. (Ed.)   47.2 Shafts, follow (Ed.)   50.6 Breasts   52.7 do?   54.6 ware. (Ed.)   57.8 PARADICE: 61.2 seeen   62.5 high   65.1 *Art's:* (Ed.)   67.8 did hast.   69-70, 76-81, 89-95 F. added inverted commas.   77.2 yielding   94.4 *Christians*

Canto X.   1.8 naked *Lillies*   3.4 with renown'd   7.7 it *humid*   8.3 POPAS   10.2 *De Gama,* now   22-25, 38, 46-49 F. added inverted commas. 22.3 *Tears* (Ed.)   24.2 sung, (Ed.)   25.3 *Fortunes* were't, (Ed.)   29.7 forc't, (Ed.)   32.8 F. added !   35.8 *mattrice,*   45.1 *Stanza's* (Ed.)   52.6 ARCHICE: 54.4 out the   54.7 (And   55.2 COULET'S   55.5 MARS,   68.7 PORTU- GALLS,   73.7 those   78.8 Works   82-85, 145-156 F. added inverted commas. 87.3 F added brackets.   88.8 sweet, LUTE.
90.7,8 Those (clos'd within the Heav'ns) each other enter,
      And *both* the *Waves,* and *Earth*: the common *Center.* (1655)
F. crossed both lines out and wrote new lines below.
94.4,8, 96.8, 99.8, 100.4, 101.2, 102.6, 105.8, 135.6, F. added !   Sts. 101-3 misnumbered   111-113 (Ed.)   119.8 *Scism.*   125.1 CINGAPUX   126.4 BRAINAS 131.6 Wood)   141.8 will hide   142.8 Hair.   150.7 CHURCHMEN (Ed.)

One of the two copies in the British Museum (G.11,385) has a few corrections, probably in Fanshawe's hand.   One of them does not occur in the Leventhorpe copy: III.71.7-8 are revised to

'And bright Syene, where th'impending Sun
No shadow makes, nor past that bound can run.

Short Bibliography

Os Lusiadas de Luis de Camões . . . Lisboa . . . Em casa de Antonio Gonçalvez impressor. 1572.

Lusiades de Luis de Camoens . . . Commentadas por Manuel de Faria i Sousa . . . Ano 1639. Madrid. 4 vols. in 2.

Luis de Camões, Lusiadas, ed. Mendes dos Remedios. 4th edn. Lisbon 1924.

Os Lusiadas de Luis de Camões. (1572 text modernised). Edicão Nacional. Lisbon 1928.

The Lusiad of Luis de Camoens, trans. R. Fanshawe. Ed J. D. M. Ford, Harvard University Press, 1940.

Aubertin, J. J. Os Lusiadas de Luiz de Camões (text and trans.) 2 vols. 1884.

Bacon, Leonard. The Lusiads of Luiz de Camões. (trans.) N.Y. 1950.

Atkinson, William C. L. V. de Camoens, The Lusiads (trans.) 1952.

Bismut, R. Les Lusiades de L. de Camões (trans.). Lisbon, 1961.

Burton, R. F. Camoens: His Life and his Lusiads. 2 vols. 1881.

Braga, T. Camões, vida e obras. Porto. 1907.

Bowra, C. M. 'Camões and the Epic in Portugal' *in* From Virgil to Milton. 1945.

Pierce, Frank. 'The Place of Mythology in the Lusiads', *Comp. Lit.* VI.2. Spring 1954.

Fanshawe, Lady Ann. Memoirs, ed. H. C. Fanshawe. 1907.

Livermore, H.V. A History of Portugal, 1947.

Appendix I

(a) Important Dates and Persons in Portuguese History

B.C.

c. 238   Hamilcar Barcas entered Hispania from Carthage and founded Barcelona.

207   Hasdrubal invaded Italy from Spain to help his brother Hannibal.

c. 182   Death of Hannibal, Hamilcar's son, who subdued the Spanish tribes and defeated the Romans in Italy.

c. 154-140   Viriatus sought to avenge the massacres of Celtic tribesmen by the Roman praetor Servius Galba.

A.D.

711   Rodrigo, the Visigothic king, defeated and slain by the Muslims.

997   Bermudo II, King of Gallicia, won Oporto from the Moors.

1064   Ferdinand the Great of Leon, Castile and Galicia captured Coimbra.

1109   Count Henry of Burgundy on death of Spanish King Alfonso VI styled himself 'Count and Lord of all Portugal' (d. 1112). His wife Teresa beat off the Moors but alienated her son by her love for Dom Fernando Peres de Trava (III.29).

1128   Afonso Henriques defeated his mother and Dom Fernando (III.30-33). His tutor Egas Moniz, who to save him when besieged in Guimaraens had offered his master's homage to Castile, surrendered himself and was pardoned by the Spaniard (III.35-41).

1139   Afonso defeated the Moors at Ourique after seeing a vision of Christ (III.42-53).

1140   Portugal independent of Castile after the 'tournament of Valdevez'. Afonso attacked the Moors (III.55-56).

1147   Afonso captured Lisbon with help of Crusaders, including many English (III.57-60; VIII.18).

1169   Warring against Ferdinand II of Leon, Afonso was injured, captured, and released (III.69-74). He saved his son Sancho from the Moors at Santarem (III.75-83).

1185-1211   Sancho I, 'Builder of Cities'. Took Silves with help from Crusaders (III.85-89).

1211-23   Afonso II, 'the Fat'.

1217   Recapture of Alcacer do Sal with help of English Crusaders (III.90). Franciscan friars introduced into Portugal. Afonso interdicted for seizing church property.

1223-48   Sancho II. Ruined by favourites. Excommunicated by Innocent IV (1245) he retired into obscurity (III.90-94).

1226   Elvas captured from the Moors.

1246-79   Afonso III. Conquered the Algarves (III.94-95).

1279-1325   Diniz, 'the Worker', fostered agriculture, building, law and literature (himself a fine poet) (III.96-98).

1294   Commercial treaty with Edward I of England.

1325-57   Afonso IV, 'the Brave'. Aiding his daughter Maria's husband Alfonso XI of Castile, he defeated the Moors at Tarifa (1340) (III.98-117).

1353   New commercial treaty with the City of London guaranteeing fair dealing.

1355   Murder in Coimbra of Donna Ines de Castro, mistress of the heir, Dom Pedro, by three courtiers at the King's instigation (III.118-35).

1357-67   Pedro I, called 'the Cruel' for his revenge on Ines's murderers and his rigorous dispensing of justice (III.136-7).

1367-83   Fernando I, 'the Handsome'. Claimed throne of Castile, and was ruined by his love for Leonor Teles de Menezes, whom he married while her husband was alive (III.138-43).

1383   Regency of Leonor.

1385   Dom João ('the Bastard') elected to the throne, and reigned until 1433.

1385   The Spaniards defeated at Aljubarrota with aid of John of Gaunt's English archers (IV.24-44).

1386   Permanent alliance between Portugal and England in Treaty of Windsor. King João married Gaunt's daughter Philippa (1387); they had five sons (IV.50).

1389   The legendary tournament of 'The Twelve of England' (VI.43-66).

1415   Ceuta stormed by the sons of João and Philippa — Edward, who later codified the laws, Pedro the traveller and patron, and Henry 'the Navigator', (IV.48-49).

1433-38   Duarte (Edward). His disastrous attack on Tangier (1437) left his brother Fernando a hostage till he died in 1443 (IV.51-53).

1438   Afonso V only a child. Regency of Dom Pedro till the King wrongfully accused him and Dom Pedro was slain at Alfarrobeira (1449).

1449-81   Afonso V made three expeditions into Africa, then claimed the kingdom of Castile and was defeated in 1476 (IV.54-59).

1481-95   João II, 'the Perfect', broke power of feudal nobility (executing Duke of Braganza (1483) and himself stabbing Duke of Viseu (1484)), and fostered the arts and exploration (IV.60-65).

1494   Treaty of Tordesillas with Ferdinand and Isabella of Spain, confirmed by Papal Bull, gave Spaniards all lands discovered west of a line 370 leagues W. of Cape Verde, and Portuguese all lands discovered east and south of the line. [For Portuguese explorations see below.]

1495-1521 Manuel, 'the Fortunate', sent out many explorers including da Gama (IV.60-81) and patronised the arts. Hoping to obtain the Spanish throne, he expelled the Jews and Muslims, and married the Infanta Isabella.

1497-9   First voyage to India of Vasco da Gama.

1502   Papal Bull confirmed Manuel's title, "Lord of the Conquest, Navigation and Commerce of Ethiopia, Arabia, Persia, and India."

1521-57   João III, 'the Pious', abandoned North African possessions except Ceuta and Mazagon in order to concentrate on the Indies and Brazil. Introduced the Inquisition.

1557-78   Sebastian dreamed of conquering Morocco, but was defeated and slain at Alcacer-Kebir, 4 August 1578.

1578-80   Aged Cardinal Henry on the throne.

1580-1640 Portugal under Spanish rule.

(b) The Portuguese in the East.

1500   Pedro Alvares Cabral, after discovering Brazil on the way, reached India, found Calicut hostile and founded trading posts at Cananor and Cochin.

1502   Vasco da Gama's second voyage, with twenty ships. Cannonaded Calicut and strengthened the factories.

1503   Three squadrons reached India, under Francisco de Albuquerque, Afonso de Albuquerque, and Antonio de

Saldanha. F. de Albuquerque left a garrison under Duarte Pacheco to defend Cochin against the Zamorin of Calicut. Pacheco defeated the Zamorin against fearful odds (X.12-21).

1505   Dom Francisco de Almeida set up forts in Africa at Kilwa and Mombasa and as Viceroy of Cochin and Cananor sent expeditions under his son Dom Lourenço de Almeida from Cochin to attack the Muslim merchants (X.26-28). Dom Lourenço was killed in action at Chaul against an Egyptian fleet (X.29-32). Almeida avenged his son off Diu in 1509 (X.33-36). Afonso de Albuquerque and Tristão da Cunha (X.39) stormed Ormuz on the Persian Gulf (X.40).

1509   Afonso de Albuquerque became Viceroy and sacked Calicut before being driven off. Diogo Lopes de Sequeira sailed to Malacca.

1510   Afonso de Albuquerque captured Goa (X.42-43) and made it his capital. Executed Ruy Diaz for seducing a captive Indian girl (X.45-49). Almeida killed on his way home at Table Bay (X.37-38).

1511   Malacca annexed (X.44).

1515   Albuquerque died at Goa. His successor Lopo Soares de Albergaria captured Berberah and established a trading factory at Colombo, Ceylon (X.50-51).

1517-21 Fernão Peres de Andrade's mission to China.

1519   Diogo Lopes de Sequiera reached Abyssinia *via* the Red Sea (X.52).

1522   Duarte de Menezes punished a revolt in Ormuz (X.53). He had the bones of St. Thomas brought from Madras to Goa (X.109-19).

1524   V. da Gama's third visit, as Viceroy, but he died at Cochin on Christmas Day (X.54).

1525   D. Henrique de Menezes attacked Coulete; died young in 1526 (X.54-56). Lopo Vaz de Sampaio usurped D. Pedro Mascarenha's post as Viceroy (X.56-58), but did well, destroying Rais Ahmed (Cutiale) and his fleet from the Persian Gulf (X.59).

1529-38 Nuna da Cunha, who followed, captured Diu near Cambay, and built a fort at Bassein (X.61).

1538-40 D. Garcia de Noronha drove out the Turks of Diu (X.62).

1538   Antonio da Silveira gallantly defended Diu against Sulyman II's great fleet (X.62).

1540-2	Da Gama's son Estavão was Viceroy (X.62), reached Mt. Sinai but failed to take Suez (X.98-99).
1541	Estavão's brother D. Cristavão saved Abyssinia from the Muslims, but was captured, tortured and beheaded (X.96).
1542-5	D. Martin Afonso de Sousa, 12th Governor, had served in Brazil (1531-3), and had captured Repelim from Malabar (X.65) and aided the King of Cambay (X.64). He defeated the Samorin's fleet (X.65). He also took St. Francis Xavier to India.
1545-7	D. João de Castro consolidated the Empire.
1546	João Mascarenhas defended Diu under siege (X.68-69). De Castro's son Fernando killed by a mine; and Alvaro reinforced the garrison (X.70); D. João relieved it (X.71) and extended Portuguese conquests (X.72-73).
1548	Fernão Mendes Pinto set up a factory in Japan, near Yokohama.
1557	Portuguese factory established at Macao.
1558-62	D. Constantino de Bragança, Viceroy; a friend of Camões.
1562-4	D. Francisco Coutinho. Released Camões from prison in Goa.
1564-8	D. Antao de Noronha. Fortified Mangalore. Recalled, he died before Mozambique; Camões returned home in the ship.

Appendix II

VERSES

Spoken in the Library of the English College by two young students
(one whereof represented the Genius of Camoens) to Sir Richard
Fanshaw Envoy Extraordinary from his Majesty of Great Britain
to the Court of Portugal, &c

Genius: Swifter than the swallow's wing,
Parthian dart or stone from sling,
Or the bullet newly fled
From his flame-environ'd bed,
Come I for to see a Friend
Whom choice Arts and Tongues commend.
Tell me, gentle youth, I pray,
Is my Lord yet gone away?
If he be not (as I fear)
Go and whisper him i' the ear
Here's the Genius of a Poet
(This verdant wreath doth show it)
Whom the Portugal admires
And the Spaniard his desires,
Bred up to Mars his Drums, and to the Muses' Lyres.

Student: Genius, whence come you?
Genius: From Saint Anne's
Where my Mausoleum stands,
Humbly sueing for the bliss
My Lord's honoured hands to kiss.
If there's any crave my name,
I it was sang Gama's fame
In such words, and such a strain,
'Twill survive old Time's short reign,
And in my bright *Lusiad* shine
As an adamantine shrine —

Though I also must confess
Much he owes to th'English dress,
Proud of so rich a fashion,
Ne'er known unto our Nation,
Which no praise reaches home but admiration.

Student: I am surpris'd? What do I see?
Camoens the Great? No! it cannot be;
Time stole most of his hair away
And dyed his beard a hoary grey.
Chill Age ne'er frosted o'er your crown
Nor Spring adorn'd your chin with down.
One eye he lost in bloody wars;
Your forehead's graced with two twin starrs.
To him our dialect was unknown
Yet you pronounce it as your own.

Genius: Suspend your doubts, fond youth;
Time will unravel Truth;
Longer delays I can't allow.
By dints of sacred Laurel on his brow
I know my honour'd Lord, and must salute him now.

> Here the little student retired, and the
> Genius advancing forward, after his
> Honours to my Lord, made the fol-
> lowing Address:

Sir, whose true worth and far-renowned name
Claims a fair memory 'mongst the sons of Fame,
Whose soul is harmony, in whose candid breast
Both Mars and Pallas make a sweet contest,
And groundedly, since (I myself can show it)
You are both golden Knight and golden Poet;
    Pardon my bold intrusion. The Fates doom
Camoens should welcome you unto this room
Which, though thus fraught with books, your learning can
Swell it into a second Vatican.
How happily am I chang'd, since by your pen,
Rescu'd from death I see the world again,
And heir to Hippolytus's fate am thus
By your life- breathing lines a Virbius.
    Sorrow in one night hath made some men grey;
I'm green by th'Antiphasis of this joyful day.
Nor lack I now an Eye: you've giv'n me one

Out sparkles Argus' hundred all alone —
An English eye, and English tongue so sweet
Phoebus himself might learn to speak by it.
But this is not a time to run upon
Favours peculiar, but that general one
Your presence doth our Nation, since it brings
Joys to the best of Queens from the best of Kings,
And high caresses such whose every line
Welcomer is and wealthier than a mine.
  O that your Quill, England's select delight,
Would this Pandora draw in black and white,
Whose priceless worth all other Queens outvies
As far as Sol's noon-star Night's twinkling eyes.
Body and mind she's perfect; in her face
Is writ whole Nature's story join'd with Grace,
To whom Heav'n giving all choice gifts, 'tis fit
They should be shown the world by a heav'nly wit.
Take then the pencil, and a Temple raise
Transcending Spain's and your Escurial's praise.
Then in it place your Queen, and on each side
Raise altars to each virtue of the Bride.
By her, enthron'd in armour all complete
Join hand in hand her Bridegroom, Charles the Great,
And, whilst amazement makes th' beholders dumb,
Warble a sweet Epithalamium
Unto the Royal Pair; then, mounting higher,
From Poet's fury to the Prophets' quire,
Unroll the good yet dark decrees of Fate,
And read these Nuptials truly fortunate.
  Great is the theme, and great the guerdon which
Your temples with fresh Laurels will enrich.
  I sung unto a Nation and a King
Knew not the price of Verse, but you shall sing
To him and her who honour men of parts,
And in this dull-brain'd age encourage Arts.
  No more, great Sir. Time calls me to my urn —
Yet must I needs profess 'fore I return,
The College's resentments, now unable
With choicer viand to set out the table,
Since the best cooks are sick, and, newly rose,
Can hardly dress a homely dish of Prose.

I therefore, who supply their room, request
You'll pardon this my little and ill-dress'd,
And by a glance from your reviving eye
Lend health to their long bedrid Poetry,
Whilst I i'th' Language of a strict embrace
Take leave of you, Chief of the Poet's race.

Da veniam subitis non displicuisse merentur
Festinant Fanshaw, qui placuisse tibi.
                                    [Martial.][1]

---

[1] I am indebted to Dona Virginia Rau and Mr. T. P. Waldron, who helped me to obtain
a photostat of this piece, and to the Librarians of the University of Coimbra who kindly
gave me permission to use it and to consult this and other Fanshawe MSS. in the Library.

DATE DUE

DEMCO 38-297